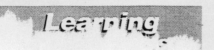

WATER BASED RECREATION
managing water resources for leisure

WATER BASED RECREATION
managing water resources for leisure

Tutor's Manual

Fiona McCormack

An A4 looseleaf tutor's manual with exercises, case studies, notes, OHPs and materials for training use with copying rights

ISBN 1 85450 152 6

The Environment Agency

In April, 1996 the National Rivers Authority for England and Wales was replaced by the Environment Agency. This was a merger of the work of the NRA and other organisations, including Her Majesty's Inspectorate of Pollution, the Waste Regulation authorities and some smaller units from the Department of the Environment. The rationale behind the creation of this new agency was to streamline environmental protection and create a 'one stop shop' for businesses.

The aim of the Environment Agency is to work towards sustainable development. It aims to achieve this through acting as an independent, impartial regulator. In terms of water based recreation, its contribution will remain the same as its predecessors. It became responsible for rod licences and provision for recreation, both on and alongside their resources.

WATER BASED RECREATION
managing water resources for leisure

by

Fiona McCormack

ELM Publications

This first edition of *Water Based Recreation: managing water resources for leisure* is published 31st August 1994 by ELM Publications, Seaton House, Kings Ripton, Huntingdon PE17 2NJ (Tel.04873-254 or 238 Fax 04873-359).

Printed by St Edmundsbury Press, Bury St Edmunds, Suffolk, England.

Bound by Woolnough Bookbinding, Express Works, Church Street, Irthingborough, Northamptonshire, England.

ISBN 1 85450 154 2

British Library Cataloguing-in-Publication Data. A catalogue record for this publication is available from the British Library.

Contents

List of Figures

List of Tables

Acknowledgements

In compiling the research for this book I must thank all those organisations who responded to my requests for information, in particular the British Marine Industries Federation, British Waterways, HM Coastguard, Thames Region NRA and The Broads Authority.

My own interest in water based recreation was nurtured by the Ocean Youth Club, who offered me the opportunity to understand the lure of the water based activities, I am, therefore, indebted to them for their early encouragement and support.

I owe my thanks to the Department of Leisure and Environmental Management at Buckinghamshire College with whose support I have been able to develop module courses in this important area.

Finally, I would like to thank David and my parents for all their help, support and advice during the preparation of this book.

About the Author

Fiona McCormack is a lecturer in Leisure Management at Buckinghamshire College, a college of Brunel University.

She is a keen water sports practitioner enjoying both dinghy sailing and yacht cruising. She spent several years working in various aspects of water based recreation, including Mate on various Sail Training Vessels and a Yacht Skipper for Island Cruising Club in Devon. She is a graduate of Loughborough University's MSc in Recreation Management and has gone on to develop several modules in water based recreation for HND and undergraduate courses.

In addition to lecturing and writing, Fiona McCormack is also working on research for a PhD in the use of recreation for young people at risk, based on her experiences of outdoor activities and sailing projects.

Introduction

Participation and interest in the management of water resources for leisure has increased greatly over the last ten years. It could be argued that this concern has been triggered by the general increase in environmental awareness. As an island we have enjoyed thousands of miles of coast to compliment our natural and man made inland water resources. For many years it may have seemed that as a plentiful natural resource water did not require specific management for leisure. The 1960s saw the launch of the National Trust's Enterprise Neptune, an initial attempt to protect the undeveloped areas on the British coastline. The 1980s have seen a dramatic increase in recreational development in coastal areas and in the provision of inland water for recreation. Increasingly leisure managers will come into contact with water based leisure provision in some form. This text will fill an empty space in the market as a course text for students studying modules in water based and outdoor recreation on leisure management degrees and HNDs. It will also be a useful reference for general leisure, tourism, countryside management students and leisure managers with a responsibility for water resources for recreation and leisure.

The text covers information required to understand the range of resources available, the needs of participants and the scope of providers. It will then analyse approaches to the management of these resources to reduce conflict among user groups and offer the optimum recreational experiences. The structure will include current statistical information about water resources in the UK where appropriate.

CHAPTER 1

Water Resources

'Water , water everywhere ....'

Britain is particularly lucky in terms of leisure opportunities, we are surrounded by a natural leisure resource - water. Continued improvements in communications mean that most residents of the British Isles live less than a three hour journey to the coast. This proximity may explain why little attention has been given to this vast leisure playground. The 'green 1990's' have resulted in a growing awareness among participants and providers of the fragile nature and value of natural resources such as the coast. There is now a need for leisure managers to address the issues for water resources that have been considered in countryside management for many years.

In England many counties enjoy a coastline boundary and every county has some inland water resources, including rivers, canals and reservoirs. With such a high density of resources we could be forgiven for adopting a *laissez faire* attitude to their management. This decade, however, we have witnessed, as result of increased environmental awareness, the introduction of a range of policies and initiatives to protect and promote one of our greatest leisure resources. Some examples of the most important water resources for recreation are shown in *Figure 1.1*, on page 2.

Figure 1.1: **British water resources**

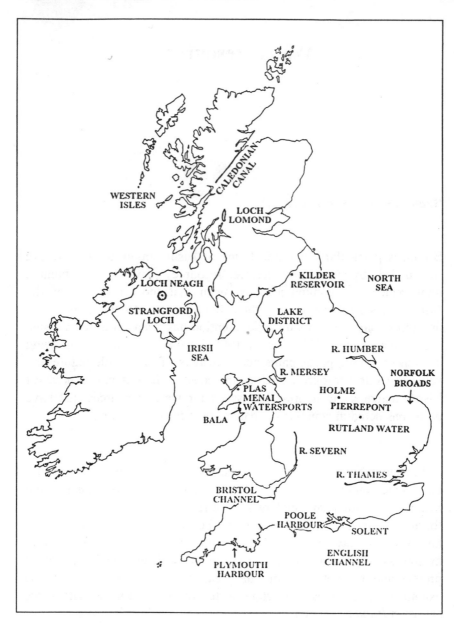

WATER RESOURCES IN THE UK

Britain enjoys some of the widest range of water resources in the world. We can choose between peaceful slow flowing rivers, silent, glassy lakes or the roar of fast flowing rapids and the powerful coastal environment. Every local authority in Britain will be able to identify some water resource in their area from the small river or stream to hundreds of miles of coastline. However small or large the resource may seem, it will have the potential to offer a wide range of leisure activities if sensibly managed. The resources can be classified in two main ways:

> Inland and Coastal
> *OR*
> Natural and man-made

Inland Water - will be defined for the purposes of this text to be any fresh water resources which either have no contact with the coast or, in the case of rivers, once they become non tidal and fresh water i.e. when they are no longer estuaries.

Coastal Water - will be defined to include all salt water areas with an outlet to the main sea or ocean.

Natural Resources - Areas which have been formed through natural geological processes for example streams, lakes and oceans. In many cases man's intervention in natural processes will mean that there is not always a clear division between man-made and natural. For example in recent years we have seen rivers diverted by man, natural resources dammed to form reservoirs and harbours constructed where no natural harbour previously existed.

Man-made Resources - exist when man has engineered the resource, either from nothing or from a natural resource to form a new water area with different characteristics than it had previously enjoyed.

3

These categories cannot be considered in isolation. *Figure 1.2* below shows that most resources will fit into a combination of both categories: man-made inland, man-made coastal, natural inland, natural coastal.

Figure 1.2: **Illustration of the overlap between water resource methods of classification**

	Coastal	Inland
man-made	marinas some harbours	canals some lakes reservoirs gravel pits
natural	beaches bays seas cliffs estuaries sea lochs	rivers wetlands streams lochs lakes ponds

Coastal Man-made Resources

As engineering technology has improved, man has become increasingly capable of constructing features on the coast which provide a water resource for both recreation and other demands where the resources would not naturally occur.

Harbours :
An early example of this type of man-made resource can be seen in the number of sea barriers constructed over centuries either to form a safe harbour for fishing fleets and other boats or, more recently, to protect property. The small Dorset former fishing town and now popular seaside resort of Lyme Regis boasts a typical man-made harbour formed by the Cobb - made famous during the filming of the *French*

Figure 1.3   **The Cobb at Lyme Regis**

Lieutenant's Woman. This early sea wall was constructed, during the reign of Edward the First, to protect fishing boats lying at anchor. Today the wall serves more frequently to protect leisure boats during the summer months and to form an important focus for the town's resort activities, such as boat hire and fishing trips. It also affords some protection from prevailing south westerly winds on the adjacent bathing area. This old sea defence, however, fails to provide suitable protection during the severe winter gales and most pleasure craft are found winter moorings in the adjacent car park. This serves the dual purpose of winter boat park and summer tourist car park.

Other forms of man-made coastal construction have become leisure venues in themselves. A clear example of this is the ultra modern Thames Barrier, now a visitor attraction in its own right. Opened over ten years ago, the barrier is a complex design feat to protect not only the busy Port of London but also the vast expanses of property in the capital city. Since construction the barrier has only been used eleven times (until 1993) to protect London. To supplement this activity a comprehensive visitor centre has been created offering a range of water's edge activities such as a restaurant, picnic area, information centre and riverside walk. This illustrates how non recreation constructions can be turned into leisure and tourism venues.

Marinas:
The 1970's saw a dramatic increase in specific man-made leisure developments in the form of yacht marinas which can be found in most areas of our coast. These marinas grew up around the existing concept of a 'car park' style facility for yachts, where the owners could pay an annual fee for a mooring or 'parking space' for their yachts. The owners benefited from easy access to their boats, walking along pontoons (floating walkways) directly onto their boats without needing to use a dinghy. Originally marinas provided services which included the basic requirements of the cruising yachtsman - fuel, access, security, boat-yard services and, often, washing and showering facilities. Gradually the number of services offered increased to include shops, bars and restaurants, thereby offering a complete

package for both resident yacht owners and visitors. The marina managers were providing a full leisure package for the yachtsman. During the boom years of the 1980s, new marinas were introduced to attract a wider market. The attraction of water and boats as a venue for water's edge leisure activities was acknowledged. Marina complexes were built, combining the yachtsman's package with shopping malls, cinemas, restaurants and bars to attract visitors. Many of these developments also offered the marina village concept of luxury housing on the water's edge with moorings attached.

Natural Coastal Resources

The coasts of England, Wales and Northern Ireland, approximately 3,083 miles in total, offer a rich and varied natural resource which owes its continued existence, in part, to activities of the National Trust who own 17.2 per cent of it. The purchase of this land was carried out under a project entitled *Enterprise Neptune* in response to fears that much of the coast line was being destroyed by man-made developments, such as factories, power stations and oil refineries (see *Figure 1.4*).

The areas which have been used for this type of development have been harmed not only by the visual eye-sore, but also by the destruction of habitat and by pollution. A more detailed study of coastal resource planning and *Enterprise Neptune* can be found in chapter seven.

Beaches :
All around our coast we can enjoy a visit to the beach. Beaches were developed as a seaside holiday bathing area in the nineteenth century. However, modesty codes dictated that bathers should be concealed from public gaze and needed to be transported to the water's edge in a bathing machine. As social codes of modesty changed, the beach became the central focus for the seaside holiday. With this a leisure market developed in accessories such as deck chairs, sun shades and the traditional bucket and spade. As the seaside holiday grew in popularity, side-shows developed such as Punch and Judy and donkey

rides to entertain children. The water resource was generally restricted to bathing activities.

Figure 1.4   **Calshot with Activity Centre, Power Station and Oil Refinery**

Since the 1950s other sports have became more popular and sea-front stores have enticed holidaymakers with lilos, basic surf boards, inflatable dinghies and snorkelling equipment. This has continued to develop and many people enjoy their first taste of wind surfing and water skiing from the beach whilst on summer holiday.

Beaches in Britain are made of a variety of substances, the most popular for holidays and leisure activities, such as land yachting, is fine sand. However, many of the early popular seaside destinations were to pebble beaches such as Brighton and Herne Bay on the Kent coast. Maybe, because neither of these substances were easy under foot, promenades were developed to allow participants to enjoy the sea air without getting sand between their toes.

The management of beaches for leisure presents a range of challenges which will be covered in detail in a later chapter. The main problems faced are visitor management (congestion), physical safety, adverse weather and pollution.

Bays:
Further naturally occurring features of the coastline are bays and coves, which often provide sheltered water for a range of leisure pursuits. They are particularly favoured by motor boat and water skiing enthusiasts. Many bays and coves also conceal a rich variety of hidden treasure, both natural and wreck, to inspire divers.

Bays and sheltered water require certain management issues to be addressed. Many do not have good access from the land, therefore, launching facilities need to be provided in order that damage to wildlife and habitat can be avoided. Other bays and coves centre on the shore with a popular beach. In these cases careful planning needs to balance any conflicts between users, thereby maintaining an enjoyable and safe environment for all.

Cliffs:
Although much of our coast offers beaches and wetlands, arguably the

most prominent features of our coast, both from land and sea, are the extensive areas of cliffs. Indeed the 'White Cliffs of Dover' have become synonymous with England, home comings and splendour. The local tourist board uses the image of white cliffs to attract thousands of visitors every year.

Cliffs naturally encourage water's edge activities such as walking and climbing, however, recent media coverage, of a hotel slipping into the sea from its cliff edge perch, demonstrates clearly the need to manage this resource in terms of erosion and damage to wildlife.

Seas:
The sea is an immense resource, Britain borders an ocean and several smaller sea areas as follows:

> English Channel
> Irish Sea
> North Sea
> Atlantic Ocean
> Bristol Channel

With such an immense resource it can be difficult to assess the need for management. However, we are increasingly made aware that pollution dumped at sea can have devastating effects on leisure venues, local economies and wildlife. For example, the collision involving the *Rosebay* off the Devon coast in 1990 caused hundreds of gallons of oil to be deposited into the sea at the begining of the holiday season. This disaster threatened the water quality for divers, bathers, fish, birds and all local wildlife; beaches and boats ready for the new season could have been left heavily stained and polluted by oil. Luckily, and with the help of modern technology, a boom deflected much of the potential damage, but this shows clearly that management of our seas is vital to the success of many coastal water based forma of recreation. Pollution is far from the only management problem and will be considered with the challenges of safety and control in Chapter 5.

Sea Lochs:
So far we have concentrated on the resources of English coastal areas, however, we must not forget the huge and popular resource of sea lochs, found mainly on the west Scottish coast. These provide relatively calm, deep water resources, cutting into the heart of inland areas. They attract thousands of day trippers every year; some to take in the dramatic beauty; others to fish, sail, and partake of a full range of water sports in one of Britain's most uncrowded and beautiful natural resources.

Estuaries:
These areas are where the rivers meet the sea, where water becomes subject to tides and is salty. These naturally occurring features form many of Britain's harbours, for example, the River Dart and Dartmouth, Chatham on the River Medway and Bucklers Hard on the River Beaulieu. River estuaries offer natural protection and often towns to allow easy access to the water.

Harbours:
Most harbours in the United Kingdom are either man-made, such as the example of Lyme Regis, or estuary town developments. There are, however, several naturally occurring harbours where not only is protection afforded to boats, but they are also large enough to be the home of a range of water sports within their confines. Examples of these large harbours are Chichester, Langstone, Poole and Portsmouth on the south coast. Many such harbours exist where a number of rivers combine to run into the sea. The diagram in *Figure 5.1*(on page 104) shows the range of activities in Poole Harbour. Harbour Authorities are responsible for controlling and managing the activities within the harbour.

Figure 1.5: **Sketch map of opportunities for water based recreation in Poole Harbour [not to scale]**

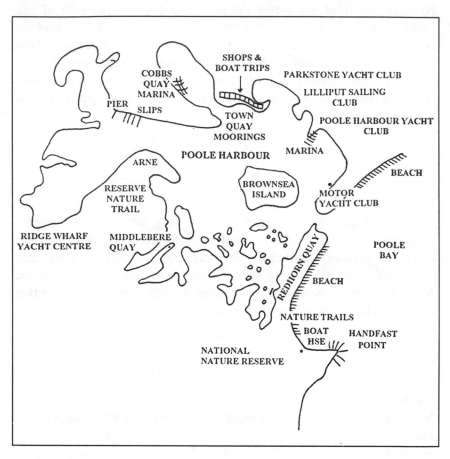

Inland Water Resources

For many of us the coast is only available for holidays and excursions. For our every day leisure needs we are forced to look for opportunities closer to home. That is not to say, however, that our inland water is only important in terms of use by local residents; many inland resources are popular holiday venues, for example river and canal boat holidays.

Natural Inland Water

Inland water exists naturally a wide variety of forms as shown in *Figure 1.1* on page 2. Most local authorities have some naturally occurring water resources in their area and, therefore, are able to offer water based recreation to their communities and attract visitor revenue in the form of tourism.

Rivers:

Rivers and streams dissect Britain, their routes, generally decided by nature, have ocasionally, been diverted by man's intervention. Indeed, recreation users of major rivers, such as the Thames, Trent, and Severn, will face man's intervention in the form of locks, marinas and tow paths. Rivers are still, however, a natural geographic phenomenon which require careful management to fulfil their role as a leisure resource whilst maintaining their natural form and beauty.

Rivers in England are mainly managed by the regional sectors of the National Rivers Authority, although some privately managed small rivers remain. In terms of leisure and recreation rivers are the historical venue for rowing and river boats. Other sports, such as canoeing, have been successfully integrated. There are also numerous river based sailing clubs despite the problems. A river is not really suitable for the sail boat since it needs to frequently tack across the river to proceed. On narrow and busy stretches this can hamper boats travelling up and down the river. On the water's edge improvements in water quality in many rivers has increased the number of anglers enjoying fishing both recreationally and in competitions. The tow paths, some long distance, attract many walkers and locks are a focus for picnics and day trips. With this range of demands careful management is required. To this end the National Rivers Authority are currently producing a River Thames Recreation Strategy.

Lakes, Ponds and Inland Lochs:

These elements have been combined to include areas of enclosed natural water, both large and small. Most large lakes and lochs are

13

concentrated in the North of England in the Lake District National Park and in Scotland, particularly the Southern Highlands. Resources such as Coniston Water and Lake Windermere in the Lake District and Loch Lomond in the Southern Highlands of Scotland offer a majestic and huge leisure playground. The physical size of such resources reduces the problems of congestion and conflict found on rivers, however, the enclosed nature of these areas makes them more vulnerable to pollution from dumping since there are no escapes and the area is more concentrated than coastal resources.

The major lakes and lochs are used for all types of watersports and frequently support large marinas and water sports centres on their banks. The water's edge activities include walking and day trips. Angling needs careful management to ensure constant stock and to prevent over fishing in some areas.

Ponds are much smaller water resources and as such are not generally used for water sports, although some larger ponds are used for casual rowing boats. They do, however, form an important focus for community water's edge activities and many children sample the delights of angling with their first rod or net in the village pond. Ponds are also an important way of conserving wildlife.

Wetlands:
Wetland areas are an important feature of the British habitat providing a home for waders and other birds. The most significant wetland area in Britain, for recreationalists, is the Norfolk Broads. The broads consist of a fenland area where peat developed on a reed base. The fens were harvested for thatching and peat until about fifty years ago, when demand for these products dwindled. What followed was a reduction in these activities which led to the destruction of some species that thrived on traditionally managed fens. The area also offers wet woodlands, waterways and marshes. The water resources present 200km of navigable rivers and 'broads'. This has made the area a popular tourist destination with approximately 1 million visitors per year and 12,000 boat licences. The activities are managed by the

Broads Authority which seeks to reduce negative impact.

Man-made Inland Water

Despite the wide ranging opportunities for naturally occurring water resources, man has developed a range of constructed resources to supplement his needs. With the possible exception of Rutland Water in Leicestershire, these developments were not constructed with leisure in mind but with industrial needs dictating their original design. With time, and as industrial demands changed, many of these resources have been developed for leisure and recreation.

Canals and Waterways:

Canals were developed in the 'Canal Age' of 1757 to the 1830's in answer to the transport demands of the industrial revolution. They were designed as arteries in the British transport system ferrying raw materials, products and people to and from towns and villages. At their peak canals covered 4,250 miles of navigable rivers and waterways, carrying 30 million tons of goods every year. The first canal to be constructed was the Sankey Brook (St Helen's Canal) in 1757. The boats were horse drawn and, therefore, transport was slow. The advent of a railway system produced a faster competitor and many boats converted to steam motor and, later, diesel engines. Thus by the 1920s the major canal management cost had changed from tow path maintenance (canal bank erosion caused by the tow horses) to erosion created by engine wash. Commercial use of the canals reduced in the 20th century leading to a reduction in the mileage to 3,250 (*source: British Waterways*).

Due to reduced commercial demands, 2,000 miles of waterway were assigned to the responsibility of British Waterways in 1963. In 1968 the Transport Act classified waterways into 3 groups:

Commercial Waterways	340 miles	Carriage of freight
Cruising Waterways	1,100 miles	Leisure and recreation
Remaining	540 miles	Maintenance

Canals have become popular venues for canoeing with several watersports centres on their banks. Tourism has developed with many companies offering traditional long boat or barge canal breaks.

Reservoirs:
Large urban populations require large amounts of water for domestic and industrial purposes. These areas in Britain do not have sufficient natural water supply for their needs. Water, therefore, has to be pumped in from other areas. To collect this water, existing (often high) natural water resources are dammed, creating man-made lakes or reservoirs to collect and store water before pumping it to the urban populations. These man-made lakes are ideal centres for watersports, although it should be remembered that their primary task is to provide a clean water supply and therefore some activities may not be possible.

Reservoirs are also found closer to the urban populations that they serve, forming temporary storage for the water either pumped from further afield or collected from nearby rivers. On the western edge of London Thames Water has a collection of reservoirs used for sailing and wind surfing, such as the Queen Mary and Queen Mother reservoirs. These present an ideal opportunity for recreation managers to bring watersports to a urban population, thereby reducing problems of physical accessibility.

Reservoirs can be seen as a direct response to urbanisation during the industrial revolution. The development in 1847 of the Longdendale Valley by Manchester City Council heralded a new type of reservoir closer to urban communities. These developments were permitted by Private Bills which also provided legislation to restrict access. In this way another 250 reservoirs were created towards the second half of the nineteenth century (Tanner, 1993).

The inter-war years saw growing pressures for access to reservoirs for recreation. However, resistance to access was strongly voiced in terms of threats to water quality for water supplies. In 1939 the Ministry of Health issued its advisory memorandum 221 which was interpreted to suggest that there should be no access to reservoirs for recreation due to the risk of contamination. However, the Heneage Committee on Gathering Grounds, a sub-committee of the Central Advisory Water Committee, concluded that there was no reason to restrict public access, providing safety measures were in place. By this time research showed that angling and sailing were creating a significant force for access, not only to the water's edge, but on the water as well. These growing pressures led to a report in 1963 by the Institution of Water Engineers suggesting, cautiously, that fishing was acceptable, sailing and rowing could be allowed where there were management controls, but that canoeing was a cause for concern, and swimming and water skiing, should be excluded (Tanner, 1993).

The Water Resources Act 1962 led to the creation of new lowland reservoirs offering extensive recreation provision. This was followed by the recreation provision requirements for water authorities in the 1973 Water Act. The 1970's and 1980's saw a steady increase in the use of reservoirs for recreation. In 1989 the ownership of reservoirs was changed to private water companies, which caused considerable concerns for the recreation interest. The legislation and effects on water based recreation will be considered in Chapter 6.

Industrial Extraction Sites:
Commonly known as gravel pits, many sites for mineral extraction, once active use is over, have been flooded for recreation use. This has proved effective with the following types of industrial extraction:

Sand and gravel	Silica sand
Slate	Sandstone
Open cast coal	Peat
Clay and shale	Chalk
Deep mined coal	Limestone

Extraction sites offer a number of benefits for recreation use. They are often close to urban populations, bring watersports to communities, and allow planning to produce an ideal solution. Examples of successful water resource use of extraction sites (sand and gravel) include the National Rowing Course at Holme Pierrepont near Nottingham and the Cotswold Water Park, both offering sailing, wind surfing, swimming, water-skiing, jet skiing, motorboat racing, fishing, horse riding, country park and accommodation.   The other great advantage of these sites for watersports is that various lakes will either exist or can be created to cater for, in designated areas, the needs of specific sports or activities.

THE SCOPE FOR WATER RESOURCES IN LEISURE PROVISION

In this chapter we have seen that water resources have a part to play in a variety of leisure pursuits.   This book will be considering the management of water resources, not only for watersports, but as a venue for leisure.   It will consider water resources and their affect on tourism, sport and passive, informal recreation.

In tourism water has formed a central focus for seaside holidays, as illustrated earlier.   The market for tourism has expanded well beyond the simple seaside break, but the importance of water is ever present. Many countryside venues have a water focus, for example, the Norfolk Broads and Lake District, where an essential element in their attraction is the splendour of the water resources.   At times this may simply be as a setting to convey the qualities of peace and tranquillity that are frequently key elements in the holiday atmosphere.   However, a growing market for internal tourism in the UK is that of activity holidays where water often offers the participant the challenge and enjoyment of outdoor activities.   Finally, the importance of cruising holidays should not be neglected, for the unskilled holiday-maker boating holidays make a perfect way to relax and enjoy the countryside.

Watersports participation is on the increase as perceptions of elitism slowly change and new production methods and provision make the sports accessible to all.   However, leisure does not stop at the water's edge and this book will not forget the need of anglers whose sport, although not physically water based, requires care and provision from the leisure industry.

Finally, as with the two previous areas, Chapter 3 will consider the demands of casual passive activities, those that frequently use water resources, as a focus for the leisure activity. The additional pressures and opportunities presented to water resource providers of walking, picnicking, shopping and entertainment should also be included for a full treatment of water resource management for leisure.

CHAPTER 2

Water as a Resource for Leisure

INTRODUCTION

One method used to evaluate the complex role which leisure plays in people's lives is to consider the theoretical outcomes of leisure activities. Several outcomes can be shown as a result of leisure which are beneficial, they have been identified in *Figure 2.1* below.

Figure 2.1   **Outcomes of leisure**

Choice	freedom to do as one wishes
Fun	enjoyment, pleasurable experiences
Challenge	testing skills and abilities
Creativity	release for self expression
Relaxation	unwind and restore strength
Relief of stress	forget pressures and problems
Social interaction	mixing with friends and family
Status	win new status within peer group
Exercise	enjoy physical workout to improve fitness

Water resources can fulfil some of our leisure needs. The sociologist Dumazedier described leisure in terms of:

> *activity - apart from the obligations of work, family and society - to which the individual turns at will for either relaxation, diversification, or broadening his knowledge and his spontaneous social participation, the free exercise of his creative capacity.*

For the purpose of this book leisure will be defined as an activity chosen freely for pleasure and which offers the participant any range or combination of the outcomes suggested in *Figure 2.2* below.

Figure 2.2   **Qualities of water as a focus for leisure**

OUTCOME	DESCRIPTION
Relaxation	Water has many soothing qualities and can help people to relax and unwind. Bathing can physically assist in relaxation.
Relief from Stress	Water Resources are often areas of peace and tranquillity which help us to forget the pressures of society
Exercise	From a walk by the water, to active participation in watersports, water offers a range of opportunities for physical exercise
Social Interaction	Water resources can form a focus for meeting and socialising
Competition	All watersports offer the chance of status achieved through competition
Creativity	Water has often been the subject of our creative instincts, painting, drawing and writing
Fun	From a very young age most children are encouraged to see water as a pleasurable tool for our leisure

WATER AS A RESOURCE FOR LEISURE: a historical perspective

The therapeutic qualities of water have long been acknowledged. Ancient civilisations developed the healing and relaxation benefits of water through baths and spa towns. The British first became interested in the healing qualities of 'taking the waters' towards the end of the seventeenth century when spa towns, such as Bath, became popular visitor centres. The British became attracted to the use of water for boating, pleasure cruises and bathing in the 18th century. At this stage, however, such activities were a preserve of the elite. For the masses water was seen as a means of transport, food and income as they had little time for leisure. The development of water resources for leisure can be categorised into three main areas.

1. Sports and Recreation

The elite developed such pastimes as rowing, yachting, and cruising to complement existing field sports and cultural activities. Watersports were developed competitively during this period and many events such as the Americas Cup, Henley Regatta and Cowes Week can trace their roots to these traditions. Participation in water based leisure was mainly restricted to the wealthy. This has coloured popular perceptions of watersports for generations and even today many watersports are seen to be the preserve of the wealthy. The development of watersports generated a new leisure industry providing trained crews and tailor-made luxury products for the sports.

2. Coastal Holidays

Coastal holiday resorts were established to cater for the wealthy as a response to growing awareness of the therapeutic qualities of the seaside. Health-restoring activities, such as sea water bathing, were first highlighted by Dr Russell in 1753. Brighton was swiftly developed as a fashionable seaside resort. It was seen as health-restoring to bathe and to walk along promenades enjoying a breath of sea air to counter the poor air quality experienced in smog filled cities and towns. This became fashionable in the late 1700s. Although the seaside resort was traditionally the preserve of the well off, it has fared better at changing its image of elitism than many watersports. Indeed the introduction of four public holidays by the Bank Holiday Act [1871] and the development of railway links, such as the London to Brighton line in 1841, popularised seaside breaks. Elitism did not of die off totally and we witnessed the development of new seaside resorts to maintain a distance between the leisure activities of the elite and those of the masses.

3. Day trips and visits to water's edge activities

Water became a focus for leisure for all of society in the form of water's edge activities such as picnics, walks and outings to rivers, lakes and ponds near to the home base. Water resources are still a popular environment for leisure whether on or off the water. Indeed the British Waterways suggest of water:

> *Whether on the towing path by the water... or on the water in a boat ... it creates a special atmosphere*

and that

> *Every year one in six of Britain's population finds peace and quiet or exercise and fun on our waterways*

Water resources, therefore, can be seen to have developed as an essential ingredient of the leisure industry in Britain today. Water can offer its users a range of experiences and challenges. It can fulfil all the outcomes suggested in the definition of leisure and its popularity, as a focus for leisure, can easily be seen in an analysis of leisure behaviour. In many of our key 'honey pot' sites for visitors water plays a vital role. In choices for holidays water is frequently a key element and, in recent years, there has been a growing popularity of watersports themselves.

FACTORS WHICH AFFECT PARTICIPATION IN WATER BASED LEISURE

As the role of leisure management in water based recreation has grown, it has become increasingly important to understand why people take part in the activities and why others are termed non-participant groups. To begin this investigation it is useful to consider some traditional leisure management models and to apply them to water activities. There are three main models:

- classification of factors
- questions of participation
- accessibility

These models can be used to explain questions about participation. They are useful since they:

- attempt to organise facts
- turn theories into a format which can be applied to situations
- facilitate our understanding of complex phenomena

Classification of Factors
This is a way of categorising a complex array of factors into sub-groups or sub-headings. Managers can then address aspects of one particular sub-group or look generally at broader issues, depending upon what they need to achieve. There are two suggested classifications: four traditional factors and George Torkildsen's revised classification. We will consider each in this chapter.

i.   Traditional Factors

1. *Personal Factors:* are mainly useful when considering an individual, however, analysis in generalised terms can lead to stereotyping.

2. *Social Environment Facts:* facts about the area or environment in which we live, e.g. rural or urban, high wealth or high deprivation.

3. *Perception Factors:* how individuals see their leisure opportunities.

4. *Spatial Factors:* proximity to leisure activities.

ii. Torkildsen's Revised Classification

In *Leisure and Recreation Management* George Torkildsen reconstructed these 4 classes into three main factors:

Personal	e.g. age, gender, ability
Social and circumstantial	e.g. income, class
Opportunity	e.g. availability of facilities, instruction

Some of these factors will be matched to participation in water based recreation later in this chapter.

Theoretical Proposition Models
In his book, *Understanding Leisure*, Les Haywood offers a different approach to the question of leisure participation patterns. The four statements or hypotheses will attempt to explain the importance of leisure for individuals. For this section we can consider the application of these hypotheses to water based leisure:

Firstly 'Choice is essential to the meaning of leisure'. Without this choice, the idea of leisure would have no meaning.

Therefore, water must offer a range of activities to be widely accepted as an important leisure resource. The types of activity must attempt to serve a variety of needs and preferences. Earlier in this chapter we have seen that water can be a focus for sport, recreation, play, relaxation, passive and active leisure. We can, therefore, expect water to attract both strong and diverse participation.

Secondly 'Choice is circumscribed by factors such as time, space, money and individual capacities and differ with personal circumstances'.

Therefore, for any one activity or target group we would need to carry out an in-depth study of these factors, what works well for one venue or activity may not apply to others.

Thirdly, 'People's leisure activity is affected by the ways in which society is structured: e.g. social class, gender age and race'.

Therefore, to attract a particular user-group we must identify their needs which can be generalised to some extent across these social structures.

Fourthly, 'People's leisure activity is related to unacknowledged conditions of existence. They are the basis for attitudes, perceptions and values which both facilitate and constrain leisure choice' (Harwood, 1989).

Therefore, to attract high participation rates we must have a strong marketing strategy to increase awareness of both facilities and activities. Since most watersports are not promoted through the school curriculum, then efforts such as the Royal Yatching Association's (RYA) Year of Youth Sailing are necessary to increase awareness of the sport.

Accessibility
This model poses the question 'Is the water based leisure activity available to us?' The conclusions of potential participants will probably be based on the following concepts:

Perception   -   how do people imagine the activity?

Physical accessibility	-	can people easily get to your venue with or with out a car?
	-	how long will it take to get there?
Financial aspects	-	how much will it cost to go in?
	-	how much will it cost to get there?
	-	how much does it cost to get the right equipment?
	-	are there lots of extras in social costs?
Social factors	-	will I meet people that I will get on well with?
	-	are the management welcoming or do they promote exclusivity?

The model of accessibility can be applied to water based leisure, resulting in some important questions for the leisure manager. Why did the seaside holiday become a traditional element of leisure for most of society, whereas traditional watersports remained a pursuit of the elite? Historically, for the mass population of the mid-industrial period of 1870-1900, *accessibility* is the answer. Despite train links facilitating physical accessibility, two main problems faced the ordinary man at this time, social and financial accessibility. The world of rowing and yachting were a reserve of elite clubs and societies with strict control on the background of their members, hence these sports were perceived as socially inaccessible for the ordinary man. If this were not enough to discourage participation, unlike the seaside holiday, watersports required specific specialist equipment. Before the introduction of mass produced items, this expense was beyond the means of the average wage earner.

Therefore, to assess the factors which affect participation in water based leisure, this historical scenario cannot be forgotten, since the ideas and experiences of our forefathers are often represented in modern perceptions of opportunities. To conclude, the water based recreation manager needs to consider the following factors when attempting to understand participation rates in water based activities:

- The way people see your activity (perception)
- A range of social factors which may constrain people's ability to become involved
- The knowledge and awareness of your water based activity
- The location, ease of access and journey time to your facility

These factors can be studied in order to assist the manager in improving participation in their particular water based activity.

HOW DO THESE FACTORS AFFECT PARTICIPATION IN WATER BASED LEISURE?

The first conference on Water Based Recreation, in September 1993 at Southampton Institute, included a workshop session on participation in watersports. The conclusions were as follows:

1. Problems of physical accessibility, including lack of resources and management conflict.
2. Environmental impacts of watersports limit participation.
3. Equality of opportunity.
4. Health and Safety issues.
5. Elite image of the sports.
6. Lack of statistical data about participation to analyse.

In this section points 3 and 5 will be considered in detail. Other points such as environmental issues will be considered in later chapters.

Social Factors
Frequently these factors are outside the control of the individual or the leisure manager, but the manager can identify some factors which may constrain leisure participation and attempt to resolve them. For example, many young mothers find it difficult to take part in leisure away from their children. The watersports manager wishing to attract more women with children could provide a crèche or complementary children's classes. To examine these factors further:

28

a. Gender

Watersports are male dominated, with 60-70 per cent participation by men and only 30-40 per cent of women taking part, on average across a sample of general watersports data available. The watersports manager, therefore, needs to identify the reasons why so few women take part in these activities. A major influence on many women dropping out of sports participation is motherhood. Child care can be difficult to find and expensive; most watersports require considerable time spent in both the activity itself and in preparation. Clearly these factors can make it particularly unattractive for women. The answer, as suggested previously, is for the watersports centre to provide some child care. Unfortunately this is costly and with new legislation under the Children Act 1989 it requires purpose built facilities and trained staff.

Children can only be one reason for mothers in the community not taking part in watersports. Other women may be deterred by the male environment, preferring more feminine activities. A successful method of increasing female participation has been demonstrated by several sailing schools on the South Coast. Having identified that fewer women were attending RYA cruising courses, sailing schools looked for the reasons. It was discovered that many women become frustrated by dominant males on the courses and that the male instructors could be off-putting. The solution, therefore, was to introduce the 'women only' course, providing female instruction to an all woman crew. This proved very successful in cruising. Feedback from courses suggests that women enjoy the less competitive and aggressive approach achieved in this way. The 'all women' approach can be criticised for taking the sport away from the real mixed world, but it has been particularly successful with middle-aged women and has the potential to attract those from ethnic minorities.

b. Age

Images of canoeists paddling down foaming white water rapids and young men on jet skis can portray the image of watersports as an activity for the young and fit. Equally, many young people see pipe-

smoking gentlemen at the helm of slow moving yachts and narrow boats and feel that watersports cannot offer the excitement they are looking for. These examples, however, show that watersports are suitable for everyone and that most individual sports can be practised fast and competitively or in a relaxed, recreational form. The watersports manager needs to ensure that his/her programme caters for a range of tastes and that classes are offered for different age groups. Older people can feel reluctant to join a class of teenagers and the method of delivery will require a different emphasis. Adults may need a well planned and explained introduction with time for questions, youngsters on the other hand may need to get out on the water as soon as possible and to learn by trial and error rather than by classroom techniques.

The opportunity for young people to experience watersports is less than many other curriculum-based activities, but voluntary organisations such as Scouts, Sea Cadets and Sail Training organisations have done much to increase these opportunities. The RYA acknowledged the problem in 1993 by launching a 'Year of Youth Sailing'. Sailing clubs around the country were encouraged to publicise and run courses for young people. Unfortunately, although attendance was high on many of these schemes, the number who continued was fairly low illustrating the problems of maintaining enthusiasm by offering continued opportunity.

c. *Class*

As discussed previously, many watersports developed as activities of the wealthy. All the main governing bodies of sport have worked hard to alter this image with participation campaigns such as 'Get Afloat, Get A Boat' run by the British Marine Industries Federation (BMIF). The sports of yachting and rowing have found the image hardest to alter, possibly because yachting still requires a perceived capital outlay and many older yacht clubs can apear stuffy and uninviting. Rowing is the traditional sport of Universities and Public Schools, events such as Henley Regatta and the University Boat Race have served only to reinforce this privileged image. Other watersports have fared better at achieving cross-class participation, possibly assisted by the availability of many such activities during beach holidays abroad.

d. Ethnic minorities

Watersports are not a traditional recreation for many of the ethnic groups in the UK. Lack of knowledge about the activity could be a major contributor to low participation rates. The development of country parks such as Lee Valley close to urban areas has improved accessibility. Many of these parks have also run publicity and courses directed specifically at informing ethnic groups.

e. Disabled

Twenty years ago opportunities for sport for the disabled were very rare. Watersports were no exception. The last ten years have seen huge advances in many watersports. The work of the Jubilee Trust in building a traditional sail training vessel specifically to take disabled people to sea was unique in its concept. The ship allows people with a range of physical and mental disabilities to take as full a part as possible in the activities of the ship. This includes hoisting and lowering sails, and steering with the help of audio compasses for the sight-impaired crew. The work of the *Lord Nelson* has opened new opportunities for disabled people from all walks of life.

Other sailing initiatives include the RYA Seamanship Foundation, which arranges sailing holidays on volunteer boats during the summer months for blind sailors. They have also developed a sailing trimaran, the *Challenger,* suitable for use by disabled sailors. The Island Trust has, for some years, provided dinghy sailing weeks for children from Exeter School for the Deaf.

What about other sports? The National Water Ski Federation has done much in recent years to promote water-skiing as an activity for physically disabled people. The British Disabled Water Ski Association was formed in 1979 to promote and assist disabled participation in water-skiing. Their work includes special courses and advice on equipment design.

Perception and Image:
Whilst considering some examples of social factors that may affect participation, frequent mention has been made of the mental picture or image that people have of watersports. This is based on information from friends, the media and personal observation. Negative perception and images may prevent people from actually trying the sport. The watersports manager, therefore, needs to work in two ways:

1.   To create a positive image for the sport.

2.   To change existing perceptions of the sport.

Watersports, like many other sports, suffer from poor image and bad press. Some of these negative images are: too old; too young and male dominated. How can the leisure manager overcome these images? See *figure 2.3* below for some examples.

Figure 2.3:   **Methods to overcome negative perceptions of watersports**

Perception	Solution
Britain is too cold for watersports.	Always run novice courses in the summer months. Provide good and suitable equipment to keep novices warm. Do not keep people standing around outside if they are cold and wet, finish the debrief in the warm. Keep people active. Provide a warm dry environment after the activity. Illustrate all these points in your publicity.
The clubs are snobby and unfriendly.	Encourage club open days for members of the public.
Too expensive to get started.	Publicise schemes and courses which provide all of the specialist equipment. Provide a notice board for second hand items.
The activities are too dangerous.	Display clear safety information. Always ensure safety rules are kept. Display safety records to show the low chance of accidents.

Awareness:
People's leisure habits frequently reflect past experiences, activities they have tried at school, in the family or with friends. Unfortunately, for watersports managers, schools can rarely offer watersports as part of the curriculum, so, unless people find out about the activity through friends or family they are unlikely to know much about them. It is, therefore, the responsibility of watersports providers to increase the knowledge and awareness of their particular sport. This can be done:

    a. nationally

    b. regionally

    c. locally

National governing bodies can increase youth participation by working with schools and youth groups to promote the activity. Teachers and youth leaders can be useful targets for information about opportunities for visits and local contacts. The BMIF produce a leaflet describing general opportunities for schools in watersports.

On a local level clubs and centres should visit schools and youth clubs to talk about their activities. They should also contact the local leisure services department, who probably produce a directory of leisure providers and clubs. The local leisure services may also run sports 'taster days' which are a good opportunity to make contacts of all ages in the local community. Finally, all clubs should make sure that their local library has details of the activities available, together with a contact address.

On a regional level, specific sports may run training courses to encourage participation. Regional venues, such as country parks, should ensure that the relevant Tourist Information Centre keep details of the activities available. These are just a few ideas to encourage participation. Increasing awareness, positive publicity and partnerships are the keys to success.

Physical Accessibility:

Water resources cannot move to the people but the watersports manager can improve physical accessibility in a number of ways.

1. *Car parking* - since many people do have access to a car and will arrive by car ensure that the venue has ample parking which must, of course, be well sign-posted and maintained.

2. *Non Car users* - many non participant groups have little or no access to personal transport and rely on public services. Find out how the centre can be reached from a selection of local destinations by public transport and offer these details on all publicity. Make sure that the information is kept up to date. As public transport is not always available, compile a register of members willing to offer lifts.

3. *Sign-posts* - ensure that the entrance is clearly marked and visible from both directions on approach roads. Many water resources remain hidden for local residents due to poor sign-posting. Ideally the sign should be **bold** and offer the following information:

    Name of club/centre

    Activities provided

    Enquiry contact

For an example of sign-posting see *Figure 2.4* on page 35.

Figure 2.4:   **Entrance signs for two sailing centres**

a)   Clear name supported by information about services available, together with contact telephone numbers

b)   Clear name, but no further information to encourage new participation

Financial Accessibility

As purchasing equipment for watersports is dictated by market forces there is little that the watersports provider can do to alter these prices. There are several points that the provider can consider, however, in order to extend financial accessibility to a wider group:

1. Clubs can reduce costs of membership by carrying out some maintenance themselves in 'working parties'. This can also create a sense of belonging.

2. Clubs can offer an introductory subscription to encourage people to try the sport.

3. Clubs can offer discretionary rates for groups with less disposable income, e.g. students and retired members.

4. Centres can offer equipment for hire, including clothing and accessories.

5. Clubs can negotiate bulk discounts for members, either with mail order equipment companies or local suppliers.

6. Provide 'for sale' notice boards for second hand equipment.

7. For sports which require a partner or a number of partners, a notice board or register can be used, e.g. to match non-boat owners with owners needing a crew. Crew registers exist in many sailing clubs around the country.

8. National Governing Bodies for sports could purchase some equipment to be loaned for introductory courses around the country.

TRENDS IN PARTICIPATION IN WATER BASED LEISURE

This chapter has concentrated mainly on management issues connected with participation in watersports. Watersports do, however, only make up a small percentage of total participation in recreation with a water focus. This section will, therefore, construct a picture of current participation in water based recreation, looking firstly at individual areas; watersports, water's edge activities and tourism. A comparison will then be made between these areas.

Participation in Watersports

Recreational boating and watersports are, at present, a minority interest but have a substantial market in the leisure industry with some 3 million people taking part. Despite this fact, it is still difficult to comment in detail on watersports participation since there is still a lack of in-depth analysis of behaviour in the market. The most comprehensive and recent study on the subject was produced in 1989 by Leisure Consultants, *Boating and Watersports in Britain - Market profiles and Prospects*. Other sources of data used in this section include the *General Household survey* and the *Digest of Sports Statistics*. For the purposes of this study regular participation is to be four occasions or more in the year 1988/9.

All data shows sailing as the most popular of watersports with 1.5 million enthusiasts, approximately three and a half per cent of the total British adult population. Total participation in watersports was estimated, in 1988 by Leisure Consultants, as 3 million adults. Little data is available on junior participation, but estimates suggest 200,000-400,000 children under the age of sixteen take part in some watersports activity, mainly as part of a holiday. After sailing, research by Leisure Consultants shows that power boating and canoeing are some of the most important activities with a participation rate of 2.3 and 1.8 per cent respectively. At the lower end of the spectrum, their survey indicates activites such as sub-aqua and jet skiing attracted only 0.2 per cent participation in 1988. The survey's total estimate for watersports participation was that 6.8 per cent of the population in 1988 took part in water based recreation.

Basic quantitative data on participation does little to assist the leisure manager in assessing the needs or demands of the market. For this work more detailed information is required, profile indicators for leisure usually include: age; gender; occupational status and geographical region of residence. Some information is available for 1988 on each of these areas:

Age Composition

As stated earlier little information is available for casual participants under 16 years of age. Data for individual sports membership of affiliated clubs can be the only guide. For example, 25 per cent of members of clubs affiliated to the British Water Ski Federation were under 16 years old. Royal Yachting Association membership data show that yachting and cruising attract an older average age group. However, overall data show that over half of participants are under 25 years and that there is a sharp reduction in the 25 to 34 year age range.

Gender:

Watersports show a very strong male domination of 2:1 over women within the sport as a whole. Sailing data again shows a greater balance across the sexes.

Male	62%
Female	38%

(Source: BRBM survey 1988)

Regional Differences:

British geography should allow for equal opportunity of access to water of some kind in all the areas. Research into the main areas of high watersports participation indicates that there is a concentration in the South East and a low participation in the Midlands. We would expect that coastal recreation would be lower in the central counties of the Midlands, but there is still a wide range of inland resources. The distribution shows some correlation with the percentage of total population living in each area, but the participation as a percentage of the total is 10 per cent higher in the South East and Anglian regions.

(See *figure 2.5* for details). The results of Leisure Consultants' report in 1989 show that people in the South East are least dominant in jet skiing and water skiing; that power boating is particulary popular in Scotland; wind surfing is the most popular water sport in the Midlands; and, finally that canoeing has a higher participation in the North.

Figure 2.5: **Geographic distribution of water sports participation** [% total resident polulation in brackets]

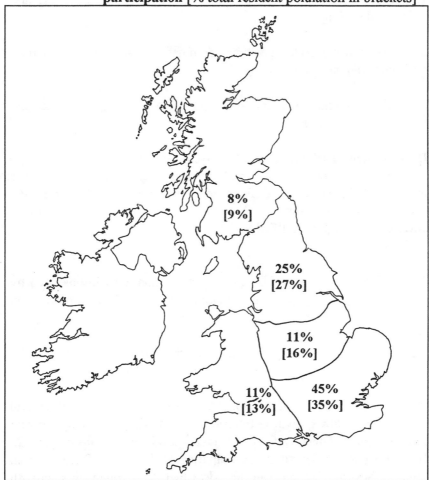

8%
[9%]

25%
[27%]

11%
[16%]

11%
[13%]

45%
[35%]

Source: Data from *BMRB survey* for Leisure Consultants, 1989

Socio-Economic Group:
Watersports participation in general shows a strong bias towards white collar workers which can, in part, be explained by traditional perceptions of the sports and the current reasonably expensive nature of many of the activities. Further study by Leisure Consultants of individual sports highlights:

1. Professional and managerial dominance in jet skiing, sailing and wind surfing.

2. Other white collar positions dominate rowing, power boating, canoeing and water skiing.

3. Skilled manual workers favour sub-aqua, canoeing, board sailing and power boating.

Development of Watersports Participation:
As with data on specific participation rates, lack of detailed information has made it difficult to substantiate any trends in the development of watersports. Nonetheless, some characteristics in its development can be identified.

1960s - Early 1970s -   Boom in participation, possibly assisted by the development of GRP as a production technique for boat building.

Late 1970s onwards -   Slower growth, possibly explained by recession in the early 1980s.

Statistics from the *General Household Survey* for 1980, 1983 and 1986 show a slow growth in traditional sports such as sailing, rowing and canoeing. Other watersports have shown slightly faster growth, from 0.6 per cent of adults participating in 1980 to 1.3 per cent in 1986. Several factors can be identified to explain this growth throughout the 1980's. Firstly, there was a growth in leisure-time throughout the period. Disposable income is an important factor in leisure participation and during the 1980s many people's disposable income increased. The sports attract younger people (15-24 year age group), the 'baby boom' of the 1960s is found in this age group during the eighties. Awareness, through campaigns, of the importance of a healthy lifestyle have promoted many out-door sports. Technological advances have reduced production costs of watersports equipment. Finally, many more holiday destinations, both in the UK and overseas, offer opportunities for casual watersports participation.

A change in any of these factors could cause a reduction in the growth of the market, and figures for the early 1990s are likely to show stagnation or small growth due to economic factors (including the recession). Other factors which can be seen to prevent growth are image, shortage of appropriate moorings and constraints on the use of water created by the range of uses as covered in chapter 5.

THE IMPORTANCE OF WATER AS A FOCUS FOR OTHER COUNTRYSIDE OR OUTDOOR RECREATION

Analysis of casual trips to countryside locations was carried out in 1985 by the Countryside Commission. The data, unfortunately, does not always show whether a trip was made to a water resource or other countryside venue. Despite this problem it is possible to observe that water's edge activities may have a potentially significant audience, as shown in the following table.

Table 2.1: **Participation in Countryside Activities**

Activity	% of trips
Drives, outings and picnics	19
Long walks	18
Sea coast	8
Country parks	4

Source : Countryside Commission 1985

In terms of inland water's edge participation the British Waterways estimate that each year they host 7,280,000 visitors for informal use together with 980,000 anglers. These trends in participation can be explained by the accessibility of waterways for casual use, 26,000,000 people live within 5 miles of one of the waterways administered by the British Waterways. The Broads Authority estimate that they receive one million visitors annually.

CHAPTER 3

Water based leisure activities: an introduction

The scope for water centred leisure activities can be divided into two distinct areas both sharing common interests in tourism activities; watersports and water's edge activities. This chapter will analyse these activities, considering the history, structure, provision for, and needs of each activity and will conclude with a summary of these demands and the implications for leisure management.

DEMANDS CREATED BY WATERSPORTS

As demonstrated in the previous chapter, participation in most watersports has seen a steady increase over the last decade. Most watersports' needs could be summarised simply by the availability of a water resource. However, a statement of this type would only serve to over simplify a complex and differing range of demands. In this section all major watersports will be analysed individually including dinghy sailing, wind surfing, surfing, canoeing, water skiing, sub-aqua, rowing, yachting and power boating. Two smaller areas will also be mentioned, jet skiing and dragon boat racing. Trends show there has been an increase in popularity and participation in both of these activities.

Dinghy Sailing:
Because dinghy sailing is comparatively inexpensive it is often the recreational sailor's first experience of sailing. Second-hand boats can

be purchased for as little as £100 - £200. Dinghy sailing is also more accessible to people based away from coastal areas. Inland clubs are found on mineral extraction sites, lakes, reservoirs and rivers throughout the country. Dinghy sailing can either take the form of cruising or club racing. Many recreational sailors choose to sail in 'class' boats which are produced to a standard specification and can, therefore, race against each other on equal terms. For many inland water sailors racing offers a focus and a test of skills, as small lakes offer little scope for interesting cruising. Approximately 60,000 dinghies and keelboats race regularly in the UK according to *The Digest of Sports Statistics*.

Many of these inland recreational sailors sail at recognised clubs affiliated to the governing body, the Royal Yachting Association. The RYA's responsibility is to promote the sport and maintain standards as follows:

1. Provide a structured training scheme.
2. Assess and approve instructors to teach the courses.
3. Assess and approve sailing schools to teach the sport.
4. Run an affiliation scheme for clubs.

Any centre wishing to provide dinghy sailing courses should apply to the RYA for registration and employ qualified instructors. The RYA approved centre provides a structured teaching approach in a safe and well equipped environment. The training scheme for dinghy sailing is structured in five levels or stages, from starting sailing to advanced skills thereby offering progression for new participants. Sailing in general is more popular in the south of England and least popular in the Midlands and the North. Dinghy sailing is more successful in these areas than yachting and power boating as reflected in the 24 approved sailing clubs and centres in the West Midlands alone (RYA Affiliated Clubs).

In addition to a management structure, provided effectively by the existing governing body, dinghy sailing needs access to water resources. In coastal areas clubs have developed providing members with all-weather launching slips, storage parks for dinghies, changing and shower facilities, safety or rescue boats, and social areas as a focal point. Increasingly prime frontage is becoming expensive even in coastal areas for new clubs wishing to be established. For inland dinghy sailing the physical requirements are the same though there are other considerations. Many inland water areas are shared by a number of activities. Sailing and wind surfing are compatible, whereas power boating and motorised sport are not and time zoning is, therefore, required.

Wind surfing:
This is a comparatively new watersport its popularity as a world-wide water activity has developed since its acceptance as an Olympic event in 1980, (part of the seven event yachting schedule). Originating in California, the first board was marketed in the States during 1969 by Hoyle Schweitzer. By 1979 his company, Windsurfer International Incorporated, was selling 700 boards per week. The sport was introduced to the European market in Holland during 1973. It is estimated that there are now several thousand wind surfers in the UK.

Wind surfing was conceived for US coastal areas to combine the simplicity of surf boards with the additional power source used by sailors, the wind. Wind surfing, therefore, combines the skills of balance required in surfing together with wind awareness and general sailing ability needed for sailing. For many participants the attraction of the sport may be the sun-bronzed image, for others the accessibility of the design. The equipment consists of four simple, low maintenance components as shown in the diagram in *Figure 3.1* on page 46. The entire equipment is fairly light and is easily transported on a car roof rack.

Wind surfing in Britain is represented by the Royal Yachting Association which approves 200 centres both in the UK and, more increasingly, in popular sunshine locations such as the Sunsail centres in Turkey and Greece. Their approach to maintaining standards is very similar to that of dinghy sailing and many centres offer both sports. Training can be followed in a 5 level or stage scheme taught at RYA approved centres by trained instructors. One of the problems in encouraging wind surfing participation in Britain is, unfortunately, the weather; beginners tend to fall into the water frequently. A technique to reduce initial teaching in the water, thereby avoiding the cold and enabling pupils to concentrate, is to use a simulator where basic techniques are demonstrated and attempted on dry land.

Figure 3.1:   **Basic Parts of a Windsurfer**

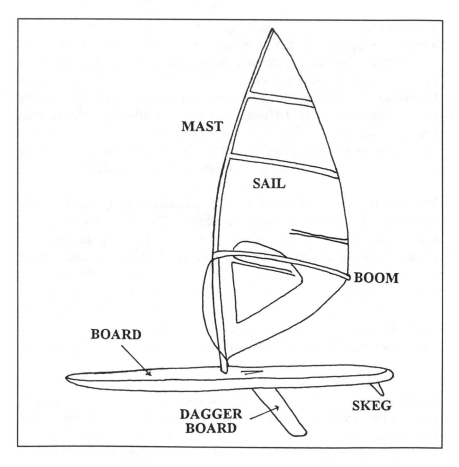

Wind surfing centres, as with sailing centres, cannot combine motor boat sports. In terms of equipment required the sailing model will cover most requirements. The centre wishing to include board sailing will need to provide racks to store the boards off the ground in order to limit accidental damage. Many wind surfers do not need to use specific centres and more confident sailors will look to launch from beaches. The only problem arising from beach launching is congestion on summer days. To overcome this a launching zone (apart from bathers) could be provided.

Offshore Yachting:
Although some small yachts are sailed and raced on Britian's larger inland waters, such as Lake Windermere in Cumbria and Loch Lomond in Scotland, yachting, for the majority, is a coastal sport. Unlike wind surfing, yachting is a sport steeped in tradition and history. Developed as a pastime of the wealthy, yachting still carries the reputation of being an elitist sport. Participation surveys indicate that most participants, (40-70 per cent) hold skilled manual, administrative and managerial positions (Martin, Mason and Smith, 1989). Yachting is an expensive sport, despite the introduction of some smaller trailable yachts, e.g. the MacGregor 26, which offers a new yacht for under £12,000. The advantage of this option is that marina or mooring fees can be avoided when the boat is not in use.

Yachting combines the areas of sail boats and motor craft and is most popular as a cruising or recreational sport. The introduction of several class racing designs, capable of combining cruising and racing such as the Sigma range, has developed class racing in several clubs. It is no longer necessary to own a yacht to enjoy sailing. The Yacht Charter Association has a membership of companies who hire out boats for a day, week-ends or weeks. This, combined with flotilla holidays in the Mediterranean, has opened opportunities for recreational yachting to a wider market. Aspects of chartering and flotilla holidays will be considered in the tourism section of this chapter.

Before commercial enterprises opened up the market, many voluntary clubs were created to offer sailing experiences to non boat owners. The most famous of these is the Little Ship Club where boat owning members take other members onto their boats. Interest in sailing matters are encouraged by meetings and talks. Despite the large number of yacht clubs many more recreational sailors do not join clubs but sail with other yachts from local marinas or boatyards. Another non-site specific club is the Cruising Association which, among other activities, helps to match crews with boats. The Cruising Association has its Headquarters, newly developed for 1994, in the London Docklands area, making it easily accessible to members who live and work away from their sailing venue.

Yachting is concentrated in the south of England with over 50 per cent of moorings and marinas being located in this area. A recent survey put the number of marinas at 159 nation-wide, 70 per cent of which have been constructed since 1970. Marinas offer the yachtsman high density mooring, convenience and facilities, but at a high price. Dramatic price rises in the late 1980s led to concern that marinas, rather than increasing yachting opportunities, have increased the financial constraints.

Despite this criticism, marinas provide an ideal location for many of the sailing schools and centres in the UK. As with previous sports, yachting is governed by the Royal Yachting Association which run specific training schemes for both motor boats and sailing yachts. The newcomer can be introduced to sailing on a safely equipped yacht with a highly qualified skipper/instructor at any one of the approved schools around the British coast. The scheme offers progression through both practical and shore-based courses to the Ocean Yacht Master standard. Regulations controlling instructor qualifications changed in 1994.

Rowing:
The year 1829 witnessed the first boat race at Henley between Oxford and Cambridge. This type of competitive rowing is what most people think of when they picture rowing. It is important to remember that recreational rowing became very popular, as early as 1857 when

several river guides were published to promote the activity. Rowing, however, like yachting, has an early and elitist background, illustrated by Sydney Crossley in 1899 when he described rowing as *the most aristocratic and scientific of sports*. Competitive rowing is still seen by many as a sport of public schools and traditional universities.

The reduction in the number of school-based clubs in the last decade has been used to help explain a slow-down in growth of participation in recent years. This, however, has not detracted from performance. The 1992 Olympics saw rowing, once again, come to the forefront of British sport when their rowing team won five gold medals. The success continued into 1993 when Britain took home eleven world gold medals helping the Amateur Rowing Association to make the claim: *Britain's Most Successful Sport!*

Rowing can be considered in terms of:

Competitive events	- a range of races for individuals, pairs or teams of both men and women usually held on flat water river courses.
Traditional boats	- old working boats and skiffs rowed both recreationally and competitively, for example the Cornish Gig races.
Recreational rowing	- rowing is a good way to get fit, relax and enjoy the countryside.
Touring	- using both traditional and modern boats to explore Britain's rivers.

Rowing is represented by the Amateur Rowing Association which registers both individuals and clubs, there are over 200 'open' clubs in England although research illustrates an imbalance in accessibility, with London and the south east dominating participation with 45 per cent of total participation in the sport in this one area. The ARA trains coaches who run a range of proficiency courses at centres throughout the UK. Many rowing centres have now been developed on a 'pay as you play' basis thereby encouraging new participants. Examples of these centres are the Women's Rowing Centre and the London Docklands Rowing Centre.

Rowing centres need water's edge accommodation with a paved area (to avoid mud in winter) for launching and retrieving boats and also boat storage, together with changing and socialising areas.

Figure 3.2   **Traditional Boat Houses on the River Thames**

Note the gently sloping front and the high ground floor to allow easy storage of boats

For safety and training a support boat is often used. However, a walk along the River Thames in the early morning will illustrate the continued use of the bicycle and megaphone as training tools. In addition to the regional centres, the Sports Council has successfully developed a rowing competition course on a disused gravel pit at their National Watersports Centre, Holme Pierrepont in Nottinghamshire.

Water skiing:
It was in 1922 on Lake Pepin, Lake City, Minnesota, USA that the first water skier, 18 year old Ralph Samuelson, combined snow skis with water. Having first experimented with being towed on wider boards around the lake, Ralph, unsuccessfully, tried a seven foot pair of snow skis. This lead him to shape two pine boards, eight foot by nine inches, with attached made-up bindings and enjoy the world's first ever water ski ride. He developed, at the same time, the start position still taught today. Water skiing arrived in Britain after the second world war and has rapidly grown in popularity. In their report Martin, Mason and Smith (1989) estimated that there were 400,000 reasonably active water-skiers in the UK.

Since 1992 water skiing has developed as both a competitive sport and recreational pastime. For competition there are three main disciplines:

Tournament	-	slalom, ski jumping, trick skiing
Barefoot	-	slalom, trick skiing and bare foot jumping
Ski-racing	-	circuit and point to point racing

These basic disciplines have recently been developed to include *knee boarding* where the competitor kneels on a small board, and *cable skiing* which may prove particularly useful where water space is limited.

The national governing body for water skiing is the British Water Ski Federation, founded in 1951. The BWSF seeks to encourage new participants, promote the sport and to retain and preserve water ski sites. Water skiing appears to have been one of the hardest hit water sports with regard to the provision of space. The sport requires a rectangular area in excess of 10 acres of flat, sheltered and reasonably deep water. Competitive skiing requires ramps and slalom courses to be created and maintained at centres (see *Figure 3.3* below). Due to noise and the incompatibility with other water sports, for example, sailing, many local authorities restrict water skiing, thereby causing a shortage in availability of sites. This has resulted in a high level of latent demand, highlighted by the fact that 25-30 per cent of clubs have a waiting list (*Digest of Sports Statistics*).

Figure 3.3: **A water ski centre**

Despite this shortage, the BWSF has been successful in its promotion of the sport, with the number of affiliated clubs increasing from 10 in 1950 to 170 in 1990. The sport appears to attract younger people with a recent survey showing 50 per cent of participants in London and the south east aged between 20 and 30 (Elson 1989). In 1960 an amputee, Tony Edge, made his first attempt at water skiing. He went on to found the British Disabled Water Ski Association in 1979 which has established six regional centres to teach water skiing to the disabled.

Sports Boating:
Sports boating has increased rapidly over the last decade, assisted by advances in equipment and the wide range of craft available. Sport boats are usually of open and light construction and are easily towed by a family car. Sports boats are fast and sleek, thereby attracting younger people.

There are three main types of sports boats:

Personal water craft	-	Jet skis and wet bikes
Inflatable sports craft	-	rigid or normal
Rigid sports boats	-	12-24ft in length, powered by inboard or outboard motors

The sport is represented by the Royal Yachting Association, which has set up a sports boat training course to educate newcomers in good practice and the potential dangers of a high speed craft. Many sports boat users prefer to launch with the freedom of the sea, although some inland waters are open to them. Due to the potential danger to other water users, together with the noise and wash created, many harbours and inland waters impose speed restrictions on these craft.

Canoeing:
The roots of canoeing can be traced back to the essential use of canoes for hunting and trapping by North American Indians. The sport in

Britain can be traced to the foundation of the Canoe Club in 1866, however, its popularity developed during the mid 20th century with membership of affiliated clubs growing from 1,200 in 1950 to 13,677 in 1987.

Canoeing has developed into a wide range of related disciplines:

Spring racing	- an inland flat water race for singles (K1), pairs (K2) and fours (K4), first introduced in 1867
Canoe sailing	- the canoe-style hull fitted out for sailing
Slalom	- a race between hanging poles over rapid water
White water racing	- racing straight down wild water courses
Marathon racing	- a race of stamina over a long flat course, e.g., the annual Devizes race
Canoe polo	- often played in indoor swimming pools in the small *bat* canoe
Canoe surfing	- coastal canoeing, riding waves as they reach the shore
Canoe orienteering	- a water based version of the established sport particularly suited to gravel workings.
Touring & expeditioning	- any thing from a day trip to a major voyage, such as the one undertaken by John Ridgeway around Cape Horn.

From this extensive list it is possible to conclude that canoeing offers something for everyone. The equipment has become less expensive, opening the potential market to a wide range of people. Many youth groups and clubs find it possible to provide canoeing as an activity for their members and canoeing has become a popular ingredient of the outdoor activity holiday. Canoeing can utilise a wide range of water resources including swimming pools, the sea, canals and rivers, thereby making it an easily accessible water sport.

The sport is environmentally friendly but, due to increased pressures on limited resources, some conflict has developed between anglers and canoeists. This will be discussed in detail in the next chapter. Canoeing takes place from many activity centres and initial courses are run at local swimming pools. The provider needs to consider storage (if necessary, transport for the canoes) and a suitable launching site, (preferably with a firm bank or pontoon enabling safe transfer from the edge to the canoe). The British Canoe Union, formed in 1936, is the national governing body for the sport and provides a structured training scheme. All employed canoe instructors should hold the BCU certificate.

The sport enjoys a few specialist facilities for international events - the National White Water Canoeing Centre at Bala and an artificial slalom course at Holme Pierrepont in Nottinghamshire. Problems facing canoeing can be mainly summarised as those of access, particularly to white water in rivers that are usually privately owned.

Surfing:
This sport has enjoyed growing popularity since it was first introduced into Britain in the 1950's. The sport involves riding waves, on a board, as they reach the shore and consists of three main disciplines:

Knee boarding
Body boarding
Long boarding

In 1990 the national governing body, the British Surfing Association, estimated that there were 10,000 regular participants, although, given the free nature of the sport, surfing participation is difficult to estimate. Surfing tends to attract participants who do not wish to join clubs or societies but who prefer to enjoy the sport for the freedom and independence it offers.

Surfing requires a suitable beach with a long gradual slope, facing open sea and offering a rhythmic swell of moving water. These locations can be unreliable in Britain but the best areas are found on the north coast of Cornwall and Devon, South Wales and north east England. Surfing requires little management, except for possible zoning on crowded beaches.

Dragon Boat Racing:
This is probably the newest water sport to be introduced into Britain, originating in China over 2,000 years ago. Dragon boats are 40 feet long and carry a crew of 22 people, 20 to paddle, one to steer and one to beat on a large drum to keep the paddlers in rhythm. The first competition was during 1976 in Hong Kong and has now spread to nearly 30 countries. In Britain the Dragon Boat Racing Association was founded in 1987 and has grown from one event with 440 competitors to 50 events with 8,000 competitors in 1990.

Dragon Boat Racing requires no previous skills and both able-bodied and disabled people can compete on equal terms. Currently the sport is dominated by males in the 20-40 age range. In terms of provision, Dragon Boats race on a 500 metre course which can be in two sections of 250 metres. The sport is popular with spectators and has been successfully developed in inner-city dockland areas, such as the Albert Dock in Liverpool and Millwall Docks in London.

Sub Aqua:
Humans have explored the surface of the water for many years and in a wide variety of crafts, as illustrated so far in this chapter. It would, therefore, seem only natural that, over time, we would seek further adventure and new areas of exploration. Sub Aqua has allowed us to explore the sea-bed and a whole new fascinating world. This world was brought to public attention by the television programmes of Jacques Cousteau, who not only brought this exciting new area of discovery into our homes, but in the 1950s developed the compressed

air regulator system and opened up a new water sport.

The sport has grown in popularity from about 50,000 in 1984 to between 60,000 and 70,000 in 1990, 75 per cent of which are males aged between 20 and 40 years. The sport has been governed since 1953 by the British Sub Aqua Club which has, attempted to improve the accessibility of the sport by recommending the creation of common regional stores. To provide a sub aqua centre the manager needs to invest in a range of expensive equipment, including an air compressor and a boat with outboard motor. Initial courses are run in indoor, heated swimming pools. The BSAC has central equipment to help new clubs to get established and there are some regional centres, such as Fort Bovisand in Plymouth.

Sub Aqua requires access to suitable inland and coastal waters, plus the use of swimming pools for training. In Britain problems have been encountered with conflicts between divers and fishermen and tourists. This will be discussed in the next chapter.

The Scope of Demand for Water Sports

This chapter has outlined a wide range of watersports, their management structure and requirements. Students interested in any particular sport should follow up the references at the end of this book to obtain more in-depth information. The main demands of the sports can be summarised as follows:

Specialist Equipment

Clubs and Centre for focus, competitions and instruction

Access to suitable water.

The individual sports are represented by their governing bodies as described in this section. Overall representation for sport in England is made by the Sports Council. The Sports Council is a quasi-autonomous government organisation, (QUANGO), created by Royal Charter in 1972. The aims of the Sports Council are for all sports, but their research and campaigns have contributed greatly to watersports over the last decades. The aims are fourfold :

- To increase participation in sport
- To increase the quantity and quality of sports facilties
- To raise standards of performance
- To provide information for and about sport

The Sports Council have a National Watersports Centre at Holme Pierrepont in Nottinghamshire. This centre will be discussed in Chapter 8.

A second central body representing sport is the Central Council of Physical Recreation. This is an independant body whose members include national governing bodies and other interest groups. The CCPR considers its role to be *The Voice of British Sport*. Members of the CCPR are divided into sub groups according to their specific interest area. The division of interest in this book is the Water Recreation Division. The members of this division are shown in *Figure 3.4* below.

Figure 3.4   CCPR Water Recreation Division Members

Amateur Rowing Association
British Association for Shooting and Conservation
British Canoe Union
British Dragon Boat Racing Association
British Long Distance Swimming Association
British Sub-Aqua Club
British Surfing Association
British Water Ski Federation
Hover Club of Great Britain
Model Power Boat Association
Model Yachting Association

National Federation of Anglers
National Federation of Sea Anglers
National Rescue Training Council
Ocean Youth Club
Royal Life Saving Society
Royal Yachting Association
Salmon and Trout Association
Standing Conference of Consultatives (Fisheries)
Surf Life Saving Association

DEMANDS CREATED BY WATER'S EDGE AND RECREATIONAL WATER BASED ACTIVITIES

The previous section has considered a range of activities on the water where there is an established competitive structure. The next section will consider a range of water's edge activities, both sporting and recreational, for example, picnicking, walking and angling and some, non sporting, recreational water based activities such as boat trips and punting. The activities to be discussed are shown in *Figure 3.5* below:

Figure 3.5   **Water's edge and recreational water activities**

WATER'S EDGE	RECREATIONAL WATER BASED
Picnics	Boat Trips
Walking	Entertainment Boats
Painting	Punting
Spectating	Narrow Boats
Beach holidays/visits	Casual Boat Hire
Angling	Holiday Cruisers

Many of the activities listed in this figure would show significantly higher participation rates than watersports. Unfortunately little information is available as to the true levels of participation and most ideas can only be based on observation.

WATER'S EDGE ACTIVITIES

As shown, in *Figure 3.5* on page 59, there are a range of popular activities which do not necessitate entry onto or into the water but are an attraction to the water's edge. Because these attractions bring extra income to the venues and create initial interest in watersports, leading to possible future participation, it is essential that leisure managers, responsible for water resources, are aware of the scale, needs and management implications of these users.

Picnicking:
A family wanting a day out, including a picnic, is often attracted to the open space of a countryside location. Many day trippers choose their open space with a water focus, both for interest and for its peaceful qualities. These locations include canal banks, country parks, river banks and lakes. The participants often arrive by car and, therefore, put extra demands on parking spaces usually taken by watersports participants. If sufficient car parking is not provided, then approach roads can become blocked for trailers and wider vehicles.

As most of these visitors will be inexperienced in water recreation, it is essential that clear notices are displayed, explaining the dangers of drowning, and life saving equipment should be readily available. Areas where boats are launched or busy locks need to have restricted visitor access to prevent conflict and accidents. Picnics create two problems, rubbish and noise. The first problem can be helped by the careful positioning of litter baskets and notices requesting that all rubbish should be disposed of carefully. The second is less easy to control and careful planning is required to prevent conflict with other users. Interests of all visitors must be valued and require careful management.

Walking:
Walking has continued to be the most popular sport for people in Britain with 19 per cent of the population in 1986 taking part regularly (*People in Sport*, Sports Council). The waterways not only offer a rich and varied cruising ground, but the tow paths provide extensive

walking, including several long distance trails. These paths are very popular with older walkers as they often cross flat and level ground. The British Waterways own the greatest system of long distance footpaths in Great Britain offering 1,500 miles of walking.

The Countryside Commission is also developing the Thames Path which, once completed, will allow the walker to cover 175 miles from the Thames Barrier to its source. To increase and maintain interest in this activity, managers should not ignore the maintenance of footpaths, sign posts, stiles and gates.

Spectating:
Major regattas and competitions attract thousands of visitors every year. Event organisers, from major events such as Henley Regatta, to the local sailing club open meeting, should ensure that the spectators can be safely and comfortably catered for. Provision will need to be made for car parking, together with competitors' enclosures to allow for their preparation. The spectators present a potential source of income, if catering can be provided. Any event attracting spectators should attempt to attract new participants by making further information available.

Not all spectators attend specific events, but enjoy watching the activity at locks, harbours and other water venues. A manager will need to ensure the safety of these people and may wish to provide seats, toilets and refreshments to satisfy their needs.

Painting:
Water landscapes have always formed an important part of British art. Another user, therefore, of water resources will be the artist and photographer. Their needs differ little from the needs of other water's edge users.

Angling:
Recreational fishing or angling could fit into any one of the previous

sections. It is indeed a sport, but not exactly a water sport, although some angling is done out at sea and from boats, so the subject can be considered under a range of headings. Recreational angling is distinguished from commercial activities by three factors - the personal angler, the sporting element and the use of a hook and line.

Angling can be classified under three main headings :

Coarse fishing - fresh water fish
Game fishing - salmon, sea trout, brown/rainbow trout fishing
Sea fishing - inshore, from jetties and piers or deep sea

Most angling is a water's edge activity. It was the 15th most popular sport in Britain according to the results of the General Household Survey 1987. The National Angling Survey 1979 suggested that 3.4 million people had been angling that year. The majority of participants are male and, unlike other watersports, angling attracts participants across a wide socio-economic group. In Britain 60 per cent of anglers take part in coarse fishing. It is easier to obtain these figures as club membership is reasonably high. The reason for club membership is often to obtain access to local water.

Coarse fishing is governed by the National Federation of Anglers, which is the second largest governing body of sport, with 431 affiliated organisations. Coarse fishing takes place on slower reaches of rivers, lakes and ponds. Improved water quality in the River Thames has greatly assisted access for this sport. Anglers conflict with other water and water's edge users, and this will be outlined in the following chapter. There are also environmental concerns of over-fishing and the damage caused to wild life, particularly to birds, by discarded equipment.

Bathing from Beaches:
Every year thousands of people head to the coast for either a day visit or for a longer holiday. Many of these swim in the sea, relax or play on the beach. These visitors are of crucial importance to the seaside

resorts for the short holiday season. Their needs are simple but require management to balance their demands with those of other users.

Generally, the casual beach user requires car parking facilities, toilets and refreshments. Access to the beach needs to be provided with minimum costs in terms of cliff erosion. Notices or flags should be displayed indicating whether it is safe to swim and to mark areas regularly cut off by the tide.

WATER BASED RECREATIONAL ACTIVITIES:

Details in *Figure 3.5* on page 59 also indicate that there are some water based activities which are not true sports but are still important to the leisure manager as they attract participants otherwise not interested in water based leisure.

Boat Trips:
The highlight of many days out and holidays is a boat trip. The duration of such tours is for anything from an hour to whole days, attracting sightseers and other participants merely seeking an enjoyable cruise. The boats are usually set up as sightseeing tours, using the advantage of water transport which affords an uninterrupted view of buildings and countryside. A popular venue for such cruises is the River Thames between Henley and Runnymede, allowing tourists to enjoy the sights of Windsor Castle, Eton and stately homes, such as Cliveden. Other popular areas include major harbours. Poole, Portsmouth and Plymouth harbours all offer such a service. Fishing trips are also provided for the amateur angler from many seaside resorts, such as Lyme Regis. Participants require vessels to be safe and need easy landing stages to embark and disembark.

Figure 3.6   **Pleasure Cruisers**

These boats need a good level ramp to increase physical accessibility,
clear notices to show cruises on offer and the time of the next cruise

Entertainment Boats:
On a similar theme to boat trips, many boats are now fitted out for entertainment. River boat companies in particular run disco and party trips in the evenings along many stretches of river. These trips are particularly popular around Maidenhead and Windsor. The implications for managers must be to consider safety, particularly the risk of passengers drinking alcohol and accidentally falling overboard. Accidents, such as the one on the River Thames in 1989 involving the *Marchioness,* have further raised questions on the professional conduct and safety of such cruisers.

Despite these concerns, pleasure boats are an important source of income and employment. The British Waterways licence 120 day trip and restaurant boats on their water alone.

Punting:
Punts are the traditional Thames craft used for leisure purposes since the late 19th century. Punting is also closely associated with Oxford and Cambridge Universities. It is in these cities that punting mainly survives today, serving the needs of old students and visitors wishing to sample traditional life while exploring the quiet backwaters. During the summer months, hire companies do good business along the banks, using temporary pontoons to access the punts. Although a pleasure craft for the majority, the Thames Punting Club also organises races.

Narrow Boats:
Traditional narrow boats have become increasingly popular for holiday homes and for cruising on the improved canals and waterways system. Many people have purchased narrow boats and restored them as homes and cruisers, learning and revitalising traditional crafts. More people are satisfied to charter a traditional narrow boat for a short break or longer holiday. There are companies who specialise in traditional boats and many existing river cruiser companies have added narrow boats to their fleets. The Inland Waterways Association promote and organise events and working parties on the inland network.

Casual Day Boat Hire:

Many 'honey pot' inland sites and coastal harbours offer both powered and rowing craft hire. The hire period is often as little as one hour and people are attracted to the idea of seeing a different view of the locality. Windsor and Oxford have large numbers of these hire boats during the summer months. The leisure manager, responsible for introducing this type of enterprise, should be concerned with the amount of safety equipment that should be provided.

Holiday Cruisers:

Including narrow boats, the British Waterways estimate that 1,206 self drive boats are licenced on their waterways. These modern cruisers are particularly popular for river cruising and for use on the Norfolk Broads, where their width does not restrict access. These boats offer comfortable accommodation in a shorter length, thereby reducing overnight mooring fees.

IMPLICATIONS FOR TOURISM

The growth in popularity of both watersports and water based leisure has led to an increased potential for tourism and the development of new markets. This section will cover some points for tourism arising from the activities described above.

Activity Holidays:

Outdoor pursuits or activity holidays have provided a growth market for tourism during the last decade The activity holiday market offers a range of challenges for young and elderly alike. Water based activity holidays are provided by watersports centres, such as Plas Menai in Wales, for all ages.

Training Courses:

Most of the watersports centres, described in the first section, run training courses, as approved by their specific governing body. These courses can often be completed within a week's continual course or in regular day sessions. Water sport centres should be aware of the potential holiday market for running week-long courses on a residential or non residential basis.

Seaside Holidays:
Water is the natural focus for seaside holidays, but leisure managers in British coastal holiday sites are increasingly aware of the challenge of overseas resorts who can guarantee good weather. Ventures, such as Center Parcs, should be considered as they can provide an enjoyable, water focused holiday whatever the weather.

Waterways Cruising:
Whether on narrow boats or modern cruisers, waterway holidays have suffered some decline due to competition with other warmer locations. Hoseasons now offer French and other destination cruising holidays. One response to this could be to promote British waterway holidays more effectively in foreign markets.

Yacht Chartering:
The Yacht Charter Association has members throughout the UK offering good quality yachts for skippered and bare boat (self drive) holidays. However, yacht chartering in British waters has suffered recently from poor summers and potential clients often choose flotilla holidays abroad with guaranteed sunshine.

Overseas Holidays:
A growth market for most watersports, British companies such as Sunsail now offer wind surfing, yachting and dinghy sailing from sites around the world.

To conclude, water presents a focus for many leisure activities and tourist opportunities. This chapter has summarised the demands made by these activities. The following chapter, will consider other water users and evaluate conflicts between user-groups, together with environmental concerns.

CHAPTER 4

Managing a Range of Demands on Water Resources

The recreational activities described in the previous chapter are not the only demands on water resources. Water has been a traditional source of transport and food since primitive civilisations, not forgetting that water itself is essential to life. In this chapter examples of other water users and demands will be investigated, identifying and analysing potential conflict between these users and leisure users and, finally, the conflict that exists between various leisure users as noted in the previous chapter.

OTHER USERS OF WATER RESOURCES

Water is essential to healthy life and the British economy. Over the last decade billions of pounds have been raised through the extraction of North Sea Oil, thereby supporting other important marine industries.

Fisheries industry:
During 1991, the value of fish landed in Scotland from UK vessels was approximately £246 million, making it a substantial contribution to British economic activity. Fish farming is another important industry and salmon farms in Scotland alone produced £150 million income in 1991 (McIntyre, 1994). Fishing has been a traditional British industry creating a superb range of small, sheltered harbours around our coastline.

Unfortunately, two main problems have beset the industry in recent years, causing a decline in many harbours. Firstly, surveys have shown that fish stocks, in British waters, are dwindling. The once seemingly inexhaustible supply of fish is now threatened. This threat has led to controls and restrictions on the amount and type of fish that can be landed. Further to this, government legislation now restricts the number of days that fishing vessels can go out to sea. These pressures have forced many fishermen out of business. Secondly, concerns about pollution and water quality have lead to fears about the safety of fish, both farmed and landed. For example, the *Braer* oil tanker disaster off the Shetlands in 1993 caused massive damage to the surrounding fish farms, both in terms of actual pollution and in creating concerns about the quality of the fish.

The British fisheries industry has suffered from many problems over the last decade and, as a result, there has been a reduction in the number of fishing fleets. The additional pressures of recreational water users and, in particular, their mooring areas have put further pressures on an already-troubled industry. It can only be hoped that this traditional livelihood survives today's pressures and continues to offer colour and character to the many fishing villages around the British coast. See *Figure 4.1* on page 70.

Marine Commercial traffic:

In terms of shipping movements, the seas and oceans surrounding Britain are still some of the busiest in the world. The business of cargo transportation by sea still proves to be the most cost-effective method of transporting many bulk products and raw materials. British ports, such as Southampton, have declined, in terms of size and number of ships, partly due to a decline in the demands for this form of transport and partly to the increased size, capacity and speed of modern ships. As a result, the dock areas in these traditional ports have been scaled down and are now used frequently for infill sites, industrial building, shopping malls, housing and marinas.

Figure 4.1   **Traditional Fishing Harbour**

Despite this scaling-down, our shipping lanes remain busy and ports, such as Southampton, still enjoy regular shipping movement in their crowded waters. In 1990 the Port of Southampton saw just over 25 million tonnes of cargo landed (*World Shipping Statistics* 1990). The Dover Strait, a narrow stretch of water between England and France serves a wide variety of transport needs, as shown in *Figure 4.2* below. It is possible to see, from the pie chart, that the dominant users are the cargo ships, accounting for over three-quarters of the total number.

Figure 4.2   **Types of users of the Dover Straits**

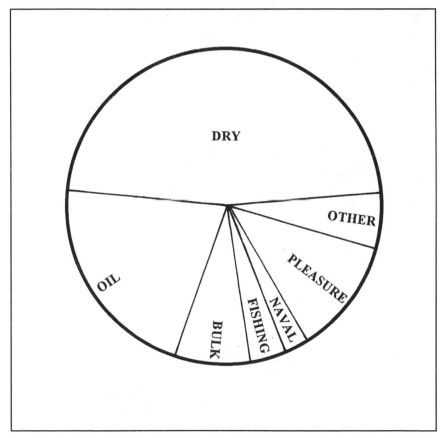

Source: HM Coastguard CNIS Dover

The management problem for such a narrow stretch of water is not only what the ship's purpose is but also its size, (which affects mobility), its speed and direction. The seas have always been regarded as a place of freedom, but in narrow and busy areas it is necessary to implement a separation scheme rather like motorways (see *Figure 4.3* below). The scheme organises shipping, travelling up and down the channel, into two lanes, eastbound and westbound. Not all shipping, however, travels east/west; ferries from Dover to Calais and Boulogne travel north/south. When crossing east/west lanes the ship or pleasure yacht must do so as quickly as possible, at right angles to the lane, and give-way to ships using the east/west channel. These schemes are monitored on radar and have done much to reduce the number of accidents or collisions, the last being in 1979.

Figure 4.3   **Traffic Separation Scheme - Straits of Dover**

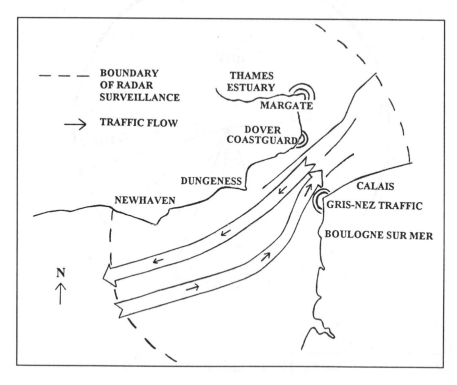

Inland freight traffic:
The use of the British canal system for freight transport has dwindled, (unlike Holland) despite the need to reduce the pressure of freight on British roads. British Waterways have worked hard to attract freight back to the waterways using the arguments of reduced congestion, cost and environmental friendliness. Currently four million tons of freight travel along British waterways, reducing the number of lorries on the roads in the north east of England by approximately 200,000.

Water supply:
Water is essential to life and many of the major towns and cities in the south east do not have sufficient water supply for their residents. Water, therefore, has to be collected and pumped around the country to those areas with a shortage. The average domestic consumption of water in 1990 in England and Wales was about 140 litres per person per day. Domestic use, however, is only a small part of the total demand. Metered water is supplied to industry for cooling and other functions. Water is also essential to agricultural areas for crops, to assist rainfall and the natural irrigation processes.

The supply of water is not limited to surface water alone, some of the water supply is provided by abstraction of ground water. Estimates from the National Rivers Authority show the regional difference in water supply throughout England and Wales in 1990. From this it is possible to identify that Northumbria enjoys the biggest surplus - 94 per cent. It is estimated that demands in this area will increase by 20 per cent by the year 2021, leaving a healthy surplus of 74 per cent. The story in the Thames region is rather different. In 1990 there was a surplus of only 4 per cent and, if predictions for 2021 are correct, water consumption will rise by 26 per cent in this area leaving a deficit of 22 per cent. The Thames area will, therefore, need water from other areas, such as Northumbria. This has led to increased pressure to conserve water by reducing accidental loss. The water supply is controlled by private water companies under the scrutiny of a government controlling body, Ofwat. The primary concern of these companies is to provide cost-effective, clean water for both commercial and industrial use. Water resources have frequently been developed for recreation causing some conflict.

Power Supply:

Although much of Britain's power is supplied by other processes (i.e., traditional generators, gas generators and nuclear reactors), some power supply is provided through hydro-electric generation. Hydro-electric power generators need water resources that are high above sea level and are, therefore, restricted to regions, such as Scotland and Wales. Hydro-electricity is also an important power source in Scandinavian countries, such as Norway.

Hydro-electricity is generated by the continuous flow of water through turbines created by the control of the natural flow of water via a dam or barrage, thus creating a lake (see *Figure 4.4* on page 75). This method of power supply is popular due to the low impact on the environment. It also creates new lakes which can be managed for water recreation.

Emergency Services:

British water resources are used in emergencies such as fire and flooding. Fire services pump water from rivers and canals to fight fires in the area. In times of flooding, less full water resources receive flood water to relieve damage.

Passenger Transport:

Both coastal and inland water provide transport for passengers on both business and pleasure. A range of passenger vessels are in operation, linking different parts of the country and reducing, in some cases, the distance travelled on roads. These forms of transport include:

Channel Car Ferries - larger boats with the capacity to carry vehicles. Some are very large and cross the North Sea and English Channel. Other smaller ferries take a few cars with the passenger remaining in the car, for example the services between many Scottish Islands (the Skye to Kyle of Lochalsh service).

Figure 4.4   Hydro-electric Power Station

Lake water resource - good for water based recreation, unfortunately the pipes mar the hillside

Passenger Ferries - are often small boats that sail between towns separated by a harbour, for example, the Gosport to Portsmouth passenger service.

Chain Ferries - cross short distances, often where strong currents or tides prevail, for example, the chain ferry that crosses the Medina River on the Isle of Wight.

Hovercraft - are car carrying, such as the Dover to Calais service and other passenger services, offering a high-speed alternative to ferries.

Catamaran - another high-speed option, either car and passenger or passenger service, for example, the popular commuter service, Southampton to Cowes, on the Isle of Wight.

Ferries are an important feature of our transport network, creating employment and income in many areas like Dover, where there were an estimated 15,044,000 passengers to/from the UK in 1989 (Department of Transport, *Transport Statistics Report - Cross Channel passenger and Freight Traffic*).

Mineral Extraction:
The discovery of North Sea Oil and Gas supplies has been an enormous contribution to the British economy. In Scotland alone oil sales in 1990 produced an estimated £1.7 million income (McIntyre, 1994). Offshore extractions have created employment for thousands of people in service industries. Unfortunately the production platforms and drilling rigs are unattractive and have caused complaints when they have been located inshore, for example Poole in Dorset.

Inland mineral extraction of sand and gravel has created opportunities for man-made recreation sites. Sometimes this is on completion of all activity, in other cases, by creating a dam or barrage, a lake can be used for recreation, while extraction continues on a neighbouring site, (see *Figure4.5* on page 77).

Figure 4.5   **Summerlease Gravel Pits in Maidenhead**

Waste Disposal:

Millions of tonnes of waste are poured into the sea around Britain every year, including by-products of industry and sewage. In recent years there has been growing concern for this use of water resources and stricter regulations have been passed. They have, however, provided difficult to enforce.

Defence:

Traditionally one of Britain's greatest strengths in terms of defence has been her coastal boundary. Historically, the power and influence of Britain has been dominated by her Navy. Despite recent cut-backs in the British Royal Navy, their activities still dominate some areas of coast. The Ministry of Defence (MOD) use harbours around the British Isles for their naval operations. Many of these ports have developed historically as naval ports and today are able to attract tourists to enjoy the maritime and naval heritage. Portsmouth offers a range of attractions for visitors, including the warship *Warrior*. The main naval bases are shown on the map in *Figure 4.6* on page 79. Mentioned in the next section, MOD firing practice from cliff-sited firing ranges also has an impact on other water users.

CONFLICTS BETWEEN USERS

With such a wide variety of uses and so many differing objectives, there are likely to be areas of conflict. These conflicts may be between one commercial user and another, for example, fishing fleets may be an obstacle to cargo ships and coasters. Conservationists feel strongly that the activities of toxic waste disposal at sea are extremely detrimental to the environment and the public health. Conflicts also frequently occur between recreational and commercial users.

Figure 4.6 **Major defence sites on the British Coast**

Maintaining clean water for water supply:
Many water sports are environmentally friendly, leaving little in the way of negative impact in terms of water quality. Therefore, dinghies, wind surfers, canoeists and rowers are welcomed onto many inland lakes and reservoirs whose primary function is the supply of water for domestic use. The water companies spend time on water treatment before use and, therefore, minor contamination can be eradicated. Major contamination, however, is not so easily controlled and there has been resistance to motorised water sports and live-aboard boats using reservoirs as there is a risk of greater polution.

Disposal of pollutants by industrial processing:
The use of water resources for waste disposal has caused concern amongst water sports participants. The nature of the waste has health implications. Water sports enthusiasts run the risk of ingesting quantities of polluted water or becoming infected, if they sustain any open cuts or grazes, or can suffer skin irritation by just being in contact with polluted water. Surfers who are concerned about the disposal of raw sewage from the beaches where they surf, have formed a campaign ('Surfers Against Sewage') attempting to increase public awareness of the problem and to persuade the water companies to adopt more hygienic processing techniques.

Congestion in some areas:
As previously mentioned, congestion can lead to conflict and safety issues in many of the waters surrounding Britain. The Channel waters, including the Dover Strait and the Solent, are particularly good examples. Recreational users can endanger themselves and other vessels by their lack of awareness of the needs of other water users. For major shipping the time required to alter course or speed is considerable. It is important that small craft ensure that they are visible to other water users by carrying a radar reflector and displaying the correct day marks or night lights. These can reduce conflict by allowing shipping to identify small craft early and to take suitable precautions.

In areas of narrow and/or shallow water recreational users must be aware of the rules of the road and the right of way for larger vessels. In the Solent area in summer there are frequent examples of all sizes of pleasure craft endangering themselves by hampering the passage of commercial vessels. The national governing bodies must continue to educate recreational users on the needs of larger commercial vessels. The problems of congestion are demonstrated in *Figure 4.7* below. The cargo ship not only has to negotiate a narrow channel, but also to avoid small yachts which are not giving way.

Figure 4.7   **The Solent**

There are also cases of conflict between coastal cruisers and fishing fleets. For example, when fishing vessels have their nets out, other craft must give a wide berth and, in many cases, recreational users have been unable to recognise fishing vessels, strayed too close and caused damage to nets. In crowded harbours conflict can occur when yachtsmen moor alongside fishing boats and go ashore, leaving the fishing boats trapped on the inside and unable to go to sea. All of these conflicts can be reduced by good management and education of recreational water users.

Access:
Although there are vast areas of water resources, particularly on the coast, there are frequently insufficient access points. Many of the access points, such as harbours and slipways, were designed and built for the needs of the commercial user. Growth in water sports has, in many cases, been faster than the growth of suitable access provision which, in turn, leads to congestion by the recreational users of facilities primarily designed for commercial use. The commercial users have in some cases resented this intrusion into their provision and conflicts have occurred. A particular example is the conflict between divers and the fishing fleets in south west England.

The use of water resources for defence purposes have served to reduce access in some areas. Here it is considered that the access must be restricted for reasons of national security. Defence work, and, in particular, firing ranges out at sea, further restrict close inshore access during firing practices at many sites along the coast, including Wembury Bay near Plymouth and the Dorset coast at Lulworth.

Unsightly development:
Water sports enthusiasts and water's edge participants are attracted to water for peace and quiet. However, many industrial and commercial uses have resulted in unsightly development spoiling the pleasant environment for recreational users and have detracted from the recreational potential of some areas. Examples of such developments include the oil refinery at Calshot in the Solent and the power station at Cap de la Hague in France.

CONFLICTS BETWEEN LEISURE USERS

With all the demands on a scarce resource it is expected that sites available for water based recreation will have to serve a number of different and sometimes conflicting demands. In sites specifically managed for water recreation these differences can be zoned or controlled to allow different sports access. Other sites, either not managed for recreation or private venues, may cope with these differences or conflicts by excluding certain activities completely. As pressure on water resources increases it will become even more important for managers to adopt zoning to allow equal opportunities for all water sports.

The main issues which are the basis for these differences or conflicts can be summarised as *safety, noise, attitude* and *disturbance*. These points will be considered below, followed by examples of actual conflicts between recreational user groups.

Safety:
Many outdoor pursuits and sports involve an element of risk or danger; this forms the attraction for many participants. The degree of danger or risk of the activity itself should be assessed and managed. Precautions should be taken by participants to reduce or remove the possibility of an accident. This is usually accomplished by individuals wearing safety equipment or the club abiding by safety codes of practice. The issue of safety will be covered in more detail in chapter twelve.

Running individual activities can reduce risks to participants. When a number of activities are run in a small area at the same time though, new risks are created. These new risks are the potential danger that one activity can present for another. This is particularly the case where motorised sports are involved. Speed boats and water skiers present a danger to slower moving craft and, therefore, water resources are usually dedicated to one type of activity, or activities are zoned in terms of space or time.
Surfing is sometimes restricted or zoned to reduce dangers to bathers on crowded beaches. In recent years some local authorities have also insisted on surfers obtaining insurance. This bye law is enforced by the local life guards.

Attitude:

Some activities are purely recreational or leisurely in nature, for example, cruising slowly down stream or across to a tiny harbour. Other activities are pursued vigorously as a very competitive sport. The attitude of the participants is radically different, one wishing to enjoy a relaxing day and the other wanting to win. When these two very different attitudes are incorporated in a confined space, conflicts and accidents can and do occur. The cruising yacht, finding itself in the middle of a racing fleet, may cause damage to the equipment of a racing boat or, at worst, be hit. Although both participants have equal rights to enjoy the water in their own way, many racing fleets assume right of way over cruising craft.

Noise:

Many water users are attracted to the resource for peace and sports such as sailing, angling and canoeing, can provide a quiet and tranquil experience. Other participants, however, are looking for excitement and do not worry if this includes noise. The most obvious example is the noise generated by power craft such as jet skis, motor boats and water skiing. The noise made by these activities breaks the peace for other water users and, in the case of anglers, may frighten away the fish. For this reason many local authorities have restricted or banned power craft sports from some of their water resources. The BWSF, however, believes that noise is no longer a major problem due to advances in technology. The modern ski boat has been developed to substantially reduce noise levels.

Disturbance:

This is closely connected to the problem of noise, for example, the groups of picnickers making such a noise that anglers cannot attract any fish. But disturbance covers more than just noise, it includes disturbance of the surface water. Fast moving power boats can create a considerable wash which is often sufficient to rock or even sink a small craft. The wash will also churn up the water and disturb the angler's chances. Canoeists also churn up water in rivers making it difficult for anglers to fish. To rectify this conflict, the British Canoe

Union and the National Federation of Anglers, with the help of the Sports Council, drew up a statement of intent in 1983. Unfortunately, due to local disputes this was never completed.

During the summer months, on beaches in the south west of England, some conflict has occurred between divers and bathers. This was first reported by the South West Sports Council in 1976 and involves the problem of access to the water. The activities of the divers was said to disturb bathers and fishermen on the slipways.

SUMMARY

In this chapter the main water users have been identified and their needs considered. If water sports are to continue to grow and flourish, then it is important that water users can share the resources harmoniously. This will, of course, mean that compromises need to be reached between all users. Recreational users should be educated in the needs of commercial users and offered clear guidelines as to how conflicts can be avoided. Many of the conflicts occur because users do not understand the problems faced by others. For example, many small craft are unaware of the problem a large ship faces when manoeuvring. Many of the same recreational users have never stood on a ship's bridge and seen how difficult it is to observe small craft, unless radar reflectors are displayed. Many of the national governing bodies of individual sports have worked hard to increase understanding between their users and other water users. If recreational water activities are to remain a pleasure, then work must continue to increase this mutual understanding.

Managers of water resources must also work to provide access to as many water activities as possible in order to offer good accessibility for all. Diversification of single sport centres will be required if all water sports are to continue to grow. Local authorities could consider an audit of their current water recreation provision in order to assess areas where latent demand may exist. Many of these management issues will be covered later, but an important technique in managing the demands and conflicts identified is Coastal Zone Management.

Coastal Zone Management:

This technique seeks to manage the diverse range of demands on the delicate coastal fringe by applying zones of operation. Zones allow, theoretically, all activities and demands to operate so that no one group is totally excluded and conflicts between users are reduced. The concept of coastal zone management also, importantly, helps to reduce environmental impacts and serves to identify and protect particularly delicate areas. The subject has been developed extensively in Britain by the University of Portsmouth and, although not restricted to the interests of recreation, these demands are playing an increasingly important role in research. Examples of coastal zone management are demonstrated by Hampshire County Council in the Solent area.

CHAPTER 5

The Impact of Water Based
Leisure Activities

Water based recreation does not operate in a vacuum. The activities of participants affect not only other water users, but also many different users of the country. Some of these effects will be positive, bringing benefits to others, others effects will be negative, harming or upsetting people and areas in which the activities are pursued. These effects are usually considered in terms of impacts or outcomes of the activities. The impact of water based leisure is wide reaching, affecting people, places, the economy and the environment.

These impacts require understanding by water resource managers in order to promote the benefits to their full potential and to identify management techniques to reduce the negative impacts, for example, bank erosion. The impacts can be classified as *negative, positive, economic, social* and *physical* or *environmental*. It is under these main headings that the impact of water based leisure will be assessed in this chapter.

ECONOMIC IMPACTS

The leisure industry, of which water based recreation forms a sector, has grown in economic importance over the last decades. The leisure industry contributes to employment, income, and export economic indicators. Parts of these benefits are directly attributed to water based leisure participation, not necessarily in proportion to the percentage of participation. Water sports are considered a minority activity in terms of total recreation participation. They do not, however, form a minority aspect in terms of consumer spending; this is possibly explained by the amount of equipment required for many water sports. This section will consider the impact of water based recreation on employment, consumer spending, associated industries and the export trade.

Employment:
Water based recreation is part of a wider service industry and, by the nature of service industries, it provides an intangible product. Water sports centres offer an experience, at the end of which, the participant takes nothing physical away. This sector of water based recreation is, therefore, people intensive, providing employment for people in instructing, safety, maintenance, and shore-based jobs. The second aspect of the water based leisure industry is the production and maintenance of equipment associated with the sports. As water sports are equipment intensive this also provides a significant employment opportunity.

The leisure industry as a whole accounts for 13.5 per cent of all UK employees. A breakdown of these figures indicate that in September 1989 sport and recreation accounted for 308,900 employees, retail leisure goods 500,000, and manufacture of leisure goods 500,000 (source: Institute of Leisure and Amenity Management). It is difficult to estimate the percentage of those that are employed in the water based leisure industry. It is likely, based on consumer spending on marine goods, that the industry contributes to a significant proportion of the figures for retailing and manufacture.

The type of employment created will vary from semi-skilled to managerial. Many of the manufacturing industries require staff skilled in boat building techniques. This has led to the creation of a range of BTEC and degree courses in boat building and design. Further details of particular jobs in the water based recreation industry and training opportunities will be discussed in Chapter 11.

Consumer Spending:

Estimates of the value of water based recreation can be made by considering the amount spent by participants on their activity. This spending can be divided into three main sections :

1. *Equipment* - including specialist items, e.g. boats and diving equipment, trailers, buoyancy aids, fuel, books, magazines and other items.

2. *Clothing and footwear* - items used only for water sports, e.g., wet suits, oil skins, sailing boots and shoes.

3. *Services* - moorings, storage, maintenance, insurance, membership fees, and brokerage.

A further area of consumer spending is on second-hand equipment. This spending has not been assessed except to the extent of brokerage fees, included under services. Despite this omission, expenditure on boats is by far the greatest aspect of consumer spending on sports goods and equipment in the UK. The UK Central Statistical Office estimates that boat purchases accounted for £1,190 million in 1989.

Leisure spending on all water based recreation was evaluated in 1988 by a research team from Leisure Consultants. Their findings indicated similar patterns, allowing the conclusion that, although water sports are a minority activity in terms of participation, the consumer spending is out of proportion and represents a high value. Unlike other sports, where spending on footwear and clothing accounts for much of the total, water based recreation spending is mainly concerned with equipment and services.

Water sports spending represents a considerable proportion of total sports spending in the UK. It remains, however, only a very small part of total leisure spending (£73,500 million - 1988) and as little as 0.2 per cent of total consumer spending in 1988. (Leisure Consultants, 1989).

To summarise this information, it was estimated that in 1988 the water sports market was worth over £520 million (Leisure Consultants, 1989). Most of this expenditure was devoted to equipment and services. With equipment purchases as the largest area, two thirds of this expenditure was on craft and essential equipment. Water based activities account for approximately 10 per cent of total sports participation, in contrast spending represents approximately 17-18 per cent of total sports expenditure.

Is the level of expenditure the same across all water sports?

Research shows that there are big differences in the level of consumer spending in individual sports. In 1988 boating dominated higher levels of consumer spending with an estimated £400 million, divided fairly equally between motor boats and sailing. At the other end of the scale, the jet ski market represented approximately £2 million. Differences between expenditure in individual sports can be explained by:

1. The level of equipment ownership

2. The relative cost of participation

3. Participation rates

Research shows rowing and canoeing represent low consumer spending while boating and sub aqua require significantly higher expenditure. Working from the estimated 3 million participants in all water sports, and accepting that some people do more than one sport, average expenditure, in 1988, was approximately £174 per person.

Related Industries:
With such a relatively high level of consumer spending, it is only to be expected that the water sports industry comprises a large number of businesses to cater for the equipment, clothing and service needs of customers. The industry consists of both large corporations and small businesses and its interests are represented by the British Marine Industries Federation (BMIF). The BMIF has a total of 1,400 member

companies ranging from boat builders to insurance companies and provides information on products and services to recreational users. The information service is offered through the operation of a free telephone information service called *Boatline*.

Membership of the BMIF only represents a small proportion of the total marine industries and further investigation into the *Sell's Marine Market Guide* offers detail on the diverse nature of the industry. The guide suggests that there are as many as 4,700 companies in Great Britain and Eire offering a range of approximately 900 products and services. Products and services such as safety equipment, cookers, paints etc. involve the largest number of companies.

Export Trade:
Overseas markets remain important for many of the larger British boat builders with nearly half the total boats built in the UK being exported. British designed power boats and canoes figure strongly in export markets. On the other hand, imports of boats, particularly some French built yachts, almost equal the number of exports. The number of imported boat sales being in excess of 25 per cent of total sales (Leisure Consultants, 1989).

To conclude, the marine industry offers a range of economic benefits. Despite the contribution in terms of total consumer spending being very small the marine industry offers manufacturing diversification and development of overseas markets. The employment created is particularly beneficial in the current state of high unemployment.

Social Impacts:
The activities of water sports and associated marine industries do not only affect water based recreation participants and the economy, but also have wide reaching implications for society. The impacts of water based recreation can be both beneficial, for example, the creation of local employment opportunities, and detrimental, for example, over-crowding. The following section will consider the positive and negative impacts separately.

Positive Impacts:
There are many social benefits for local communities where water based recreation has been developed. Water resources managed for recreation can offer a new lease of life to communities affected by declining traditional industries and serve to replenish falling population and local wealth.

New employment opportunities:
All communities benefit from increased employment opportunities, but these are particularly welcome in areas which have experienced a decline in traditional employment. Water resources, for recreation, require a relatively large number of staff if they are to be well managed. The opportunities that exist are from general site maintenance and cleaning to clerical posts. Many employees may not need specific leisure management training or can receive 'on the job' training.

In many areas opportunities for school-leavers are particularly welcomed where existing industry has reduced the intake of young apprentices. New water sports venues could improve the calibre of applicants by working with local schools and colleges to prepare students for work in the leisure industry. New venues can also help their acceptance into communities by ensuring that as many staff appointments as possible are made from the local population. By employing local residents a new centre can improve awareness of the facility simply by word of mouth and ensure a more positive reception.

Improved infrastructure:
The infrastructure of an area includes roads, buildings, facilities, and services. The development of a new water sports centre can improve these basic elements of the locality. A major venue may lead to new roads being built or improvements to public transport in the area. A well planned and produced venue will add to the opportunities in the area and, therefore, improve its image. The development of water resources for recreation in depressed or previously disused sites have altered the perception of an area from a run-down and undesirable

location into a prime site for development. A fine example of this process can be seen in the redevelopment of the Albert Dock area in Liverpool. The new apartments, shops, restaurants and bars centred around the dock moorings have attracted millions of visitors who previously may not have chosen to go there. Hence, development may bring with it increased visitors and, therefore, potential income.

This type of development contributes to attracting new companies and businesses into an area. Usually a company looking to relocate prefers to move to an area their employees view as desirable.

Increased property values:
For local residents, already living and owning property close to water resources, development can improve the value of their properties. A study carried out by Dr Ken Willis and Guy Garrod of Newcastle University on properties situated close to canals and navigable rivers indicated a positive premium associated with the proximity of residential properties to waterways. These higher prices were not just restricted to houses on the water's edge but included properties some distance away, and properties with a water frontage onto pristine waterway developments enjoyed an average premium of 19 per cent above properties elsewhere. Other properties in waterside developments enjoyed an 8 per cent premium over other properties.

Therefore, where work is undertaken to improve the waterside environment for recreation, property owners can expect to see the value of their properties increase. This is obviously welcomed by existing property owners.

Potential for secondary spending:
When a water resource is developed for recreation and leisure, marketing of the venue will obviously seek to attract new visitors. Although people visit specifically to view the new venue it is possible for local residents and businesses to benefit in terms of secondary spending. This potential will include local shops, public houses, restaurants, hotels, guest houses and other local attractions. It is

difficult to assess the amount of potential income generated for existing and new business but it can become a considerable contribution to the local economy.

To benefit, local business may need to adapt to meet the needs of these new visitors. For example, where a marina has been built yachtsmen often arrive in the evening requiring basic provisions. To capture this market a village shop may need to review its opening hours and even the types of products stocked. For the local business, which is willing to adapt and meet the new challenges, rich rewards may be gained.

New business opportunities for depressed areas:
Some work has been carried out, particularly in depressed inner city dockland areas, to develop leisure opportunities focused on a water resource alongside business parks or light industrial developments. Examples of this can be seen in Southampton with the Ocean Village leisure complex and marina village alongside office developments. Many new marina developments have included provision for waterside offices. These present a particularly attractive location for new business to the area.

Conservation of local environment and heritage:
Many water resource developments include provision for the preservation of the local environment and/or heritage sites. It is possible for investment by development companies to rescue an area from being used for fly tipping and becoming generally neglected and over-grown. The management of a resource for leisure often involves work on the natural environment. For example, British Waterways has spent time and money restoring tow paths and the natural environment surrounding the water. These restored sites can then offer new opportunities of access for local residents.

British Waterways is also responsible for the preservation of 2,050 listed structures and 135 Ancient Monuments. The diversity of this heritage ranges from the magnificent Gloucester Docks warehouses to a simple mile post. The work of water resource development is important in preserving and maintaining local heritage for future generations.

New opportunities for recreation and leisure:
Finally, the development of a local water resource for leisure in itself offers residents new recreational opportunities. A new company could encourage local residents to hold 'Open Days' or 'Come and Try It Days'. Liaison with local schools, colleges and clubs, if appropriate, could help to ensure that local people realise that the development offers wider opportunities for their leisure.

Negative Impacts:
Unfortunately the development of water resources for leisure is not without problems for local communities. Some local people enjoy the positive benefits described above and consider that the change or new development is an improvement. Others, however, find that the new resource alters their environment in ways that are, in their opinion, undesirable. These impacts are outlined below.

Seasonal nature of some employment:
In the previous section it was highlighted that a benefit of the development of water resources for recreation may be the creation of new jobs within the community. Unfortunately, in Britain the nature of such work is frequently seasonal. Therefore, for many communities all that water recreation development offers is, at best, summer employment and winter on the dole, or the influx of non-resident migrant workers in the summer months further undermining the local community.

Pressure of new development:
Where development occurs in unspoilt areas, local residents may see the resource in negative terms, being perceived as ruining the local area. Developers can avoid this local resistance by working with the environment and using construction materials and designs which are sensitive to the existing environment. For example, by providing a low level rustic club house rather than a three storey concrete construction.

Also car parking areas could be situated in a concealed location, thereby avoiding impairing the view from local vantage points.

In other areas the development can add to existing developments and place a strain on the local environment, communities and infrastructure by increasing the number of visitors that the developments, together, attract. An example of this is on the River Hamble in Hampshire where marinas have been added to an already over-developed river estuary.

Over crowding:
The development of some water resources has resulted in the creation of 'honey pot sites'. Such an area is where the new resource has been so successful and has attracted too many visitors and participants thereby over-reaching the carrying capacity of the site. This, of course, leads to problems of access (roads become blocked with parked cars), damage to the natural environment by the sheer number of people who are forced out of the designated area and loss of enjoyment - all due to overcrowding.

The problems of carrying capacity and overcrowding are complex management issues. It is often not possible by their very nature to refuse or restrict access to these sites. It, therefore, remains to increase the carrying capacity by further development, if space allows, or the careful promotion of alternatives. These overcrowding problems for local residents are clearly evident during the summer months in many Devon and Cornish towns. Here, local residents find it impossible to go about their daily life without being held up by the sheer volume of visitors and holiday-makers.

Loss of a sense of community:
The development of water resources for leisure can, as has already been mentioned, cause problems of migrant workers joining the community for the summer months. Further to this, particularly in some coastal resorts, many properties are purchased as second homes or holiday lets. This further reduces the number of permanent residents

and can result in a breakdown of community focus.

Pressure on existing business:
Some existing business, rather than benefiting from the increased sales opportunities, are pushed out of business by increased rent and competition. The local council may find that improvements in the infrastructure have led to increased demands for commercial property thereby forcing rents beyond the reach of some local businesses.

Bigger companies attracted to the area may also be able to enjoy economies of scale and offer lower priced goods and services, forcing some existing companies out of business. Some marinas only permit contractors specified by themselves to work on their premises, thereby, restricting opportunities for small local firms.

Increased price of housing:
This was described as a benefit for local residents in the last section, however there is a reverse effect. Rising property prices begin to exclude local residents wishing to buy for the first time. Holiday lets also have the effect of pushing up rent and reducing the number of properties to let on an annual basis. This can force young people away from their communities to find affordable housing.

Having studied these social impacts the manager must be careful to see the situation proportionally. For example, the development of a sailing centre, on a disused gravel pit will have few social implications except, perhaps, increased recreational sailing opportunities in the local area. It is really only major developments, such as the Southampton Docks, which will start to have such a variety of social implications.

ENVIRONMENTAL IMPACTS OF WATER BASED RECREATION:

Growth in public concern for the environment has a particularly large impact on water based and water's edge recreation. The water environment provides natural habitat in a wide variety of forms. Inland water provides natural river banks for plants, animals such as voles, spawning grounds for fish and nesting for water fowl. Lakes and wetlands are important habitats for numerous species of flora and fauna. The coast resource is home for sea birds, fish and marine aquatic life and provides cliff nesting sites for many birds.

In Scotland the marine habitats can be summarised as follows:

1. *Fringing Habitats* - adjacent to the sea including cliffs (for example, Sumburgh Head in Shetland, home to many sea birds), sand dunes (for example, St. Cyrus) and lichen covered rocks found above the high-tide level on some rocky shores.

2. *Sealochs* - deep, steep sided inlets from the sea (a result of glacial action during the last ice age), with sandy or muddy bottoms which are home to burrowing animals, such as the Norway lobster.

3. *Estuaries* - where rivers meet the sea, many contain wide mud flats and extensive salt marshes that harbour small animals (an essential food source for thousands of waders and wintering wildfowl), and act as nursery grounds for commercial fish species.

4. *Rocky shores* - the type of wildlife that these shores host depends on the degree of shelter they afford. Wild shores, subject to strong wave action, are home to limpets and barnacles whilst sheltered coasts house seaweed and possibly seals.

5. *Sandy and muddy shores* - host to burrowing animals - an important food source for other wildlife.

6. *Seabeds* - either rock (home to shell fish, fish and kelp forests), or sediment (sand or gravel) home to burrowing animals such as sea urchins, shrimps, sea cucumbers and bivalve molluscs.

7. *Open sea* - home to plankton, nekton, and thousands of species of fish and marine mammals. Scotland's seas offers habitat to 40 per cent of the world's population of grey seals, also bottle nosed dolphins, porpoises, common seals, otters and even whales reside in its waters.

A recent report by the Nature Conservancy Council, Scottish Panel, suggests that, in many ways, conservationists and recreationalists hold common concerns for the marine environment as water pollution causes problems for both marine wildlife and recreational users. Indeed there exists great potential for collaborative action on a number of issues. Generally, recreational users cause little damage to the marine environment, although harmful effects can be identified in certain 'hot spots'. For example, delicate invertebrate species may be damaged and gradually removed from popular diving areas. Sewage pollution and litter can become significant problems at frequently used yacht marinas.

The following section identifies the potential negative impacts of water recreation on the environment and analyses methods adopted to minimise or repair this damage.

Environmental Impacts of Water Sports:
Boating provides participants with the rare opportunity to visit beautiful and unspoilt areas sometimes not easily accessible from the land. Unfortunately, increasing levels of participation have led to increased pressure on these natural environments. If users are to be able to continue visiting such areas it is essential that awareness of the potential impacts is increased and that work is directed to achieve a balance. The British Marine Industries Federation has accepted this challenge and launched a campaign to ensure that the continued development of boating and water based leisure activity is achieved through a careful, beneficial and fundamentally harmonious relationship with the environment. This campaign, entitled *Steering a Balanced Course,* has five main objectives:

1. To create harmony between the UK marine industry, water sports participants, boat users and the environment.

2. To promote awareness in environmental issues amongst its members and encourage them to adopt strategies which will safeguard the environment and the future of the marine industry.

3. To project a positive attitude of the industry on environmental issues.

4. To commission an in depth Environmental Assessment of the UK marine industries.

5. To construct and promote an environmental code of practice for the marine industry.

The impact of water sports can be identified in five main areas, *water quality, dumping, birds and wildlife, physical erosion* and *depletion of aquatic species.* This section analyses each issue, separately identifying water sports which are particularly problematic.

Water Quality:
The discharge of sewage and other waste materials has led to many harbours and rivers becoming polluted resulting in low water quality. Recent years have witnessed growing environmental awareness, and work has commenced to improve water quality and reduce pollution. This has been successful in some areas. Rivers, such as the Thames, and some of our beaches have witnessed dramatic improvements. Pressure has been place on industries, such as the water industry, to rethink such processes as the dumping of raw sewage off beaches. Nevertheless, thousands of yachts and boats every week, particularly in summer, discharge untreated sewage directly into the sea or marinas.

The discharge of sewage from boats is unsightly and can lead to very unpleasant smells in enclosed harbours and marinas and brings about two problems. Firstly, it carries diseases and viruses which can affect other water users, such as swimmers, and can be carried in partially cooked shellfish. Secondly, the decomposition of organic matter uses up oxygen, potentially starving aquatic organisms of oxygen and killing them.

Many racing and cruising boats need to be protected from the growth of barnacles and green algae which, over a season, will severely affect speed and detract from presentation and, over time, undermine their structure. To reduce the growth, boat owners paint the submerged surface with a paint usually know as anti-fouling. In the early 1980s it was discovered that there were growing levels of tributylin (TBT), a toxic agent used in anti-fouling paint. The affect of TBT is detrimental to shellfish, particularly to Pacific Oysters that live in several estuaries. A law was passed, therefore, restricting the use of TBT in anti-fouling paint to vessels over 25 metres in length.

Another pollutant is washing-up water (some washing-up liquids contain phosphates) that is pumped from boats. This practice has caused foaming of inland waters, such as the Norfolk Broads, and has increased the levels of phosphates within the water.

The bilge of all types of boats collect a mixture of water, fuel and sometimes oil. It is good practice, in terms of boat safety, to pump the contents of the bilge overboard at regular intervals to avoid the intake of too much water. This is often carried out by boat users when in marinas. Fuel pollution, due to spillage, also occurs at or near filling stations. Diesel spills cover the water with a translucent film and create an unpleasant smell.

Dumping:
Boat owners and other water users are often short of space which can lead to them dumping rubbish, particularly plastics, into the water. Although, in the past, there have been many discussions on the safety of disposing of biodegradable products (rotting vegetables, cardboard and other such matter that may well decompose without adverse effects to wildlife), this process takes time and is unsightly and smelly.

Floating debris can cause blockages and even jam lock gates. Broken glass and tins can cause injury to both wildlife and humans.

Plastics are particularly dangerous by their very design-strengths. They will not decompose and when dumped from boats they either sink, float on or just blow along the surface and eventually wash up on beaches and banks. Seals and birds have been discovered with the plastic rings used to keep cans of drink together around their necks causing them at the least distress and at worst death. Many fish and birds have been known to mistake plastic for food and have choked on it.

Birds and Wildlife:
Birds and other forms of wildlife can be affected by the toxic elements of some anti-fouling paints and have been caused great stress or even killed by the dumping of waste products. However, the requirement of many water sports to share the natural habitat of many species of birds and wildlife has led to concern among conservationists that the resident population are being forced out by the recreationalists. Water skiers and wind surfers have especially been identified as they require the same type of resource (open water) that attract over-wintering water fowl. In a study of the Solent area, the activities of wind surfers and water skiers have been identified as disturbing and distressing roosting birds. The development of moorings and marinas is considered by some conservationists as having a negative impact on water fowl and reducing the amount of sites available for roosting. Langstone Harbour is home to many boats and birds and, despite the recommendations of the Boating Facilities At Harbours Capacities Group that *account must be taken of the need to preserve the feeding grounds of certain species of birds, the authors are unable to accept sufficient reason to restrict the number of moorings in this area at the present level,* the conservationists strongly opposed the provision of new mud moorings and development of marinas. The fear of conservationists was probably based on the experiences of the River Hamble - at last count offering 2,730 berths or moorings with plans to extend to a further 4,000 - but with total disregard for the promotion of species. *Figure*

5.1 on page 104 illustrates the pressures of over-development.

The impact of these particular recreational activities is not restricted to coastal waters, inland waters also provide vital habitat for water fowl. The East Midlands Water Recreation Strategy contained specific policy recommendations for conservation:

Water based recreation should not be considered appropriate to every piece of water; a balance should be achieved between all interests.

From this we are warned of the possible reverse conflict where water recreation is excluded in many sites and yet on sites for recreation wildlife is still allowed to co-exist. Birds and wildlife are affected by noise from all water users and this can drive them away from natural sites. To summarise, birds and wildlife are detrimentally affected by water users by way of dumping, disturbance and stress.

Physical Erosion:
The increase in the number of pleasure craft and, particularly, motor boats in inland water areas has resulted in considerable bank erosion. On the Norfolk Broads it is estimated that erosion has increased significantly, resulting in a loss of approximately 1.6 metres in ten years. Most of this additional damage is caused by the wash created by moving and manoeuvring boats. Further damage can also be attributed to the mooring of boats to banks in unofficial locations.

Bank erosion is caused by the breaking down of the *rond* - a popular habitat for a number of species. The diagrams in *Figure 5.2* illustrate the process of bank erosion on the Norfolk Broads.

Figure 5.1 **Over Development in River Estuaries**

The pressures of recreation development on natural estuary habitats

Figure 5.2a   **Bank erosion - before erosion**

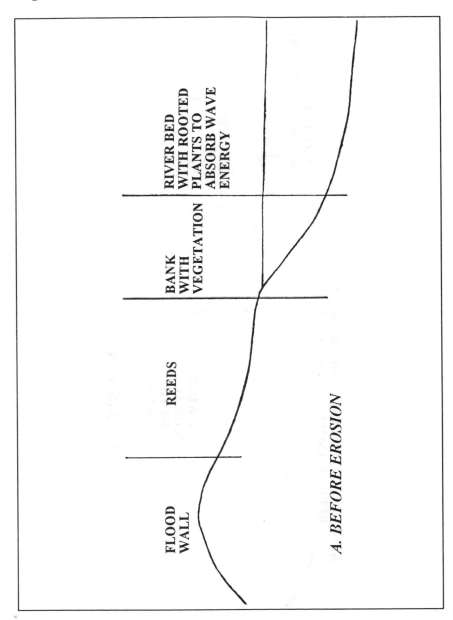

Figure 5.2b   **Bank erosion - influences**

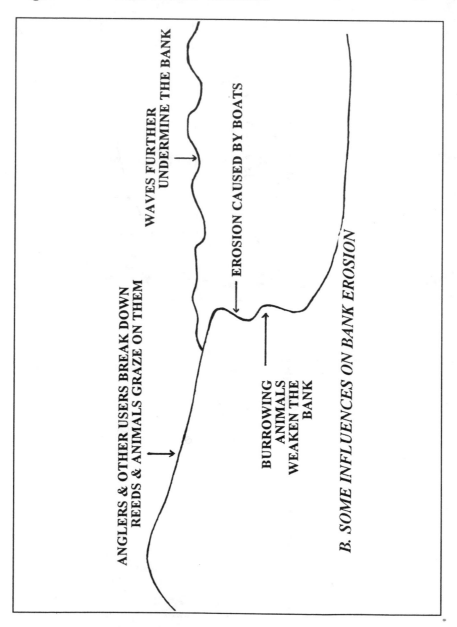

Depletion of aquatic species:
Water resources are home to many small and large aquatic species. It has already been mentioned that TBT causes problems for some shellfish. Fish, in general, are particularly sensitive to pollution and water quality. However, further impacts of water based recreation cause concern, particularly sub aqua diving.

Studies, as far back as 1979, indicate that diving can cause serious depletion of some benthic organisms. Although evidence is hard to find, concern that souvenir collecting by recreational divers leads to a reduction in species such as sea urchins, star fish, sea fans and other rare molluscs. Damage to coral reefs is also associated with the activities of divers.

The environmental impact of water's edge activities:
Many water's edge activities have similar impacts on the environment as water based activities. The following section identifies those activities particularly prone to adverse environmental impacts. It considers these impacts under the same headings as for water based activities.

Water Quality:
The main pollutant from water's edge activities is lead poisoning from anglers' discarded weights. Lead weights contaminate water, killing invertebrates, plants and animals. Swans have died from choking on swallowed lead weights. However, the problem is declining with the reduction in the use of lead weights. A further source of lead is from the shot used by wildfowlers.

Dumping:
Visitors to water resources for casual use, such as walks or picnicking, often bring food and other consumables with them. If the wrapping and resulting rubbish is not removed then it can be blown into the water thereby clogging banks and other structures. Anglers also need to beware of the danger to wild life by leaving nylon line on the bank at

the end of a day's fishing.

Birds and Wildlife:
Birds can be frightened, particularly during the nesting season, by dogs roaming out of control or simply by the noise and intrusion of humans. To afford birds the necessary peace and quiet some cliffs have restricted access.

As a result of anglers carelessly discarding fishing tackle and line on river banks many water fowl die each year, their beaks or necks become entwined in the line and they either starve or strangle themselves.

Physical Erosion:
Banks can become eroded by anglers trying to achieve a better site or vantage point. Over time banks become broken by constant access. Casual users wear down sensitive habitats if they do not keep to the allotted paths. Campers do untold damage by cutting trees for fire wood and lighting fires.

Depletion of Aquatic Species:
The collection of bait for fishing from beaches and mud flats has become extensive in some locations over the last few years. There is concern that the worms are not replacing their population quickly enough under these pressures. The worms are not only a species in themselves but also essential food for waterfowl and other wildlife.

HOW CAN THE IMPACTS OF RECREATION BE REDUCED ON THE WATER ENVIRONMENT?

As a result of growing environmental concern many organisations are working to reduce these impacts as the BMIF states: *to steer a balanced course between conservation and recreation.* There are ways that each of the identified problems can be avoided by recreational users as individuals. The management tool to introduce these practices is through education, legislation or intervention. Having analysed the methods to reduce these negative impacts, this section identifies examples of attempts to introduce them.

Water Quality:
The impact of sewage on inland waters has been reduced by legislation banning the discharge of such waste. All boats must have a holding tank which can be emptied at a pumping station. Fines of up to £2,000 are imposed on Lake Windermere for failing to obey this legislation. On many stretches of river it is also required that the outlet valve is sealed.

Unfortunately legislation banning the discharge of sewage does not exist for the coastal waters around the UK although many other countries, such as the United States of America, have laws requiring the use of holding tanks in coastal waters. To overcome this problem boat users should be encouraged to use holding tanks, all new boats could be designed to include holding tanks and marinas should be encouraged to offer convenient 24 hour facilities to reduce the need to use marine toilets in harbours.

To avoid spillage of oil and diesel boat owners can only ensure that their engines are well maintained to reduce the chance of leaks. Drip trays should be emptied ashore regularly to avoid seepage into the bilge. Some inland cruisers are now fitted with filters to reduce the chance of waste from the bilge being discharged.

Pollution by anti-fouling paint has been significantly reduced by the ban of TBT in paints sold for recreational craft. This law was passed in 1987 and means that the only anti-fouling that can be purchased is copolymer-based which produces a constant release over a prolonged period, thereby reducing the environmental impact.

Dumping:
The only solution to this is to persuade recreational users to take home all their rubbish. To further alleviate this problem all landing stages, moorings and beaches should be adequately provided with appropriate

disposal facilities. Coastal dumping has become an offence in the English Channel and North Sea, although, in practice, it is virtually impossible to enforce this legislation, which is primarily targeted at commercial vessels effectively. Responsibility for this legislation and the requirement of all harbour authorities to provide rubbish disposal facilities come under the Merchant Shipping Regulations.

Birds and Wildlife:
From the shore or banks dogs must be kept on a lead or under control, as requested. Fines can be enforce in local situations. Again, anglers need to be educated in the risks to wildlife of leaving line and weights. The National Rivers Authority provides clear guidance on this matter for anglers.

Boats should keep a distance from the banks and roosting birds to reduce disturbance. Anchoring and mooring should be away from nesting sites and at recognised landing places only. Management policy can also select particularly sensitive areas for conservation and zone other areas for recreational use. In Langstone Harbour in the Solent various areas have been designated either Sites of Special Scientific Interest (SSSI), RSPB reserves or local nature reserves. These cover a third of the most vulnerable areas.

Physical Erosion:
Accelerated bank erosion can predominately be connected to boats. To reduce erosion boat users need to reduce their speed. Research on the Norfolk Broads proved that by reducing the speed limit to six miles per hour (a reduction of 1 mile per hour) wave energy, the primary cause of bank erosion, was reduced by an average factor of 3.4. This speed limit was brought into force in 1992 and is enforced by river inspectors. In sensitive areas of the Broads wash free zones have be enforced, requiring that boats do not create any wash at all.

Once bank erosion has occurred it is necessary to adopt methods to renovate and protect the remaining bank. Many methods have been tried. Natural methods include the growing of reeds and trees such as alder and willow. Where these methods have failed man-made, often expensive solutions, have been applied, including geotextile matting, which can help plants to root and survive, wooden or steel piles, open cell concrete block work or concrete walls. Diagrams of these are shown in *Figure 5.3*.

Figure 5.3   Methods to repair and protect eroded banks

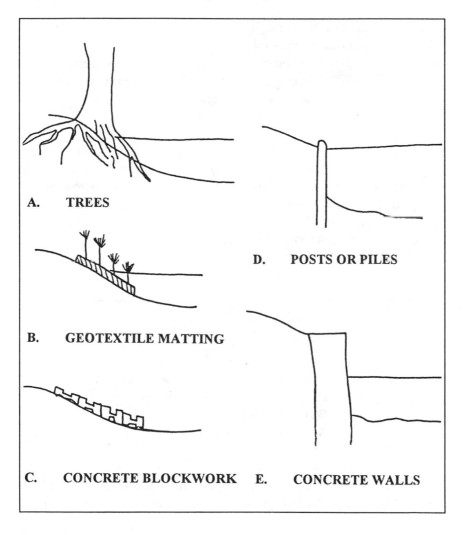

Depletion of Aquatic Species:
The best method to reduce this impact is to educate divers to look at or photograph but not collect specimens. Other methods include the designation of Marine Nature Reserves. Voluntary reserves have existed at Lundy since 1973 and Skomer since 1976. These areas protect endangered species and are designated by the NCC with help from the Natural Environment Research Council.

Campaigns to educate recreational users:
Many organisations instruct recreational users on the effects of their activities upon the environment and good practise which can reduce this impact. The BMIF 'Steering a Balanced Course' project attempts to explain the key issues to boat owners and other users and issues a free publication *A Guide to Boating and The Environment*.

Another important campaign is the one by the Marine Conservation Society who, in conjunction with National Westminster Bank, World Wildlife Fund and the Countryside Commission, have introduced a Seashore Code (see *Figure 5.4*). This code, via a poster campaign, aims to educate casual users of the shore line on how to reduce their negative impact on the natural environment.

Figure 5.4   **Marine Conservation Society**

SEA SHORE CODE
×   **Show respect for sea creatures**
×   **Take photos not living animals**
×   **Take your rubbish home with you**
×   **Drive on roads not on beaches**
×   **Be careful near cliffs**
×   **Avoid disturbing wildlife**

Further examples of these attempts to educate recreational users can be seen in the example by British Waterways. It has produced a detailed booklet laying out good practise of courtesy on the water, on the tow path and at matches, rallies and events. The information is directed towards specific interests of anglers, canoeists and boat users. The booklet, *The Waterways Code - All Together Better* can be summarised in the six point code illustrated in *Figure 5.5*.

Figure 5.5   Waterways code

SUMMARY OF THE CODE
1.   Always be aware of other users.
2.   Do not disturb boaters at their moorings and anglers while they are fishing
3.   Keep safety in mind when fishing, cycling, using locks and mooring your boat.
4.   Respect the canal environment and leave the canal as you wish to find it.
5.   Follow organisers' requests at events.
6.   Help others to enjoy the waterways too !

Source: British Waterways

SUMMARY

Boating can offer a wide range of benefits to the economy and to communities. The impact on the environment can be controlled by a combination of education, legislation and management. Indeed, future recreational users may be viewed as associates and allies to conservationists if the basic ideas of good practice can be instilled into all water users.

CHAPTER 6

Inland Water: Organisations, Legislation and Control

As identified in Chapter 1 there is a great variety of inland water resources in Britain. To ensure that these resources are maintained there is a need for legislation, management and intervention by national organisations. The objective of this has been to achieve and maintain quality, in terms of the water itself and the surrounding environment. Studies in the 1970s highlighted particular problems with the standards of water quality in inland resources. The effect of low water quality led to some water being disused and run down. It is, therefore, important to address the issues of water quality and then to consider the work of various organisations, public, private and voluntary, in maintaining inland waters in Britain.

WATER QUALITY

In 1990, 89 per cent of English and Welsh rivers and 90 per cent of their canals were of good or fair quality (source: NRA). Monitoring water quality has been achieved through the work of many organisations and is measured against standards specified by the National Water Council. These standards help all users to decide whether the water is of a suitable standard for their particular needs. The grading criteria for water quality is classified on a five point scale.

Good quality, class 1a is assigned to water resources which are suitable for drinking, water abstractions, high class fisheries, such as game, and excellent recreational value.

Good quality, class 1b is assigned to water which does not reach the high standards of 1a but whose uses can be much the same.

Fair quality, class 2 are waters which can be used for consumption but only after specific treatment and which will support reasonable coarse fisheries. This type of resource is considered to have a medium recreational value.

Poor quality, class 3 are waters which are polluted to the exclusion or sporadic absence of fish and whose main use is for industrial abstraction after some treatment.

Bad quality, class 4 refers to water which is grossly polluted and is likely to cause problems.

Research in River Quality Surveys from 1980 to 1990 indicates a small decline in the quality of rivers and canals in England and Wales. The percentage of water classified class 1a and 1b has fallen in the last decade by 5 per cent. Part of this decline can be explained by the problems caused to water quality during recent droughts. Bad quality water has remained stable over the same period. The main area of increase in decline has been in fair quality water (4 per cent).

The results of the Water Quality Surveys and the classification designed by the National Water Council is now being reviewed in order to produce a new strategy of water quality objectives as proposed in the Water Act 1989 and the Water Resources Act 1991. The water quality objectives will be introduced in England and Wales under the Water Resources Act 1991 with the purpose of ensuring that controlled waters are of sufficiently high standard to satisfy all the demands on them. The objectives are set by the Department of the Environment and the Welsh Office in consultation with the National Rivers Authority. Every water resource will have its own set of objectives together with a deadline by which time this standard must be achieved.

Water quality is also controlled by the European Community which has produced directives on a range of water quality issues. These directives are implemented by the water companies of England and Wales and by the National Rivers Authority. The directives of most importance for inland water are:

75/440/EEC	*Quality of surface water for abstraction of drinking water*
76/160/EEC	*Bathing water quality*
78/659/EEC	*Quality of water needed for freshwater fish*
91/271/EEC	*Urban waste water treatment*
91/676/EEC	*Protection of water against agricultural pollution*

These form some of the most important directives for inland water, although a study of all European directives would reveal many more which can affect the way in which water quality is managed. In order to ensure and monitor water quality, registers are maintained by the National Rivers Authority in England and Wales and the River Purification Boards in Scotland. The registers show information about discharge consents and the results of water quality samples. These registers are available for public scrutiny and would be a useful point of reference for the water sports manager wishing to ensure that a chosen site was of a suitable quality for the type of activity.

Discharges into inland water are controlled by a system of consents. Any commercial, industrial or agricultural activity which wants to discharge anything into rivers or canals must apply to the National Rivers Authority and obtain their consent. Before consent is given the authority will need to satisfy themselves that water quality will not be seriously affected. Despite these formal controls there were 29,000 pollution incidents reported to the National Rivers Authority in 1991. To assist the management of pollution Thames Region of the NRA has set up a 24 hour hotline to encourage other water users to report pollution incidents. If the incident is caught early then the impact on water quality can be reduced in many cases. Unfortunately, it has proved difficult to prosecute for pollution although an increasing number of incidents are now coming to court and, hopefully, this will act as a deterrent to potential polluters.

In Chapter 5 some of the main recreational causes of water pollution were identified. Recreational activities usually have only a minor affect on the total water quality and major pollution is usually the result of industrial or agricultural activity. The quality of water is influenced by a number of different factors: discharge from sewage works, industrial and agricultural installations. Water quality is also affected by pollution incidents such as spillage and run-off, through the ground, into water resources. Water quality can also be affected by the surrounding vegetation. The main influences identified are:

- Sewage and industrial waste

- Agriculture

- Air Pollution

- Landfill Sites

In the case of lakes and reservoirs there is no specific classification although some lakes have been measured and controlled under the river classifications and surveys. The main area of concern for water quality during the 1980s was algal blooms in lakes and reservoirs. These occur as large floating masses, on the surface of the water in the summer months, of blue-green algae. Algal blooms are caused by a combination of a long period of calm, warm weather, nitrates and sunlight. Some species of blue-green algae produce toxins which have created concerns, particularly among water sports users and clubs, as the result of its contact with the skin includes rashes, sore eyes and irritation. Ingesting the scum has caused vomiting, diarrhoea, fever and muscle pains. Many water sports centres and clubs now display notices to warn users of potential dangers as illustrated in *Figure 6.1*. It is impossible to calculate the affect that growth of blue-green algae has had on inland water sports users. However, in drought years, such as 1989, large areas of inland water were serverly affected, including Rutland Water in Leicestershire. This has resulted, on occasion, in the closure of water resources for recreation use. The map in *Figure 6.2* indicates the extent of the problem in 1989.

Another water-borne disease which has caused considerable concern among inland water users is Weils Disease. The disease is transmitted to humans via rats' urine in the water. The symptoms are flu-like but can, in some cases, become more serious. Advice to water sports participants is to avoid run-down areas where the presence of rats is suspected. Having used the water it is essential to rinse off thoroughly to reduce the possibility of becoming infected. Weils Disease is not very common, however water users and clubs are warned of the possibility and posters are often displayed to alert water users.

Figure 6.1 **Warning notice at Queen Mother Reservoir**

Figure 6.2 **Number of sites affected by toxic algae in 1989**

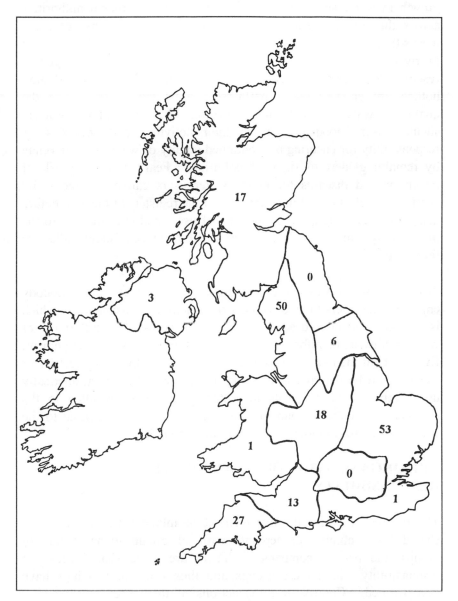

Source: HMSO

The maintenance of good water quality is essential for the continued growth in water sports in the UK. The work of national authorities across the country to improve the water quality in many resources means that now an estimated 64 per cent (1990, Water Quality Survey) of rivers and canals in England and Wales represent an excellent resource for recreation. Schemes such as the NRA Thames Region hotline are encouraging a partnership approach to improving the quality of water resources for recreation. Recreational water users should ensure good practice in their activities and accept some responsibility for ensuring the continued quality of water at their venue by remaining alert to signs of pollution. Fears about the risk of infections and diseases for inland water users can be overcome by careful site selection. If in doubt consult the register for the area before using the water, vigilance on the part of users and education as to the methods by which risk of infection can be reduced, should alleviate these fears.

Whether a water sports user, an angler or a casual visitor, nobody enjoys seeing rivers littered with debris, smelly unpleasant water which is covered with scum, dead fish and other eyesores. The importance of water quality is, therefore, critical to an attractive leisure environment. Even without the risks of infection and lack of healthy fish, most water users would be deterred from using a resource which is aesthetically unattractive. Improvements to water quality have resulted in the rejuvenation of the surrounding environment which is essential to the success of these resources as a leisure playground.

THE ORGANISATION OF INLAND WATER RESPONSIBILITY

The responsibility for the management of inland water resources is shared by a number of separate national organisations, voluntary groups and private companies. There are some shared areas of responsibility within these groups and thus some partnerships have been formed. Control over the actions of these groups is held by government. Through restrictive and permissive legislation national government control, the activities indirectly and directly through government departments.

The Development of Water Resource Management in the Twentieth Century:

The late nineteenth century saw increasing provision of reservoirs as a direct response to urbanisation. These developments were permitted by Private Bills that also provided legislation to restrict access. The inter-war years saw growing pressures for access to reservoirs for recreation. However, resistance to access was strongly voiced in terms of threats to water quality for water supplies. In 1939 the Ministry of Health issued its Advisory Memorandum 221 which was interpreted to suggest that, due to the risk of contamination, there should be no access to reservoirs for recreation.

In the late 1940s the Heneage Committee on Gathering Grounds, a sub-committee of the Central Advisory Water Committee, concluded that there was no reason to restrict public access so long as safety measures were in place. During the 1950s angling and sailing were creating a significant force for access, not only to the water's edge but also on the water. This lobby led to a report in 1963 by the Institution of Water Engineers which suggested, cautiously, that fishing was acceptable and sailing and rowing could be allowed where there was management controls. Canoeing was a cause for concern and swimming and water skiing should be excluded (Tanner, 1993).

With a new permissive policy towards recreation and access, the Water Resources Act 1963 led to the creation of new lowland reservoirs which offered extensive recreation provision. The same act replaced the 32 river boards with 29 river authorities who were allowed to provide access and facilities for recreation on their resources.

By the late 1960s water based recreation was becoming increasingly widespread and recreation provision requirements for water authorities were established in the Water Act 1973. This important Act rationalised the structure of management of water resources into ten regional authorities, these replaced the previous structure of various local authority departments and river authorities. The responsibilities for recreation required assistance and, for this reason, the Water Space Amenity Commission was created as an advisory agency. The work of the commission was difficult to assess. However, by the time it was abolished in 1983 the water authorities were providing for a wide range of water sports, even water skiing in some cases. The 1970s and 1980s saw a steady increase in the use of inland water for recreation. During 1989 the ownership of reservoirs and other resources previously controlled by water authorities was sold to private water companies.

Government Departments with a Responsibility for Water Resources:

The main department with responsibility for water resources and, in particular, water quality is the Department of the Environment's Water Quality Division. This division produced a recent code of practice for the water industry on Conservation, Access and Recreation. This covers practical guidance in respect to the environmental and recreational duties of the main water companies and the NRA. The Standing Advisory Committee produced their first report in July 1993. The results of this report indicate that, so far, access for water sports and informal recreation has not been curtailed. In fact there have been several noted improvements in footpaths and sign-posting in some regions. Other improvements included visitor centres, car parks, ramps and other equipment to assist access for disabled people. Many of these new companies appear eager to increase recreational use of their resources. The main concern, however, in this initial assessment was the shorter leases sometimes being offered to clubs when they come up for renewal. The water companies were alerted to the possibility of a reduction in grant aid to clubs with short leases. Consultation agreements have, therefore, been drawn up. A move to charge for access for major commercial events was approved if charitable events and casual access remains free of charge.

Other government organisations include Her Majesty's Inspectorate of Pollution (HMIP) and Her Majesty's Industrial Pollution Inspectorate

(HMIPI). These organisations are responsible for the implementation, in England and Wales, of a new system of Integrated Pollution Control (IPC). The IPC will be implemented in Scotland by the River Purification Authorities (RPA). The integrated pollution system was a result of the Environmental Protection Act 1990.

Scotland:

The River Purification Authorities (RPA) comprise seven River Purification Boards and three Islands Councils. They are responsible for maintaining the quality of water resources, improving the situation and controlling pollution. The RPAs hold and maintain the registers for water quality in their areas.

Northern Ireland:

Water quality in Northern Ireland is the responsibility of the Department of the Environment for Northern Ireland. This department also controls conservation practice, water resources management and pollution control, and maintains the registers for water quality in this area. A separate Directorate within this department has responsibility for water supplies and sewerage services.

England and Wales:

The National Rivers Authority was established in 1989 by the Water Act. It is an independent public body for England and Wales. The NRA is controlled by a policy making board of 15 members, appointed by Government. This board is supported by a small central staff headed by a chief executive. The NRA is a major environmental protection agency with the general remit to improve and protect the natural water environment. It achieves this on a day-to-day basis through its ten regions shown on the map in *Figure 6.3*.

Figure 6.3   **Map of NRA regional divisions**

The NRA has certain statutory obligations which can be summarised as follows:

a. Water Resources

The NRA has to achieve a balance between the environmental requirements of satisfactory flow levels with the numerous demands placed on its resources by its many users. Over-abstraction, particularly in drought periods, can result in serious environmental problems associated with reduced flow. This is achieved by close monitoring of flow rates, groundwater levels, evaporation and rainfall. The NRA has the responsibility of licensing all those who abstract water from these resources. Through careful planning the NRA can achieve the desired balance.

In the Thames Region five rivers have already dried up due to over-abstraction and the NRA is now committed to helping restore the flow in these rivers, such as the Pang and the Ver. The Thames Region has particularly high demands on its water resources and the challenge for the region is to plan for future requirement now. The work of the regions in this capacity ensures that recreational users have sufficient water to enable them to enjoy their activities all year round.

b. Pollution Control

The NRA is responsible for monitoring water quality and pollution in England and Wales. The NRA can control pollution through the registration of all who discharge waste into the water and by fining those who do so illegally. The NRA helps to maintain a pleasant environment for recreational users and ensures that areas designated for recreation do not present a health hazard for their users.

c. Flood Defence

Many areas of lowland in England and Wales are at risk of flooding. The NRA constantly monitors water levels and gives prior warning to residents if they believe that there is a risk of flooding. These warnings are very useful to water sports venues which are inevitably close to the banks and stand a greater risk of flooding. They allow time to enable boat owners to secure their craft and remove any portable items from potential damage from the flood water.

d.   Fisheries

If there are no fish in a section of water then it can safely be concluded that there may be a problem with water quality. The NRA is responsible for maintaining fish numbers in inland waters. It monitors the number, health and species of fish and maintains satisfactory levels by restocking depleted rivers. It also constructs structures to aid fish that are returning to spawning grounds.

Recreational anglers must obtain a rod licence thus aiding the NRA to monitor the rate of stock depletion whilst offering anglers access to well maintained fisheries. Management of fisheries has achieved great improvements in the amount and quality of fishing available.

e.   Recreation

The NRA is responsible for ensuring that there is satisfactory provision for all recreation users and that their activities are not to the detriment of conservation. In general, the NRA achieves this by actual provision and promotion. The NRA provides picnic areas and some riverside walks. The visitor centre at the Thames Barrier is run by the Thames Region. It also supplies public slips and launching sites for small and large craft.

In terms of increased promotion of resources, many leaflets and posters are distributed. Publications include such examples as the *River Thames Handbook,* containing general information and specific advice for anglers, campers, picnickers, divers, motorised craft users, rowers, scullers, sailors, board sailors, swimmers, paddlers, and finally walkers. This comprehensive free guide covers many aspects of safety and legislation to ensure that all water users in the Thames area enjoy the water in harmony.

The Thames Region has taken this further and is now completing a River Thames Recreational Strategy. This will include an analysis of existing facilities and suggestions for improvements.

Conservation:
The NRA understands the importance of rivers as a natural feature of the British landscape and is entrusted to conserve, maintain and enhance the environment. Rivers are becoming increasingly important in built-up urban areas as they act as linear areas of wilderness and provide homes for a complex array of species. The maintenance of these corridors, bringing wildlife closer to urban populations, is important in terms of both conservation and recreation. The availability of natural habitat close to large populations increases the accessibility of walking, bird watching, and angling for these groups.

The NRA also has responsibility for the ancient structures and buildings on its land. These may include old foot bridges, lock houses and boat houses. By conserving these buildings the NRA opens up opportunities for heritage tourism to water sites.

Navigation.
The NRA has the responsibility for maintaining and managing navigation on several rivers including the non-tidal River Thames. This role includes the physical maintenance, provision of services, registration of craft and supply of information. Physical maintenance includes the driving of piles for mooring, dredging of some stretches of river, engineering maintenance work on the many locks in its control, and sometimes entire modification of locks (Hambledon on the River Thames is currently undergoing extensive work).

In terms of navigation services the NRA mans many of the locks within its control during busy periods. This, however, is not the only service provided as explained in the list of navigation services for the River Thames:

1. *Public Right of Navigation* - maintain a fairway of specified dimensions on various stretches of river including locks.

2.   *Water Level Control* - weirs will be managed to ensure water levels in locks between an upper and lower prescribed figure.

3.   *Assisted Lock Passage* - a uniformed staff member to assist boats through locks at specified periods.

4.   *Legal and Safety* - undertakes to inspect unsafe vessels, 5 per cent of newly registered private vessels, and all vessels for hire each year.

5.   *Facilities* - bulk water supply, sanitary disposal, and dry refuse disposal.

6.   *Supervision* - patrol boats will inspect any crowded area, events, serious accidents and general river checks.

7.   *Enquiries* - handle questions from the public to agreed time scales.

All craft wishing to use a river will need to obtain registration documents from the regional NRA. This requirement includes small craft such as canoes and dinghies. On the River Thames alone 25,000 boats are registered.

The NRA has a complex role in the conservation and management of rivers and other water resources in England and Wales. Their responsibilities sometimes present conflicts such as conservation work and access for recreation, these problems are overcome through careful planning and strategic development to balance all of their objectives. The NRA has the responsibility to ensure water quality, this single area forms the most important area of their work as without satisfactory water quality many other activities will not exist.

British Waterways:
This is a nationalised industry sponsored by the Department of the Environment; the official name is the British Waterways Board. It is

responsible for all inland waterways that span England, Scotland and Wales and is managed by a board of between four and nine members appointed by the Secretary of State for the Environment. The Board was originally created by the Transport Act 1962 to replace the British Transport Commission with smaller boards responsible for specific areas of transport.

British Waterways has a responsibility for approximately 2,000 miles of canals and river navigation. Its objective, set out in 1963, is the successful management of these waterways with efficiency, economy and safety. The first problem to be addressed was to review waterways no longer viable in their current state and to formulate plans for new uses. This led to the designation in the Transport Act 1968 of commercial waterways, cruising waterways and a remainder which would be maintained or restored. This was the first indication of the growing leisure importance in the management of the waterways system.

The Transport Act 1968 was followed, in 1972, by the publication of the *Waterway Environment Handbook* which put emphasis on good conservation techniques. This has been continued in the organisation today as indicated in their environmental policy which states that a high quality waterways environment is the foundation for leisure, property and freight activities. The current environmental policy undertakes to:

1. Conserve and enhance heritage, landscape and habitat in the waterways.
2. Improve water quality and reduce pollution.
3. Set high environmental standards in all work on the system.
4. Carry out environment audits to ensure standards are maintained.
5. Promote environmental codes for developers working on their land.
6. Persuade third party developers whose activities impact on the waterways to adopt good practice.
7. Maintain the use of traditional crafts and skills where possible.

8.   To develop partnerships with other environmental agencies.

9.   To commission research to improve their understanding of the waterways environment.

10.   Improve opportunities for users to enjoy environmental aspects and in particular to encourage educational projects at all levels.

11.   To market the environmental benefits of waterways freight transport.

12.   To minimise the environmental impact of all activities.

13.   Undertake staff training to ensure that all staff are aware of environmental management issues.

The work of British Waterways is best summarised in their mission statement:

Our business is the efficient management of inland waterways system for the increasing benefit of the Nation... The waterways heritage and environment will be conserved, enhanced and made viable for future generations.

In 1978 many tow paths were opened to the public on a take-them-as-you-find-them basis. However, the work of British Waterways in the field of recreation has moved from strength to strength. Currently British Waterways is working hard to increase awareness among recreational users of the opportunities on offer. Leaflets such as *Something for Everyone* promote the great variety of recreational pursuits available in the waterways environment. Specific area guides have been produced to illustrate the activities available, such as the *Try out the Trent* promotion, which includes a pictorial map indicating locations where watersports, boating, angling and walking are available. This work is an essential contribution to awareness, particularly in inland areas such as the Midlands, of the proximity of watersports and other activities.

In 1989 the Environment Committee of the House of Commons reported on an enquiry supporting the wish of British Waterways to change and become more commercially oriented and responsive to users' needs. From this, in 1990, the British Waterways' Integrated Business Strategy was endorsed offering greater freedom to develop their waterways assets. This approach is illustrated by the customer research carried out in 1991 to assess the satisfaction of boat owners with British Waterways. This survey covered satisfaction with overall facilities, which showed that 77 per cent of boat owners rated the facilities as satisfactory or better. The survey illustrates the growing concern among national organisations to improve their service to recreational users.

Since its formation in 1963 British Waterways has encouraged an extensive restoration programme in order to increase recreational opportunity. British Waterways is unable to commit funds to restoration projects and, therefore, encourages the work of local authorities and other organisations. Under this arrangement the British Waterways Act 1983 reclassified the following restored waterways to cruising status:

- Ashton Canal (Manchester)
- Lower Peak Forest Canal (Dukinfield)
- Caldon Canal (Leek)
- Erewash Canal (Long Eaton)
- Monmouthshire and Brecon Canal (Brecon to Pontypool)
- Grand Union Canal (Slough)

Work in this area continues in Scotland, south west and northern England. This activity is essential to enable recreational opportunity to increase with demand and reduce the chance of over crowding in some areas.

British Waterways offers extensive opportunities for water based recreation close to, or within, urban areas. This is important in increasing the physical accessibility of water sports. Waterways offer opportunities for casual water's edge activities, sports, competitions and, very importantly, tourism. Improvements in the water environment has led to huge increases in the scope for canal holidays touring both peaceful countryside and crossing the old industrial developments of bygone years, satisfying increased demand for leisure breaks centred on our industrial heritage.

Other organisations with responsibility for water resources:
The authorities outlined above are government supported bodies with the responsibility for supervising the inland water resources in the UK. Other organisations play a vital role in the maintenance and accessibility of water resources for recreation in inland areas.

Water Companies
Before 1989, the responsibility for the supply of domestic water, the processing of sewage and all other associated services lay with the ten regional water authorities of England and Wales. The Water Act made dramatic changes to this provision, privatising the water authorities (to manage the utilities, water supply and sewage), and creating the National Rivers Authority to provide other services, such as pollution control and navigation. Concern among recreational users and conservation groups was voiced over the creation of these privatised companies. Under the water authorities the value of conservation and recreational access, where possible, had been an established objective and many inland sailing clubs and water sports centres were located at reservoirs and lakes managed by these regional authorities. It was feared that, by creating private companies, recreational use would either be restricted or that higher prices would be demanded for land rent and access, thereby pushing out smaller voluntary sector clubs. To reduce the chances of this happening the Act imposed the responsibility on the new water companies to have regard for the desirability of maintaining public access to water and surrounding countryside for recreational purposes. The Act also restricts the sale of land by water companies without entering into a convenant with the Secretary of State for the Environment, thereby protecting established public access onto the land.

So far the creation of the new water companies has had little of the feared impacts on recreational access. Established sailing clubs, such as Datchet Water Sailing Club on Queen Mother Reservoir, now owned and managed by Thames Water (see *Figure 6.4*), continue to flourish. Some now believe that these earlier fears were unfounded, others that the Act has successfully protected the recreational interest, whilst others are still worried about future developments. Regional water companies do not have recreational responsibilities, but have so far, continued to offer opportunities where they already exist. It could be speculated that since recreational activities have a commercial value then in future years increased and new opportunities may be available. However, as the new companies are independent there may be regional differences in policy and attitude towards recreational provision. The map in *Figure 6.5* illustrates the geographic areas of responsibility.

Figure 6.4   **Water companies now dominate ownership of major reservoirs**

Figure 6.5   **Water Service Companies in England & Wales**

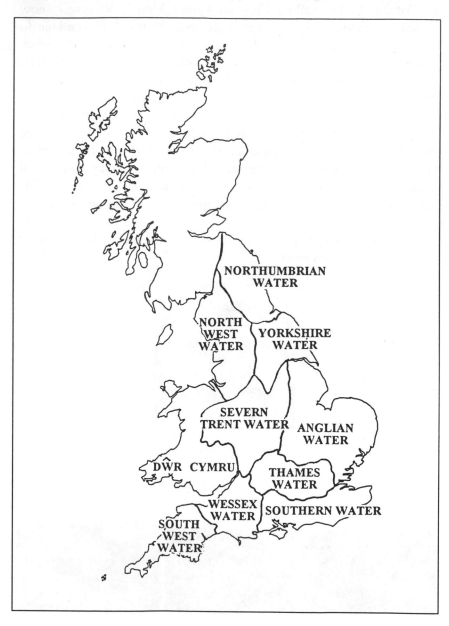

National Parks [particularly Broads Authority & Lake District]

Much of the land now owned by the new water companies falls within national parks. National parks are designated areas within England and Wales which have been selected for protection from further developments to maintain their conservation value and recreational opportunities. These areas were selected as beautiful and relatively wild countryside. National Park status offers protection to the natural environment and wildlife, access for open air activities and promotion of agricultural uses. This designation was formally created by the National Parks and Access to the Countryside Act 1949. (See *Figure 6.6* for current designated parks).

Although recreational interest within national parks is mainly with outdoor pursuits, such as walking and rock climbing, all of these parks offer opportunities for water based recreation and are an important resource for water sports within a preserved and natural environment. The resources include reservoirs such as Ladybower Reservoir in the Peak District, and rivers, particularly fast flowing, for canoeing such as the River Dart at Dartmeet in the Dartmoor National Park.

The Lake District National Park has, of course, particular interest in terms of water based recreation as it is the largest protected collection of natural inland lakes in England. Although many visitors to the Lake District go to climb its many majestic mountains, many others enjoy water based recreation on any one of its twelve main lakes (see *Figure 6.7*). Windermere is the largest of the lakes in this National Park, offering a wide range of water recreational resources including marinas, pleasure boat trips boat hire, water's edge picnic sites and a visitor centre. The Lake District offers the water sports enthusiast a huge array of opportunities from gentle tours to roaring rivers for white water canoeing or rafting. Hence, it forms an essential element of water based recreation in England.

Figure 6.6   The National Parks of England and Wales

Figure 6.7 **Main water resources in the Lake District**

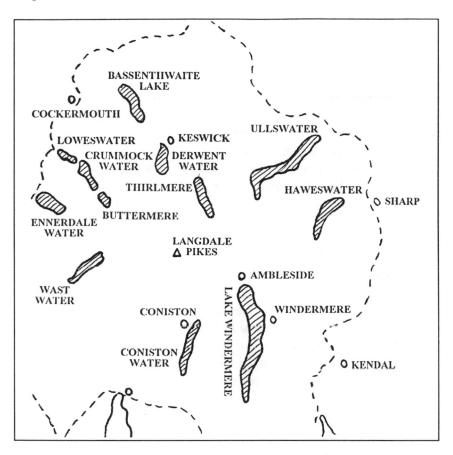

The newest of the designated areas is the Norfolk Broads, another particularly important area for inland water based recreation in England. The Broads Authority was created in 1989 with similar features as the existing National Parks but with not quite the same status. The Broads Authority was formed under the Norfolk and Suffolk Broads Act 1988 and consists of 35 members representing various interested authorities such as Anglian Water and Great Yarmouth Port and Haven Commissioners. The objectives of the Broads Authority is to:

1.	conserve and enhance the natural beauty,

2.	encourage public pleasure use of the Broads,

3.	protect navigation.

The Authority has certain powers over landbased recreation in the region, including the provision and management of open spaces. It also ensures the provision of accommodation and other services including camping and caravanning sites. The Authority has the power to encourage tourism whilst protecting existing structures and the natural environment. The Authority, therefore, has powers to ensure that water's edge recreation is satisfying for the participants whilst its impact is reduced on the area itself.

In terms of water based recreation the Broads Authority has certain navigation powers. It provides moorings, controls by licence, maintenance work, maintains facilities such as landing stages, registers all vessels on the water and generally improves the waterways. The Broads enjoy some delightful and historic cruising grounds. However, these areas have become eroded under the pressures of boats and tourism. The Broads Authority, uniquely, has the power to protect the environment whilst promoting recreational use.

Scottish Parks:
Scotland enjoys a much wider variety of inland water and wild countryside than England and, therefore, national parks have not been seen as a requirement. Regional parks have been developed, often near large populations, to include water resources for recreation. A most famous example is the Loch Lomond Park comprising 160 square miles, close to Glasgow and centred around Britain's largest inland water area, Loch Lomond. The Loch Lomond Park Authority is responsible for conservation of the natural and heritage value of the park whilst promoting enjoyment of the area and to balance these aspects with the needs of the local community.

Recreational opportunities for visitors include a range of water sports supported by several marinas, boat yards and specialist water sport centres. For the unskilled water enthusiast there is a range of cruises and ferries available. For recreational users attracted to the water's edge but not wanting to get their feet wet there is the West Highland Way, for keen walkers, and the Balloch Castle Country Park and Visitor Centre.

Examples like the Loch Lomond Park show the importance of managing areas that are particularly suitable and accessible to large populations for water based recreation. Without active encouragement many people would fail to grasp the benefits of water based leisure.

Country and Water Parks:
In response to the need for accessible recreational opportunity in Britain, country parks have been developed as centres for outdoor activities and, particularly, water sports. Country parks aim to provide a wider opportunity for countryside recreation and to protect more vulnerable areas. They were introduced in the 1966 White Paper, Leisure in the Countryside. Subsequently the Countryside Act 1968 allowed local authorities to purchase land for country parks. The Countryside Commission paid 50 per cent of the total price to local authorities and 75 per cent to private enterprises. Country parks have mainly developed in regions of dense population and with poor access to the national parks. For example, the Midlands and south east England have 53 parks each.

When country parks were first introduced the Countryside Commission set the following objectives:

1. Large number of visitors.

2. Offer a wider range of sporting activities.

3. Restore derelict land.

4. To provide a gateway to explore a wider countryside beyond.

An example is Wellington Country Park (south of Reading in Berkshire) covering 350 acres. The Park offers easy parking, picnic areas, barbecue sites, shops, nature trails, and deer park. All centre around a lake that offers water sports including sailing, wind surfing, and fishing.

Country parks have seen rising numbers of visitors since 1989 and offer several benefits, including excellent opportunities for outdoor recreation within a hour of urban areas. They have been particularly good at providing water sports.

Countryside Commission:
Although with no direct responsibility for inland water resources the Countryside Commission, founded in 1967 as an independent government sponsored organisation, is involved in various initiatives particularly connected to water's edge leisure. The Commission sets out to combine conservation with recreation by promoting understanding, research, experimental work, policy advice, designation, case work, technical advice and grant aid. Its work in recent years has concentrated on developing rights of way.

This has involved the development and funding of the Thames Path which is the first long distance route to follow a river, and runs for 213 miles from Kemble in Gloucestershire to the Thames Barrier in London (see *Figure 6.8*). The walk is suitable for short excursions, all age groups and abilities. The path was designated by the Secretary of State for the Environment in September 1989 and will be officially opened in 1994 with some sections awaiting completion. This is an important example of the work of the Countryside Commission for water recreation managers as it serves to illustrate the overlap between the activities of various organisations.

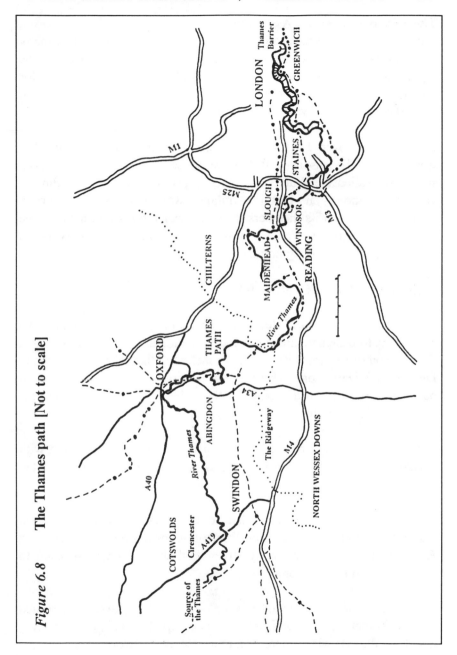

Figure 6.8   The Thames path [Not to scale]

The Inland Waterways Association:

This is a voluntary organisation founded in 1946 at a time when many of Britain's canals and river navigations were derelict. The organisation has since fought to keep the waterways open and alive, for both recreation and economic reasons. The IWA liaises regularly with official organisations which have an interest in waterways.

It has raised over £1 million towards the restoration of derelict waterways. To ensure that this work continues the IWA has a sub-group called the Waterways Recovery Group which co-ordinates voluntary labour on Britain's inland waterways. This group communicates with its members through local groups and a magazine *Navvies*. It also runs canal camps enabling enthusiasts to work on larger projects as working holidays.

SUMMARY OF LEGISLATION

1949 National Parks and Access to the Countryside Act - created the legal right to designate areas of land as national parks. It resulted in the creation of several National Parks including the Lake District, Peak District and Dartmoor. These areas are now important sites for all outdoor recreation but in particular the Lake District is of interest for water based recreation.

1962 Transport Act - replaced the British Transport Commission with smaller boards to cover specific types of transport. As a result the British Waterways Board was created.

1963 Water Resources Act - led to the creation of new lowland reservoirs which offer extensive recreation provision. The existing River Boards were replaced by River Authorities with permission to allow access for recreation.

1963 Report by the Institution of Water Engineers - suggested cautiously that on reservoirs fishing was acceptable, sailing and rowing could be allowed where there was management controls, canoeing was a cause for concern, and swimming and water skiing, it considered, should be excluded. (Tanner, 1993)

1966 White Paper, Leisure in the Countryside - introduced the idea of Country Parks as an important facility and development of the popularisation of water based recreation.

1968 Countryside Act - allowed local authorities and private companies to purchase land (with available grants) for Country Parks close to large populations.

1968 Transport Act - designation of commercial waterways, cruising waterways and a remainder which would be maintained or restored.

1973 Water Act - imposed responsibilities on Water Authorities for recreation and conservation. Water Space Amenity commission was created to assist with these responsibilities.

1983 British Waterways Act - reclassified the following restored waterways to cruising status:

Ashton Canal (Manchester), Lower Peak Forest Canal (Dukinfield), Caldon Canal (Leek), Erewash Canal (Long Eaton), Monmouthshire and Brecon Canal (Brecon to Pontypool) and Grand Union Canal (Slough).

1988 Norfolk and Suffolk Broads Act - created the Broads Authority which consists of 35 members representing various interested authorities such as Anglian Water and Great Yarmouth Port and Haven Commissioners.

1989 Water Act - Introduced the privatisation of water authorities and created the National Rivers Authority.

1990 Environmental Protection Act - introduced the Integrated Pollution Control.

1991 Water Resources Act - set objectives for water quality.

SUMMARY

The history of inland water resources is long and complex. Britain now enjoys a variety of resources for recreational use. Changes in the management and ownership of water resources have, at present, not affected recreational users substantially. The problems for inland water recreation managers in the future will be increased pressures of use, due to the rising popularity of many sports and the control of water quality particularly where algal blooms are concerned.

CHAPTER 7

Coastal Water: National Organisations, Ownership, Control and Policy

One of the greatest delights of life in Britain has been described as the island status; this allows seaside visits to be accessible from every inland town. The island geography has been an important factor in building Britain's historical seafaring traditions. For centuries fishermen have made a living from the wealth of marine assets. In more recent years, oil and gas have presented a new dimension to the value hidden in the surrounding seas. The coast has presented a natural deterrent to potential invading forces and has enabled Britain to build a strong and safe economy.

The delights of the coastal resources are equally important for the water based recreation manager, for whom Britain's endless seas present infinite challenges and opportunities. Many epic voyages started from British shores including Claire Francis' single handed circumnavigation of the world. There have been hundreds of attempts to be the first, fastest, and smallest boat to successfully cross oceans and accomplish the impossible. The seas around Britain have provided a training ground for some of the world's most famous sailors and yacht designers. The sea offers humans one of the greatest of the worlds challenges, to harness its undoubted powers and to cover ground not previously encountered. Challenge is an important quality of people's leisure, people who are possibly trapped in boring or mundane work during the week. The sea presents unpredictability, a force which humans cannot control and a scope for presenting seemingly infinite numbers of challenges. Recently John Ridgeway, who previously could be assumed to have faced all the challenges of the sea, set out in a canoe to round Cape Horn, one of the most notorious stretches of sea in the world.

Most participants of water based recreation find that Britain's seas offer ample scope for challenge and discovery. On Friday evenings during the summer months, thousands of dedicated recreational sailors and water sports enthusiasts from London and the Home Counties, head south to the Solent and other coastal water resources. Many go to cruise and relax on boats, others to wind surf from the many beaches and still more go just to relax on the beaches or stroll round the coast absorbing its magic atmosphere. With so many recreational users' in confined areas it is essential that both the environment and the users activities are managed to reduce conflict and the environmental impact. This chapter identifies the main organisations responsible for this management.

Access to the shoreline and the beds of estuaries is owned by the Crown. There are common-law rights to the access of foreshores and the seashore for bathing and other activities. In tidal waters there is a public right to navigation but there are mooring and anchoring restrictions. Many coastal and estuary areas are dominated by private water's edge properties which can restrict access to and from tidal water.

Firstly, it is important to consider the quality of the resources that are on offer. Quality can refer to the actual cleanliness of the water, the coastal environment and the beaches. Growing concerns about pollution have led the argument that many beaches around Britain's coast no longer present safe bathing areas.

WATER QUALITY IN COASTAL AREAS

In 1990 the level of sewage sludge dumped into the seas around Britain was estimated as 9 million tonnes, representing approximately 30 per cent of all UK sewage sludge. The sewage is often discharged into the sea through coastal outfall pipes leaving sewage close to the shore and bathing beaches. The results of this discharge can be seen on many of the beaches in Britain. Beach owners, managers and local businesses, dependent on the tourist trade, have expressed concern that this practice is driving customers away and destroying the associated trade. Some private owners in north Devon and Cornwall have resorted to the expensive process of cleaning their beaches regularly to prevent the discharged sewage debris being found on their beaches. The problem of disposing raw sewage at sea close to beaches and seaside towns is threefold. Firstly, the sewage washes up onto the beaches and floats in the sea. It is an unpleasant sight for tourists. Secondly, poor water quality causes concern regarding the potential for infection and disease that could affect bathers. Thirdly, raw sewage creates an unpleasant smell and drives holiday makers away from beaches.

All water sports users are affected by these discharges in some way, at the least by detracting from a pleasant environment and at worst for divers, wind surfers and bathers, regularly submerged in water, the risk of serious infection and disease.

Many groups have begun to campaign against sewage discharge near bathing beaches. The most famous has been the surfers campaign 'Surfers Against Sewage', formed by keen surfers whose enjoyment of their sport was being reduced by the unpleasantness of swimming alongside sewage waste and the after-effects of stomach upsets and rashes. Their campaign has received extensive coverage and has achieved improved awareness.

Bathing Waters and Beaches:
The increased level of public concern about beaches and water quality has lead to various legislation and controls. Although the problem of sewage appears the most emotive subject for bathers, the proven risks of serious infection are low compared to other forms of pollution. The 1975 European Community Directive 76/160/EEC set standards in microbiological terms which must not be exceeded in bathing waters.

These are defined as areas where bathing is not prohibited and which are traditional sites for large numbers of bathers each year. Most sites have been defined where car parking, toilets, staff and other facilities exist for recreational use. The guidelines check for 19 different physical, chemical and microbiological parameters which may affect bathing water quality and, in large quantities, present a public health hazard. To ensure that these standards are met at all times (one sample may prove the water is clear but further investigation may show contamination at regular intervals during the summer season) a minimum of 20 samples must be taken from mid-May to the end of September. These dates change slightly on northern coasts to reflect the shorter bathing season. The samples are carried out by the National Rivers Authority in England and Wales, the River Purification Boards in Scotland and the Department of the Environment in Northern Ireland. A bathing area is approved if 95 per cent of the samples meet the requirements.

The affects of bathing in water contaminated by sewage was discussed in a report by the House of Commons Select Committee on the Environment, published in July 1990. This report concludes that, although the chance of serious infection is very small, bathing in such water can lead to minor infections affecting ear, nose and throat, gastro-enteritis and skin irritations. Clearly it is, therefore, important for the leisure manager that coastal beaches and bathing areas are clean if customers are to remain satisfied and enjoy their water based recreation.

The results of the European Community Directives in 1991 were that, out of 453 bathing waters in Britain, 343 complied with these standards. The degree of success varied across the regions with Northern Ireland enjoying the cleanest bathing water with 100 per cent compliance. Beaches in the north west of England fared worst with only 30 per cent of their beaches offering suitable water quality. The results of these tests have led to increased efforts to clean up bathing waters. The British record has improved since 1988, when only 66 per cent of its bathing areas complied to the directives, compared to 76 per cent in 1991.

Leisure and recreation managers can inspect the results of these tests, when selecting a suitable beach for water sports projects, in registers held at the regional offices of the NRA in England and Wales, RPB in Scotland and the DOE in Northern Ireland. Careful site selection will help to ensure that the unpleasant after-effects to water users are avoided, that fears on the part of potential customers can be relieved and, therefore, happy customers should be the result.

For the casual beach user consulting registers is time consuming. Most will not bother to establish where better bathing areas exist if this is the only source of information. Therefore, in 1991 the UK launched a poster scheme for local authorities encouraging them to display water quality information in prominent sites. The information should be presented in an easily understood format avoiding technical jargon which some leisure users may not understand. Virtually all local authorities participated in this scheme for the first time allowing the leisure user sufficient information to avoid contaminated areas. The result of this may also serve to encourage areas of lower quality to improve their standards.

The European Directive is not only concerned with the water quality but also with the whole beach environment. In order to identify beaches which offered high overall standards, the Foundation for Environmental Education in Europe launched the Blue Flag campaign in 1987. The Blue Flag is awarded annually to beaches which comply with the EC directive on water quality and satisfy a broad range of criteria including good management, safety, facilities and information for recreational users. British beaches won 17 Blue Flags in 1992 (as illustrated in *Figure 7.1*). The Blue Flag campaign has provided status and a goal, in terms of quality, for beach management. Many local authorities and private beach owners have been forced to adopt a more professional approach to the management of their resources. The prestige and publicity afforded to beaches displaying the award encourages new visitors. Holiday makers may perceive that beaches without the award are poor in quality. This competition has successfully improved maintenance and quality of the beach experience in Britain.

Further to the Blue Flag awards the Tidy Britain Group introduced Seaside Awards in 1992. Beaches apply for the award which is judged on the water quality directive standards and associated facilities. They can receive an ordinary or premier award. In 1992 there were 107 applications of which 96 awards were presented of these 36 were for premier status inferring tougher standards had been met than for the Blue Flag Award.

Although designed to complement the Blue Flag scheme the existence of two different award schemes can be confusing for prospective holiday makers.

Britain is now aware of the importance of maintaining quality at beach locations. Many owners are committed to improving the facilities that they offer to compete with their European neighbours. The information provided is essential for decision-making in recreation planning and can be used to market resources if presented to customers in a user-friendly format.

Water Companies and Sewage discharges:
New requirements under the EC Directive have resulted in the necessity for water companies to clean up their act and revise current methods of sewage disposal around the coast. Currently South West Water is undertaking a project called 'Clean Sweep' designed to achieve EC standards on all bathing beaches in the their region. The scheme will cost an estimated £900 million and is made up of 33 projects benefitting 81 beaches. The completion date for these projects is set as 1995.

Figure 7.1   **1992 Blue Flag award winners**

Source - HMSO - UK Environment

An example of one of the 'Clean Sweep' projects can be seen at Lyme Regis in Dorset. The outdated sewage system was built at the turn of the century and can no longer cope with the town's population and the thousands of summer visitors. This system means that raw sewage is discharged through short sea outfalls close to beaches and has led to the failure of Lyme Regis to comply with EC standards. The new system will be able to cope with the capacity required during summer months, treating all sewage before finally discharging disinfected water through an outfall well clear of bathing waters. The benefits of the scheme will be to ensure that bathing water reaches EC standards, that water in the River Lim is improved and the holiday environment, heavily dependant on summer tourism, becomes more pleasant.

Improvement work by water companies around the country will help to win more Blue Flags for British beaches if combined with improved beach management. In this way British beaches will be able to compete successfully with other countries well into the twenty first century, thereby, maintaining the age-old tradition of British seaside holidays.

Management of other coastal pollution:
Water quality around our coasts is not solely affected by sewage discharges although they are often the most obvious and unsightly. Other sources of pollution include industrial discharges, dumping of waste from ships at sea and oil discharges most commonly from oil platforms. Estuaries have the second biggest recreational significance after beaches. Usually easily accessible, estuaries are becoming increasingly crowded with water's edge activities, launching and all number of powered and non-powered water sports. Estuaries are surveyed for water quality in similar ways as rivers and canals and the results of such surveys have shown that, of the estimated 2,700 km of estuaries in England and Wales, 90 per cent were classified as good or fair, making them accessible for recreational use (source: NRA).

There are many organisations with an interest in the quality of the marine environment:

a. *UK Fisheries Departments* - monitor the quality of the marine environment to ensure that it meets international requirements. This monitoring is carried out by the Ministry of Agriculture Fisheries and Food (in England and Wales), the Scottish Office's Agriculture and Fisheries Department and the Department of the Environment in Northern Ireland.

b. *The Marine Pollution Monitoring Management Group* - also monitors water quality and is made up of government experts and other organisations with a responsibility for the marine environment. Their proposals, made in 1991, set up a national monitoring programme to bring British water in line with international standards.

c. *North Sea Conferences* - set up to agree policies to protect the marine environment. The second conference in 1987 agreed to limit, by 50 per cent in 1995, the number of 'red list' substances contaminating the sea. The third conference, in 1990, agreed tighter controls on the discharge form ships to protect the marine environment. These controls also cover pleasure craft and it is now illegal to dispose of any waste from boats with fines and penalties imposed on culprits.

d. *International Council for the Exploration of the Seas* - acts in the interests of marine science to advise conferences and other interested groups in developing sustainable use of seas.

e. *The Oslo* and *Paris Conventions* - introduced, from the Oslo convention in 1974, motions to prevent the dumping of waste from ships. The Paris convention is concerned with the dumping from land sources.

f. *International Maritime Organisation* - is concerned with the safety of the seas and controlling pollution from ships thus protecting the marine environment.

g. *Marine Conservation Society* - formed in 1983, is concerned with raising public awareness of marine conservation issues.

Some water sports have become concerned in general marine pollution issues. The British Sub Aqua Club are currently working, through their members, with the Marine Conservation Society to build up a database of marine water quality in diving areas. The Divers for Clean Waters campaign is currently surveying members of the BSAC for information on water quality, type of pollution present, effluent pipes, related health problems and damage to the sea bed caused by scallop dredging, aggregate dredging, and trawling. This illustrates the growing relationship between conservation groups and recreational users. To reduce concerns about the environmental impact of water sports governing bodies and other organisations could seek to improve existing links and forge new relationships to increase public awareness of the positive aspects of recreational water use.

THE QUALITY OF THE COASTAL ENVIRONMENT

The attraction of the coast as a venue for leisure and recreation is, in part, due to the outstanding natural beauty often associated with these areas. Visitors enjoy cliff walks, the wildlife that lives in these areas, the feeling of freedom, open spaces and the uninterrupted views. Unfortunately, as pressure from these leisure interests and other developments grow, concern for the coastal environment increases. In the past is was assumed that the coast would be there forever, as a place of beauty and wilderness. However, as seaside developments, ports and towns begin to sprawl, it is realised that the coastal environment is at risk of losing the very qualities that make it so attractive.

The National Trust and Enterprise Neptune :
In the early 1960s much of the coastline was under private ownership. In 1875, the National Trust's first property was four and half miles of cliff above Cardigan Bay. The Trust continued to obtain coastal land and by 1965 it had acquired 187 miles of unspoilt coast in various locations such as Blakeney Point in Norfolk, Brownsea Island in Poole Harbour and the Giants Causeway in County Antrim. The National Trust had become increasingly aware of the growing pressure from the

leisure market and for development. In 1963 it commissioned a study in 1963 of the British coastline. The results of this survey, of approximately 3,000 miles of coast, was that one-third was already developed beyond the possibility of conservation, another third was judged to be of little scenic or recreational importance but the remaining third was considered to be of outstanding natural beauty and worthy of protection. This area covered approximately 900 miles of coastline at a time when the National Trust owned only 187 miles.

In order to protect the areas identified in the study the Duke of Edinburgh launched *Enterprise Neptune* in 1965 with three clear objectives:

1.   To obtain coastline identified in the survey for protection and public access for recreation.

2.   To increase public awareness of the threats to the British coastline.

3.   To raise £2 million towards the purchase of this land.

Once purchased, the National Trust applied management techniques to preserve the existing natural beauty. Sometimes it had to remove existing buildings and persuade farmers to alter their practices. In the first year the Treasury pledged £250,000 towards the appeal and the first land purchased was Whitburrows in South Wales, an area of salt marshes and sand dunes. At the end of the first decade the National Trust celebrated with the purchase of the Needles Headland on the Isle of Wight. This is a popular visitor location for holiday makers on the island and a welcome landfall for many yachts entering the Solent. Unfortunately the National Trust failed to purchase the land at Lands End which has since been developed as a major leisure venue and tourist attraction. By the end of 1992 the National Trust owned 530 miles of coastline and had raised £17.5 million to protect and preserve the recreational and conservation value of the British coastline.

The coastline continues to be managed sympathetically by wardens of the National Trust, balancing the needs of recreational users with conservation. Paths and access points are maintained as unobtrusively as possible. Camp sites and car parks are added but screened to avoid spoiling the aesthetic appearance. Areas such a Newtown Creek on the Isle of Wight are managed as a nature reserve and a popular mooring place for many thousands of yachts each year.

Heritage Coasts:

The concerns of the National Trust were followed the following year by the National Parks Commission who began a study of coastline protection. This study resulted in the publication by the Countryside Commission in 1970 of two reports, *The Coastal Heritage* and *The Planning of the Coastline*. These reports suggested, in line with the work of the National Trust, that certain areas of coastline required protection for conservation and recreational purposes. The recommendation was that selected lengths of unspoilt coastline should receive the designation Heritage Coast and be provided with a management plan, to be drawn up by the Countryside Commission. The government approved these ideas in 1972 and since this time over 900 miles of coast have been designated Heritage Coast. They are now afforded protection from development. The designated areas form some of the finest stretches of coast in England and Wales and act to protect, effectively manage and resolve conflicts occurring in these areas.

The objectives defined for Heritage Coasts were set out in the original 1970 proposals and are:

1. to select the areas of coast which are suitable for protection

2. to cover all aspects of their management and conservation

3. to offer opportunities for public access and enjoyment through active promotion with due regard for their conservation needs.

The management of Heritage Coasts is invariably the responsibility of the local authority concerned, directed by the Heritage Coast Management Plans drawn up by the Countryside Commission. The original objectives were enlarged in 1991 by the policy statement *Heritage Coasts Policies and Priorities*. This statement was reissued in 1992 when the Sports Council joined with the Heritage Coast Forum to review sport and recreation management issues on these coasts. A publication *Sport and Recreation on Heritage Coasts* assesses the management plans for every coast in the light of recreational demands and makes recommendations for further alterations. Current objectives for the management of these sites are landscape, nature and heritage conservation, public access, sport, recreation, education and tourism, environmental health, sustainable development, local communities, agriculture, forestry and fishing. Many Heritage Coasts are in wild and inaccessible places (see *Figure 7.2*). However, those areas which are more easily accessible support a wide range of water's edge recreation and water sports. Many of the coasts do not yet have a plan to include the management of sport and recreation. However, certain case studies by the Sports Council have highlighted the importance of the following management issues:

1. Agreement is needed for access to reduce the impact on wildlife.
2. Information should be freely available concerning recreational opportunities and restrictions.
3. Since there are often more than one organisation involved, managers must seek to improve the multi-agency approach for co-ordinated efforts.
4. Sports activities should be zoned to reduce conflict.
5. Rangers are important in increasing public awareness of conservation problems and enforcing compliance with any restrictions.
6. Community involvement in site management programmes can reduce problems of vandalism.
7. Codes of Conduct, [similar to the Waterways codes mentioned in Chapter 5], encourage responsible use.

Figure 7.2   **Some Designated Heritage Coasts**

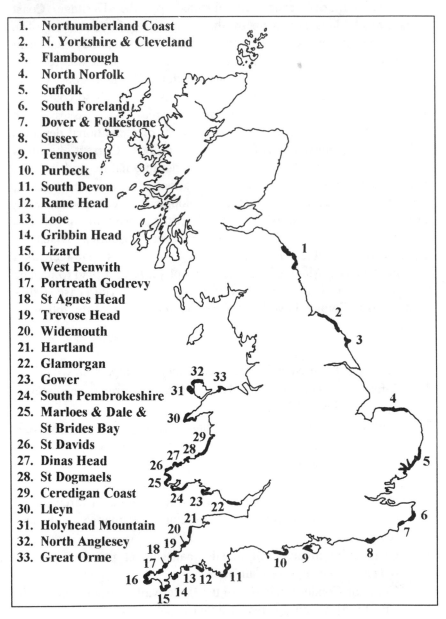

1. **Northumberland Coast**
2. **N. Yorkshire & Cleveland**
3. **Flamborough**
4. **North Norfolk**
5. **Suffolk**
6. **South Foreland**
7. **Dover & Folkestone**
8. **Sussex**
9. **Tennyson**
10. **Purbeck**
11. **South Devon**
12. **Rame Head**
13. **Looe**
14. **Gribbin Head**
15. **Lizard**
16. **West Penwith**
17. **Portreath Godrevy**
18. **St Agnes Head**
19. **Trevose Head**
20. **Widemouth**
21. **Hartland**
22. **Glamorgan**
23. **Gower**
24. **South Pembrokeshire**
25. **Marloes & Dale & St Brides Bay**
26. **St Davids**
27. **Dinas Head**
28. **St Dogmaels**
29. **Ceredigan Coast**
30. **Lleyn**
31. **Holyhead Mountain**
32. **North Anglesey**
33. **Great Orme**

8. Consultation and involvement of sports clubs and societies in the management issues ensure that all needs are understood.
9. Monitoring should take place to assess the environmental impact of various levels of use.
10. Recreation plans can be used to ensure an integrated approach to site management.

Examples of some of these points can be seen in the case of Blakeney Point. This is a popular site for water skiing and other watersports. It is also a breeding ground for terns. The problem identified was the disturbance caused to the terns from landing by water sports users. To counter this problem the use of the area has been zoned to move landing away from breeding grounds and to avoid critical seasons for the birds. This illustrates the use of zoning and inter-agency participation as the agreement was achieved with co-operation from the National Trust and Blakeney Boatmen's Association.

THE MANAGEMENT OF ACTIVITIES ON THE COAST

With over 3,000 miles of coastline and a wide range of demands, there is a need for some co-ordinating organisations to manage those areas which are particularly crowded, such as harbours and estuaries. It is also necessary to ensure that all activities in British waters are carried out legally and safely. There are several organisations - some government, others independent - which deal with these issues.

Ports and Harbour Authorities:

All ports and harbours in Britain need to be managed effectively to balance the needs of a wide variety of users. The maintenance of harbour facilities requires significant funding and staffing. This is frequently provided by an overall body, either the Harbour Authority for small harbours or the Port Authority - usually for major commercial and naval bases with substantial dock areas and higher numbers of commercial shipping movements.

The authority of the harbours is controlled by the Department of

Transport within the framework of the Harbours Act 1964. Each harbour has rights and powers bestowed upon it by individual local Acts and harbour orders. A harbour can create bye laws and has the first responsibilty to enforce these rules so long as they are allowed by the particular harbour order. There is no one framework for identifying the responsibilities of harbour authorities. They will vary from harbour to harbour. However, it is usual for the harbour authority to control the management of navigation, mooring and facilities within a harbour, and it is part of the local authority. In smaller harbours the responsibilities may include the provision of moorings for permanent and visitor use. The fees for using the moorings are collected on a regular basis by the harbour master or his/her assistant from visiting boats and by clerical staff from permanent moorings. The harbour master is usually kept busy in the summer months with visiting pleasure yachts which moor overnight to piles, mooring buoys, pontoons or harbour walls, as provided. If there are a number of visitor moorings in the middle of the harbour the harbour master usually collects fees by visiting each boat either on arrival or the following morning. The harbour master is often in a recreational management role. He offers advice and information to visiting water users. The harbour master also controls where visiting boats can moor and all visiting boats should receive permission to moor in the chosen location before leaving the boat unattended. In busy harbours, such as Yarmouth, the harbour master's team directs boats to moorings on entry to ensure that the optimum number of boats can moor up safely.

The harbour authority often provides shower and toilet facilities for visiting boat owners on the quay. If many of the visitor moorings are in the centre the harbour, the authority may chose to provide a taxi service or allow a private company to set up offering this service. In any case the harbour will need to provide a landing stage for the tenders to the visiting and resident yachts.

Harbours are required by law to provide waste disposal facilities and they usually provide water. Some harbours supply or subcontract the supply of diesel and petrol. For dinghy and other small craft harbour authorities usually supply a slip for launching and retrieving craft. The harbour authorities are increasingly assuming a recreation management role, providing services for cruising yachts on similar, although more basic, lines to yacht marinas.

Harbour authorities are often a useful source of information for recreational users. They provide weather information and details of local conditions on notice boards at the harbour office. Staff will usually be able to assist with more complex enquiries about local services and facilities.

Port Authorities invariably cover much larger areas and offer a much wider range of commercial services for cargo vessels. A major port authority is the Port of London whose responsibilities include the management of both commercial and pleasure traffic. Its responsibilities include pilotage services to help big commercial vessels negotiate the complex and narrow entrance to the River Thames. However, the Port of London also works hard to promote recreational interests. It produces a series of leaflets regarding rowing, canoeing, water skiing and jet skiing opportunities within the Port of London.

Many port and harbour authorities are members of the trade association and the British Ports Authority. The Harbour and Port Authorities contribute considerably to the accessibility of water based recreation through the provision of reasonably priced moorings and visitor services. They also make an important contribution to reducing potential conflicts between water users through careful management of the varied demands in confined harbour spaces.

Her Majesty's Coastguard:
HM Coastguard is part of the Maritime Directorate of the Department of Transport assigned the role of co-ordinating all civil maritime search and rescue operations around the British coast and for 1,000 miles out into the Atlantic. HM Coastguard is made up of a uniformed staff who co-ordinate facilities such as the RNLI, Royal Navy helicopters, inshore teams and other services. HM Coastguard run their own team

of inflatable rescue craft for inshore emergencies at Sumburgh in the Shetlands and Stornaway in the Outer Hebrides. There are rescue helicopters stationed at Lee on Solent. HM Coastguard also manages the Channel Navigation Service and assists the Marine Pollution Control Unit of the Department of Transport.

HM Coastguard employs over 500 regular officers and appoints over 6,500 Auxiliary Coastguards to form a local backup network. These Auxiliary Coastguards are volunteers who provide a range of part-time services. HM Coastguard co-ordinates approximately 7,000 incidents each year involving around 11,500 people. For recreational water users HM Coastguard provides essential information services in the form of leaflets, regular weather information on the VHF radios used by small craft, assistance on channel 67 for all maritime traffic and a register of yachts and pleasure craft.

The Coastguard was established in 1822 to crack down on smuggling operations around the coast. Until 1923 the Coastguard had no specific responsibility for the protection of lives. In 1923 HM Coastguard was officially given the responsibility of search and rescue under the control of the Board of Trade. In the 1970s a major reorganisation took place which led to the current situation with the controlling power altered to the Department of Transport.

The work in search and rescue is dominated by pleasure craft as shown in *Figure 7.3* which analyses assistance rendered to boats during 1992.

Professional seagoing activities account for 20 per cent of casualty figures. Many of the call-outs to pleasure vessels could be easily avoided by good planning - boats running out of fuel accounted for 70 incidents in 1992. Incidents to people showed the highest call-out for medical evacuations, closely followed by people cut off by the tide.

Other work of HM Coastguard includes safety information in response to enquiries from the public, investigations into safety, public relations work to increase awareness, media information, and surveillance. In the field of humane work HM Coastguard rescues stranded animals. It also assists the work of HM Customs. Further details on the work of HM Coastguard in water safety is covered in Chapter 12.

Figure 7.3   **Coastguard co-ordinated assistance to boats [1992]**

Type of Craft	Number of Incidents
Powered pleasure craft	1059
Sailing Craft	873
Merchant Fishing	665
Sailboards	366
Small Craft - dinghies and canoes	349
Inflatable Craft	185
Merchant Vessels	83
Other	78
Military	9
TOTAL	3667

Source : HM Coastguard 1992

Royal National Lifeboat Institution:
Considering the number of recreational craft using the coastal waters there are very few serious incidents each year. However, Britain enjoys the exceptional services of a charitable organisation - the RNLI. Lifeboats are located around the coast to respond to emergencies at sea. These may include lifting injured crew to safety, escorting vessels to a safe harbour or, in the most extreme cases, rescuing crews from stricken vessels. The RNLI provides both offshore and inshore service around the coast, responding to calls for help 24 hours a day 52 weeks a year. The rescue service is manned mainly by volunteers and supported by charitable donations. Fund raising is a continuous process. Every year a week is reserved by local groups for a door-to-door collection. To increase interest in their services the RNLI has a club for adults called Shoreline, and one for young members called Storm Force. Storm Force provides members with a badge, stickers, competitions, posters, puzzles and stories.

Her Majesty's Customs:

HM Coastguard was originally set up to reduce smuggling around the coast. The responsibility for this area has now moved to HM Customs. The work of HM Customs in ensuring that goods do not enter Britain illegally is a complex one. When consideration is given to the number of vessels entering and leaving harbours every day it appears an impossible task. Indeed many illegal goods have been discovered over the years entering the country on pleasure craft. Before the European market all yachts leaving Britain were required to complete a customs form declaring the identity of the boat and details of all crew members. These forms were deposited at customs boxes on the shore before departure. On returning to British waters, boats were required to report to HM Customs. HM Customs then reserved the right to visit the boat within two hours to inspect it. After two hours, if no customs official appeared, the skipper simply completed a customs declaration and posted it in to the customs box. Although obviously open to abuse, this system allowed HM Customs to keep track of most of the activities of pleasure craft.

Since Britain's entry into the European market British yachts have been able to travel to and from Europe without these checks. This makes the work of Customs Officers increasingly difficult. It is to the recreational users' advantage for good and vigilant customs procedures to be adhered to. This will discourage some of the dealing and piracy operations that have made some North African waters dangerous for pleasure craft.

SUMMARY

In order to preserve our coastal heritage for future generations the problems of usage and management of approximately 3,000 miles of British coastline have been addressed by the formation of government organisations together with the introduction of various pieces of legislation. This chapter analyses a number of the key issues for recreational users. The main factors in the management of coastal resources are:

1923 HM Coastguard officially assigned life saving responsibilities

1965 National Trust launched Enterprise Neptune

1970 Countryside Commission proposes Heritage Coast Designation.

1970 Reorganisation of HM Coastguard to current structure

1972 Heritage Coasts approved

1975 European Community Directive 76/160/EEC set standards in microbiological terms for bathing water.

1987 Foundation for Environmental Education in Europe launched the Blue Flag campaign

1991 Revised objectives for Heritage Coasts

1992 Tidy Britain Group introduced the Seaside Awards

CHAPTER 8

Specific Venues for Water Based Recreation

AN INTRODUCTION TO CURRENT DEVELOPMENTS

With the general boom in the leisure industry during the 1980s came a boom in professional provision of facilities for water sports and water based recreation. The commercialism which took hold of the leisure market could not ignore a potential market where, despite lower participation, average spending was high. The developments, which are a result of this boom in leisure industry investment, can be seen to have followed two main types. The majority of commercial ventures have developed the elitist image of water sports by developing exclusive venues for the discerning customer. High quality, often at a high price, with many marina developers being criticised for taking yachting and boat owning further from the grasp of ordinary person. It is not uncommon for a 26 ft. family cruiser to be faced with an annual bill for marina moorings on the south coast in the region of £1,700. This figure does not include day-to-day running costs and mooring fees at cruising destinations. This could thus make sailing, once more, a pursuit of the well-off.

Other enterprises have remained committed to mass participation with the development of several purpose built water sports centres on disused gravel pits and in country parks. Even more developers have tried to achieve the financial benefit of mass participation combined with the premium value of exclusivity through the development of marina leisure complexes such as Brighton Marina, Port Solent and The Albert Dock. This has been achieved with varying levels of success.

This chapter considers the development of water sports centres and examine the ways in which various types of development seek to meet the needs of their target market. It commences with an analysis of traditional water sports venues, still a very important and significant provider of opportunities today. It then looks at a range of newer style developments including the growth of marinas, the marina village concept, the leisure venue concept, the exclusive sports club, the marina as a part of urban regeneration, water sports centres and country parks.

TRADITIONAL WATER SPORTS VENUES

Clubs and Societies:

The historical base for many water sports was the voluntary members' club. These clubs attracted members with a shared interest, for example, rowing, canoeing or sailing. The members paid an annual subscription to funds to cover the costs of running the club. Most water sports clubs needed to set up in a fixed venue close to the water's edge. Some clubs, such as rowing clubs, can use the existing water resource without modification. Other clubs, such as water skiing, may need to have overall control over the water resources, as well as the club house, in order to maintain suitable jumps and launching areas.

Clubs and societies were at first the main source of access to water sports as few venues catered for a pay-as-you-play basis. The benefits of a club structure for water sports participation are that generally the costs are lower because the organisation operates on an non-profit basis and management decisions are controlled by the members for the members. Clubs are managed by non-leisure professionals formed into an elected committee. The committee is responsible for such tasks as social events, membership, treasurer, secretary, maintenance, bar, competitions and training. Committees are usually chaired by the Captain (or Commodore in many sailing and yacht clubs) who, in turn is supported in his/her duties by a deputy or vice-commodore. This tried and tested structure attempts to ensure that work-loads are evenly distributed by members and it is usual for committee members to be re-elected on an annual basis. Unfortunately, the problem faced by many small clubs is that the work falls on the same people year after year. Other members seem reluctant to contribute to workings of the club, only wanting to enjoy the facilities provided.

Water sports clubs range in atmosphere, size and age with some examples of elite and luxurious clubs established many years ago and examples of new clubs with only a handful of members struggling to get started in very basic accommodation. The traditional yacht club remains popular today, providing for the traditional market in luxury and quality service. These clubs are usually established in superb facilities and are run by a committee for decision-making but are staffed on a regular basis by a professional team of bar mangers, chefs, boatmen, and maintenance teams. These clubs offer status with membership, for example, the Royal Yacht Squadron in Cowes, Isle of Wight or the Royal Cornwall Yacht Club in Falmouth. Members pay premium rates to mix with the established names in the sport, to enjoy traditional quality service and the opportunity for social and competitive events.

These elitist clubs are decreasing in number as more clubs try to attract mass membership. Newer clubs are often established in run-down or prefabricated buildings but offer an entry point into the sport with training events, low-level competition and social events which are often designed to raise funds for the club itself. Both types of club have an important role and serve to meet specific demands from various sectors of the market. There are similarities in structure and organisation with a non-profit making aspect that is important to the success of each facility.

Water sports clubs have historically been an essential element in promoting participation in water based recreation. This is frequently ignored by public sector provision leaving alternatives to the private sector where prices may restrict levels of participation. Affiliation of clubs to the national governing bodies allows for communication and competition across the sport to be more easily established. This affiliation has allowed many clubs to grow and become more significant in the provision of water based leisure. The facilities provided by these clubs will also vary from sport to sport.

A.   Sailing Clubs

Most sailing clubs, usually found at the water's edge on either coastal or inland resources, now offer wind surfing membership in addition to sailing dinghies. Some coastal clubs offer cruising membership. The club house usually provides changing facilities and showers, basic catering facilities and a bar area for social events. Outside the club house sufficient space is required for boat parking (see *Figure 8.1*). The size of membership of inland clubs is usually controlled by the size of the boat park, not by the size of the lake itself, as all boats are removed from the water after use. The club will require all owners to be covered by third party insurance and will need to provide a launching slip, often surfaced in concrete, and a pontoon or floating walkway for boats to wait on whilst retrieving or launching is in progress.

To ensure safety, the club will need to provide rescue boats with outboard engines to assist craft and, if necessary, return them to the shore if they get into difficulties. The club may also need a race control room with good vantage over the whole area together with a committee boat to start and end races. Wind surfers are usually stored on racks as shown in *Figure 8.2* on page 171.

Figure 8.1   **Boat Park**

The need for shoreside space for dinghies can restrict the membership capacity of clubs more than the size of the water resource

Figure 8.2 **Windsurfer Store on a Rack System**

B.   Canoeing Clubs

Some canoe clubs thrive without a base, merely acting as a focus for excursions to venues and events. Other canoe clubs exist with a club house, boat storage and launching facilities along similar lines to those required by rowing clubs. Additional equipment occasionally required is a rescue boat with outboard motor and a road trailer to allow larger numbers of boats to be transported around the country. Some canoe clubs have boats and equipment of their own for use on introductory courses.

C.   Water Ski Clubs

most water ski clubs have sole use of their water resources or occasionally share with jet skis. Water ski clubs need a site of relatively flat water surrounded by gently slopping banks. For competitions and training the clubs may need to set up permanent jumps and other structures. Many of the tow boats arrive by trailer but some clubs keep a tow boat either ashore, on the trailer or on a mooring in the lake. The club house will have similar facilities as sailing clubs but covered storage may be desirable for equipment.

D.   Yacht Clubs

Usually located on the coast, most yacht clubs simply offer a social focus for yachting activities. Catering and bar facilities are traditionally available for members and visiting yachtsmen. The clubs sometimes own minimal mooring rights on a river or harbour. This offers members an extremely cheap mooring option when they finally get to the top of the inevitably long waiting list.

E.   Sub Aqua Clubs

Sub aqua clubs can again, simply be a collection of like-minded people who travel to various sites. The formation of a club can help to share the cost of more expensive equipment and offer improved safety in diving expeditions as a group. Some clubs do, however, have basic club house facilities.

F.   Rowing Clubs

Rowing clubs traditionally grew up along the major rivers of England, particularly the River Thames.   Most modern boat houses are of a similar design to traditional ones illustrated in Chapter 3.   The requirement is usually for a large open plan covered area, similar to a garage, for the storage of boats and equipment with social and changing facilities above (see *Figure 8.3*). Many rowing clubs are now open to canoe members enabling the spread of increasing financial costs at prime riverside locations.

Figure 8.3   **Modern-style Boat House**

The need for more capacity has led to outside storage

G.   Angling Clubs

Most anglers join clubs to enjoy fishing rights to well stocked resources. Many clubs, therefore, have no specific facility but merely retain the right to fish in a particular area.

Boatyards and Mooring Companies:

An alternative to club membership, for some sports, was the use of boatyards and mooring company facilities, possibly the forerunners of the modern marina company.   Boatyards were usually established around traditional maintenance skills on both inland and coastal waters. These businesses saw the opportunity to expand by allowing boat owners to keep their boats at the property in exchange for a fee or rent. The facilities offered by such yards were usually basic, either mooring buoys and piles in the rivers, half tide berths, where access was limited to times when the tide was in, and alongside moorings at the yard itself (see *Figure 8.4*).   The yards offered few extra services, possibly basic toilet facilities but little else.   Mooring companies developed on this concept but often have no actual boat yard base and merely hold the rights to lay moorings in a harbour or on a river and rent them out to boat owners.

These unsophisticated mooring facilities remain busy to this day partly because the prices charged are often significantly less than for marina or water sports centre berths.   In comparison to the £1,700 suggested earlier for a marina berth, a similar yacht using a mooring company mooring on the south coast could expect to pay as little as £600.   This significant cost reduction has led many boat owners to stay with the basic facilities on offer.

Boatyards and mooring companies still play an important role in offering financially accessible opportunities, particularly for boating and sailing.   However, throughout the 1970s, it became increasingly apparent that some boat owners would pay higher premiums for convenience and comfort together with a pleasant environment.   This had led to a rapid growth in the number of marinas.

Figure 8.4 **Types of Moorings**

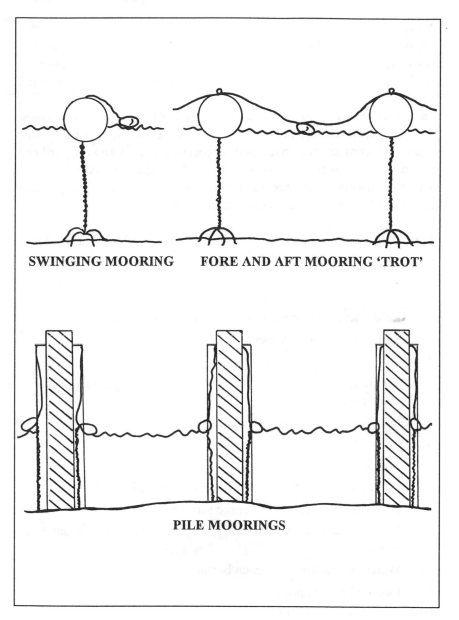

SWINGING MOORING   **FORE AND AFT MOORING 'TROT'**

PILE MOORINGS

MODERN WATER SPORTS FACILITIES

Marinas:

Many marinas developed from boat yards which, over the years and in response to demands from their boat owners, began to improve facilities. This process may have started with building a new toilet and shower block the cost of which meant that the boat yard owner either needed to increase mooring fees or increase the density of moorings. Pontoon berths became popular with both boat owners and boatyards. They offer convenience, in terms of access, for owners and the yard can increase the density of moorings from that which is possible with swinging moorings (see *Figure 8.5* on page 177 - showing a pontoon section and a typical layout of finger moorings).

From this marinas grew to offer a complete yachtsmen's package. These days marinas offer the following services:

1. Easily accessible moorings via pontoon walkways.
2. Safe car parking facilities.
3. Shower and toilet blocks.
4. Security, frequently now 24 hour in response to growing levels of marine crime.
5. Boat yard maintenance services.
6. Sail makers.
7. Engineers.
8. Equipment sales, often in the form of a chandlers outlet.
9. Boat sales, through a brokerage service.
10. The services of a marina management team ensuring the safety of boats.
11. Water and electricity to each berth.
12. Fuel and gas supplies.
13. A club bar or social focus.

Figure 8.5   **Pontoon and Finger Moorings**

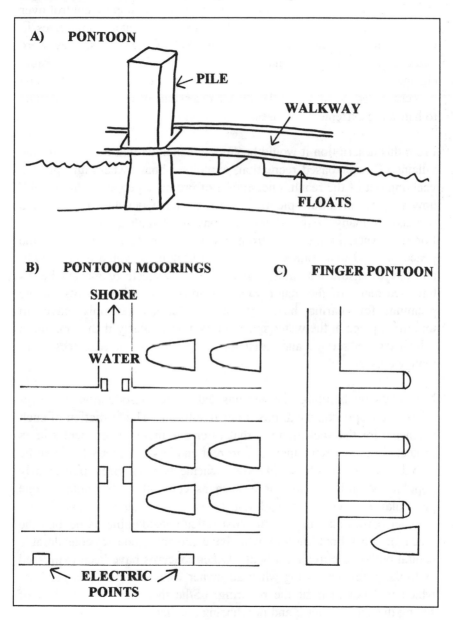

With this extensive range of services boat owners need look no further to satisfy their needs and the marina can operate monopoly control over the business. Many marina berth holders have formed committees in response to concerns that, towards the end of the 1980s, they were being exploited by huge increases in mooring fees with little visible changes to services. These committees appear to have had some success, aided possibly by the recent recession, in persuading marinas to halt these extreme price rises.

From this description it would be easy to conclude that marinas are the villains of water based recreation, exploiting boat owners and putting yachting out of the reach, once more, of ordinary people. This would, however, be an unfair picture. Marinas have developed to meet a demand by many boat owners for convenient high quality moorings. For the owner, living away from his boat, a marina berth offers the peace of mind that trained staff will be keeping a watch over it night and day to ensure it's safety. Indeed, these aspects of marina berths have led many of the major yacht insurers to offer discounts on the premium for marina based yachts. Marinas certainly have an important place in the water sports market particularly if they maintain a high quality service and resist the temptation to increase fees more than necessary.

New ideas on berthing charges has led to the introduction in recent years of the opportunity to buy a berth outright. The attraction of such a scheme for the yachtsman is that after one major investment s/he is protected from extreme increases in rent and has an asset which can be resold if required. In reality this scheme has not been particularly popular, possibly because it is seen as committing the boat to one particular marina and would not be easy to change in the future. Another reason may be that the cost, often considerable, is beyond the reach of most boat owners who have already gone to considerable capital outlay to purchase a boat. Other concerns have been expressed as to the problems arising when an owner wishes to buy a larger boat which will not then fit the mooring. S/he then has the problem of selling the existing berth and purchasing another.

Marina Villages:

The concept of housing with a mooring at the end of the garden first became popular in England during the late 1960s along the River Thames. Here many modern 'town house' style buildings were sold affording limited river frontage with a berth for a cruiser or dinghy. Examples of these buildings are shown in *Figure 8.6.* These houses sold for a premium and were very popular. However, the concept took time to transfer to coastal locations.

It was in the 1980s that the marina village concept began to take off with the construction of Hythe Marina by Marina Developments and Brighton Marina. Marina villages were designed to offer the ultimate in living accommodation for boating enthusiasts. The villages consisted, generally, of prestige modern houses or flats surrounding a marina focus. Some of the houses had a berth at the end of their garden or patio, others had access to berths in the marina. Early developments proved popular in the boom years of the 1980s, and encouraged new developments all round the coast. Marina Developments, one of the largest companies involved, produced villages at Millbay in Plymouth, Hythe in Hampshire, Ocean Village in Southampton and many more. They were not alone in this expansion and, unfortunately, the proverbial bubble burst with the onset of recession in the late 1980s. Many reasons can be found to explain the failure of some of these developments. The houses were unrealistically priced, some developers became greedy and, instead of providing quality accommodation, the size and standard of the accommodation fell. The market was saturated by too many projects for the number of potential buyers. Finally, the companies were simply hit by one of the most severe recessions of this century.

However, some developments have succeeded, for example the inland marina at Buckden in Cambridgeshire, where Watermark Leisure developed a selection of homes. Hythe on the coast has proved to be popular. It remains for managers to identify the ingredients of success in this field. Possibly the coastal developments targeted the main home market in locations where many potential customers would not find

Figure 8.6 **Waterside Properties with Moorings**

employment, the second home sales drive of Buckden overcame these objections. In many cases the marina villages have become little more than exclusive estates, some distance from town services and facilities, which lack community spirit.

Marinas as a focus for leisure complexes:
Many marinas were developed in the 1980s in an attempt to attract non-water based leisure participation. These centres often took the form of shopping malls around the edge of a marina. This is a style of development is popular in other parts of the world. The boutiques were supplemented by restaurants and bars. Some of these developments have been hugely successful. For example, Port Solent on the edge of Portsmouth, attracts thousands of visitors each weekend during the summer. Others have found it more difficult with outlets finding problems in raising sufficient income to cover the high rent charged.

To supplement the leisure experience, many centres have added multi-screen cinemas, hotels and business accommodation. It is probably not a fair time to judge the success of this, as many of the venues reached completion as the recession hit. Certainly the concept has proved attractive for developers to diversify their product base. Casual leisure users appear to be attracted to the interest of marina activities, supplemented by good access and parking and a broad choice of food and entertainment. Port Solent, for example, offers traditional pubs, Italian, Mexican, French and barbecue restaurants within a short distance of each other. For yachtsmen the venues can bring mixed feelings, for some the life and entertainment value is a pleasing bonus. For others the venture brings disturbance to the peace of boating and it's environment.

Marinas in Urban Regeneration:
In an effort to improve the infrastructure of the urban dockland environment several projects have be completed which convert disused docks into marinas and leisure venues. Examples of such developments vary. St Katherine's Yacht Haven, in the city of London, has created a popular centre for social events with thriving restaurants and bars.

Similarly, in Liverpool the Albert Dock was successfully redeveloped to provide a shopping mall, public houses and restaurants. All of these attractions are housed in the original dock buildings on the banks of the Mersey. To increase the attraction two of the city's main museums were sited within the development, the Tate Gallery and the Maritime Museum. This project has been successful in attracting visitors to the area and in improving its image. Similar projects are underway in Newcastle and Southampton.

Although these projects are successful in cleaning up previously depressed and run down areas some arguments suggest that these developments push out and exclude existing residents. Alternative policies could be to develop water sports centres in the docks thereby providing recreational opportunities for local residents. Examples of these projects include the Liverpool Water Sports Centre and several similar projects in the London Docklands. These projects are seen to offer the young people of the area new opportunities. However, they do not truly regenerate the area, attract new business or improve the infrastructure. Further problems may be faced by dockland water sports centres in terms of water quality; dock areas are frequently the home for rats and, therefore, may incubate Weils Disease and other infections.

Arguments for and against commercial dockland regeneration programmes are often summarised in terms of social concerns versus economic interest. The commercial solution, if successful, attracts tourists and visitors, new business and employment. Recreaton programmes can improve the infrastructure of the area, facilitating a change in the way the public perceives its status. These benefits can help local people by creating new jobs, improved amenities and increased prosperity. As the needs of commercial traffic change, increasing numbers of disused dockland areas will become available for development. Other options for these areas include infilling and building housing and offices on a similar theme to elsewhere. The current trend of water side development has advantages for the interests of water based recreation, widening opportunity for participation. By centring activities around areas where people live and work these developments can be seen to increase interest in and awareness of water based recreation.

Management issues raised by the docklands-style development, as with the leisure development, include problems of security. If marina and water sports centres are within a centre open to the public, increased security problems are created. These can be managed by the use of security coded gates at the entrance to pontoons and water access points. Furthermore, the disturbance to boat owners by the public leaving bars and clubs requires the imposing of careful time limits and effective monitoring of the site.

Water based recreation groups may find that these types of developments are the perfect place for promotions and campaigns to increase participation. Effective projects have included 'Get Afloat, Get a Boat' days and individual sports demonstrations. If these centres serve to bring more people into contact with water based recreation then, in terms of increasing water sports participation, they will prove to be essential.

Monitoring the Quality of Marinas:
With the rapid growth in marina development there is a need to monitor the quality of facilities available. This is currently achieved through an anchor award scheme. Marinas are assessed on the quality and range of facilities and service available. Marinas can be awarded a number of anchors, similar to the star scheme for hotels. This gives the potential visitor a guide to the quality of facilities which can be expected. Unfortunately, the scheme has yet to become popular with few marinas displaying this information. Once established the scheme can act as an incentive for marina managers to maintain high levels of service on their sites. It will also allow premium rates to be charged by those marinas achieving the highest recommendation.

Maritime Heritage and Marinas:
Further to the opportunities for dockland redevelopment into

commercial leisure venues, some cities, with a tradition of seafaring, have chosen to enhance the unique attraction of their site with a maritime heritage theme. Hartlepool has followed this theme when developing a marina complex. The Hartlepool Historic Quay, scheduled to open in the summer of 1994, offers a multi-million pound visitor attraction. The attraction reconstructs life aboard a fighting frigate in the year 1800. The centre includes the carefully restored *HMS Trincomalee*, Britain's oldest floating warship.

This historical slant is combined with a shopping mall and restaurant facilities offering visitors a full day's entertainment. Future plans include a site for the Imperial War Museum of the North. Hartlepool is effectively offering a very similar product to many others, a marina combined with shopping, food, entertainment and housing. However, it remains to be seen whether the inclusion of a heritage site will assist in attracting more visitors than the basic marina complex.

Inland Water Park Developments:
Earlier in this chapter it was suggested that marina village housing had been successfully developed in inland areas, such as the River Thames, long before coastal developments had gained popularity. In 1989 the Watermark Group created a new concept of water side second homes within fully managed sporting resorts. The development of Buckden Marina on the Great Ouse in Cambridgeshire, to include new leisure facilities and luxury holiday home lodges, proved to be an outstanding success. All of these homes are now sold and offer lakeside settings with their own moorings. The concept of Buckden Marina is to provide a quality leisure environment and a recent £3 million investment by Watermark has added improved marina services together with a health and leisure club. The club offers a heated indoor swimming pool, jacuzzi, gymnasium, bar and brassiere to ensure that members can relax when the weather precludes water sports. For non-boat owners, lodge owners can enjoy water skiing on a privately managed lake.

With the success to this development Watermark has launched a further development of 76 lodges and luxury facilities at the Cotswold Water

Park. This development will offer a quality holiday retreat where water sports can be combined with other interests. Water sports will include sailing, jet skiing, water skiing, angling and wind surfing. There will be provision for water's edge activities such a walking, horse riding and mountain biking.

Watermark Leisure has devised a popular and successful product which caters for those who wish to enjoy a variety of leisure activities during a short stay or holiday. Their centres offer a high standard of accommodation and facilities. This allows the customer to select leisure activities which match the weather and season. The future may well see this type of water sports venue developing in coastal locations.

Water Sports Centres:
In 1968 the Sports Council opened the National Sailing Centre in Cowes on the Isle of Wight. The centre was developed as part of the Sports Councils network of national training centres including Bisham Abbey, Lilleshall and Crystal Palace. National Sports Centres were designed to provide a national training centre to encourage excellence in various sports. Towards this goal the National Sailing Centre provided basic accommodation for residential courses in sailing and later wind surfing. The centre was located in the busy River Medina and offered estuary sailing for dinghies and access to the Solent and the English Channel for cruising yachts and more experienced sailors. The centre was set up to provide all the equipment needed for the courses and enabled participants to try sports without resorting to too much capital expense. At the time of opening there were very few sailing centres in existence. Therefore, the Cowes centre was seen to provide for an important gap in the market. The centre achieved high standards of instruction across the sport by providing instructor training schemes.

By the 1980s the work of the National Sailing Centre was under scrutiny. After extensive research and consultation with the Royal Yachting Association it was agreed that beginners' courses were sufficiently covered by other water sports centres (e.g. Plas Menai in Wales and Cumbrae in Scotland) and that the work of excellence training would be more efficient from a mainland site. The National Sailing Centre was, therefore, closed. The site was sold in 1987 to the Lister Charitable Trust which ran the centre as the UK Sailing Centre for a short time. New National Centres operate at Holme Pierrepont in Nottingham, Cumbrae in Scotland and Plas Menai in Wales.

Holme Pierrepont:

A site of disused gravel pits approximately four miles from Nottingham was selected by Nottinghamshire County Council as a site suitable for a major water sports development. This idea was expanded to include a National Sports Centre offering an artificial 2,000 metre rowing course. This led to a partnership with the Sports Council who provided all the capital cost for the buildings and now shares the running costs on a 50/50 basis with the County Council. The site is managed by a joint management committee whose chair alternates on a two year rotation between the partners. The site has now been developed to include facilities for wind surfing, sailing, canoeing, water skiing, rowing, camping, caravaning and fishing. The specialist facilities include the centre's artificial Olympic rowing course. Ski tow ropes are provided to allow people to improve their technique without the expense of a tow boat. In 1986 an artificial canoe slalom course was developed (see *Figure 8.7*). The course is 700 metres long and in three sections offering rough water canoeing up to grade 4 with ample spectator space. Sprint canoe competitions use the regatta lake. Recreational dinghy and board sailing is catered for on the main regatta lake which is 2,200 metres long by 150 metres wide. There are purpose built landing stages and equipment hire available. The regatta lake is also used for power boating and hydroplaning events under the supervision of the Royal Yachting Association.

The accommodation at Holme Pierrepont includes 66 visitor rooms with basins to service residential courses and conferences. Conference facilities were developed to include a lecture room for up to 170 delegates and various smaller meeting rooms. Delegates are catered for in a cafeteria and bar which enjoys views over the regatta lake.

Figure 8.7   **Holme Pierrepont**

Artificial canoe slalom course in use

Holme Pierrepont has hosted many regional, national and international events. International events in 1991/92 included the World Junior and European Supercup Angling Championships and the BCU Wild Water Racing Club Championships on the slalom course. The canoe slalom course design has been heralded as a success, overcoming complex hydraulic engineering problems without sacrificing functionality or destroying the landscape. The course has developed as a popular training ground attracting names such as Richard Fox and Shaun Pearce. The rowing course was chosen by both Oxford and Cambridge Universities for their winter training.

The smooth running of the centre was severely affected in the summer of 1990 when an out break of blue green algae led to the cancellation of a youth summer programme and the relocation of several major events. Further surveys of water quality concluded that the regatta lake is fed by an unsuitable water supply and work was carried out to remedy this situation. It now provides a unique inland facility for watersports situated in an area which traditionally experiences lower levels of water sports participation. It is possible for Holme Pierrepont to succeed in two ways, firstly by giving Britain a venue for international competitions and secondly by increasing local awareness and interest in water sports.

Plas Menai:
A purpose built centre in the breath-taking scenery of north west Wales. Plas Menai is owned and operated by the Sports Council for Wales. The centre offers state-of-the-art equipment and high quality instruction in a wide range of activities. The courses offered include sailing, cruising, canoeing, wind surfing and power boating. For newcomers the centre offers multi activity holidays making it possible for them to sample a range of water sports before they commit themselves to any one water sport in particular. The centre specialises in youth courses and offers courses for special needs and disabled customers.

This National Centre is aware of the need for trained professionals and has developed three and six month trainee instructor programmes.

These programmes will be discussed in more detail in Chapter 11, under staffing issues. The modern centre has a good selection of boats from children's Optimist dinghies to Westerly Fulmar cruising yachts. It provides all the specialist equipment required including buoyancy aids. At the end of the day customers are accommodated in modern well-equipped rooms and are able to enjoy the indoor heated swimming pool, a meal in the restaurant and a drink in the bar. Plas Menai is possibly the highest quality coastal water sports centre in Britain.

In 1992 a contract was awarded to Pennine Services PLC, the in-house team bid for the management of the catering and service elements under the Sport Councils policy of competitive tendering for the management of the National Sports Centres. It was, however, decided to retain the control of the management of the water sports facilities using contractors' labour. Future plans include the development of fitness training facilities, changing facilities at the boat house and public catering facilities.

Country Parks and Water Sports Provision:
Country parks have been developed as a centre for outdoor activities and in particular water sports. Country parks aim to provide wider opportunities for countryside recreation, and were introduced in the 1966 White Paper, Leisure in the Countryside. Specific objectives include attracting a large number of visitors by offering a wide range of sporting activities. In this process the parks sought to restore derelict land and have, therefore, frequently been developed on sites previously used for mineral extraction. The parks offer something for everyone, encouraging large numbers of urban populations into the rural environment. As many of the sites included gravel pits the creation of lakes and water resources has been a natural move. Many parks can offer a number of lakes for various, otherwise conflicting, activities.

Wellington Country Park (south of Reading, Berkshire) offers easy parking, picnic areas, barbecue sites, shops, nature trails, and a deer park. These land based activities are centred around a lake which accommodates the Wellington Aqua Sports Centre. This provides taster courses in sailing and wind surfing. Casual hire of boats and equipment is available including rowing boats, canoes, five types of dinghy, sailboards and pedaloes. Casual hire allows non-boat owners the opportunity to get out on the water without having to join a class. This service is vital in opening new opportunities for participation.

By increasing awareness, country parks have seen a rise in the number of visitors (including schools) since 1989. They offer several benefits, including excellent opportunities for outdoor recreation, within a relatively short distance of visitors' homes and have been particularly skilful in providing varied water sports through their ability to be able to design separate lakes to serve the needs of each sport.

Urban Parks and Water Sport Projects:
Although country parks provide tailored resources close to urban population, some travel is still required and many country parks have little in the way of public transport. Therefore, access to these opportunities is still restricted to those with cars and sufficient time to reach the park. In response to this problem two further water sports developments have begun to take place. Firstly, dockland water sport centres have been introduced. Secondly, some city councils' parks departments have become aware of opportunities to develop water sports on lakes and rivers running through their open spaces.

Dockland water sports centres offer deep water and, in some cases, the use of existing buildings. Some of these centres have been created by Local Education Departments specifically to offer water sports to young people. For example, the Avonquay Resources Centre in Bristol docks. Water sports in the docks are complemented by outdoor activity excursions to the countryside. The use of water sports in the dock means that outdoor activities can be provided without the need to transport the young people to open spaces. Although its main target groups are youth and community, the Avonquay Centre has proved successful in providing opportunities throughout the county.

In London, during 1989, the Docklands Sailing and Water Sport Centre was set up and funded by the London Dockland Development Corporation and the Sports Council. The centre offers subsidised water sports for local people who would otherwise be unable to afford market prices. Its popularity, however, means that it attracts people from as far afield as Kent and Essex. The success of these projects can be used to illustrate the high levels of latent demand for water sports provision. If existing disused resources could be redeveloped economically, then they would provide both financially and physically accessible water sports opportunities for all.

Many city parks are centred around lakes or other water resources. These water resources are not usually managed for water based recreation. However, they offer an opportunity to satisfy the high level of demand for water sports in cities and towns. An example of this type of use can be found at Stanborough Park in Welwyn Garden City. Here an existing 126 acre city park was developed to offer a boating and sailing lake in 1969. In 1985 a sailing school was set up on the lake and offers courses in sailing, wind surfing and canoeing. Many other city parks departments could follow this example and improve water based recreation opportunities in their area.

SUMMARY

This chapter illustrates the wide range of water sports provision available. Responsibility for provision is shared across voluntary, private and public sector organisations. This helps to achieve a balance between the various demands for levels of provision. Voluntary sector clubs are successful in catering for the specific sporting interests of their members, ensuring that the level and cost of provision is suited to the club members' budget. These voluntary clubs offer important provision for local competition and are, therefore, essential to the development of water sports within a competitive structure.

Private Sector companies originally concentrated on the higher cost areas of the market such as marinas and yachting facilities. They are now beginning to play an increasingly important role in other aspects of the market including private water sports centres. The public sector and national agencies continue to provide for the sport at a regional and national level. However, few local authorities have taken the lead and developed water resources for recreation with their leisure services budget.

The future of water sports centres may well be in the development of more multiple activity centres where participants can enjoy a range of leisure experiences. Demand also indicates the need for more short courses and luxury holiday homes centred around high quality leisure facilities.

CHAPTER 9

Associated Industries and Professions in Water Based Recreation

The previous chapter analysed the provision for water sports in terms of actual facilities, in particular, water sports centres, clubs and marinas. The results of this study indicate that a wide range of provision is necessary to satisfy the very disparate demands of water sports users. It is, however, important to remember that provision for recreation should not be restricted to concerns about facilities. Although facilities are the most capital intensive aspect of water sports provision, other services, sometimes included with these facilities but mainly able to stand alone as individual businesses, are important in satisfying the needs of water based leisure.

Provision is generally defined in terms of actual facilities, equipment, competitive structure, training schemes, coaches, and service professionals. It is not sufficient to merely provide a facility such as a water sports centre. To attract members other considerations need to be made. Equipment and opportunity for equipment sales, from major items such as boats down to small maintenance items such as boat paint, will be needed. If money has been spent on the purchase of the boat then it is, of course, desirable to insure the craft against accidents, theft and other unforeseen events. Insurance forms one of the many important specialist services for the water sports market. A competitive structure is important for maintaining and encouraging sports participation as well as recreational participation. The competitive structure is usually provided by a partnership between the national governing body and voluntary clubs. Training is provided at water sports centres, clubs, schools and other organisations nationwide. This chapter looks more closely at these other aspects of water sports provision, their management, structures and responsibilities. These can be summarised as tourism and training; services; equipment manufacture, design and supply; and finally water's edge heritage sites and visitor attractions.

TOURISM AND TRAINING

This is possibly the largest aspect of the market in terms of employment. It is often difficult to split tourism and training from the facility provision. Many clubs offer basic training courses for their members, the National Water Sports Centres' specific objective is to provide training for a variety of sports. Marinas welcome visiting yachts and, therefore, act as a form of hospitality service. However, further study of this complex market suggests that several supplementary activities can be identified in this field. Indeed, many of these businesses rely on the existence of facilities such as marinas as their base but constitute a separate, complementary service which can, and does, survive in its own right. These businesses are chartering, corporate entertainment services, management training courses, independent sailing and water sports schools, youth and sail training organisations, and overseas holiday packages.

Yacht and Boat Chartering:
In Britain thousands of yachts and boats of all shapes and sizes are available for hire or charter. This aspect of the industry has grown considerably in recent years and now non-boat owners find themselves presented with a wealth of boats for racing or cruising around British waters or as far afield as Australia and Thailand. The word charter has historically been used to describe the hiring of sea going craft and remains in use to this day. Chartering takes various forms, from catering for the needs of the complete beginner to those of the seasoned skipper. There are three main types of charter:

- Bare Boat
- Skippered
- Flotilla

Companies may offer only one or a combination of options depending on your ability and, sometimes, qualifications. With increasing numbers of boats on the water many charter companies now require a certificate to prove the charterer's level of competency. For the charter company this will give an idea of the suitability of the chosen boat for the charterer and enable it to advise on the most appropriate choice. For example, a family of four, whose skipper has recently passed the RYA Day Skipper Certificate, would probably be overstretched if chartering a complex cruiser racer, however s/he would cope easily with a standard family production boat. If the charter company can help to advise in these decisions it can significantly reduce the chance of accidents and also ensure that charterers have an enjoyable break. Many charter companies will accept charterers who display sufficient experience even if they do not have qualifications.

Bare boat chartering is the most common form of charter offered in British waters. Here the charterer becomes the skipper of the boat for the period of charter, being responsible for all aspects of the boat's safety and navigation. This type of charter suits more experienced people who do not own a boat but wish to spend a holiday as their own boss, no longer needing tuition and guidance to accomplish their desired level of cruising. Bare boat charter is available on most modern production boats and some traditional and racing class boats. Bare boat charters are now available in many foreign locations. However, unlike British charter companies, foreign countries have legal requirements regarding the qualifications of potential skippers.

Skippered charter is ideal for inexperienced customers or those wishing to have a stress-free holiday leaving the responsibility and decision-making to the paid skipper. A skippered charter will give the charterer a fully equiped boat together with a qualified skipper. The skipper need not be an instructor as they do not teach. However, by necessity, the skipper will demonstrate a range of sailing techniques and manoeuvres. The charterers will probably end their holiday considerably more knowledgeable than when they set out.

Flotilla charters have become very popular in the Mediterranean were charterers can take a boat out as part of a group of other boats. The lead boat is run by a qualified skipper to organise the navigation and sailing. It also has a hostess to organise entertainment during the holiday and an engineer to deal with any unforeseen problems. This type of charter offers the freedom of bare boat charter, plus the security, for the inexperienced, of a skipper in the lead boat to advise on tactics and to ensure that the navigation and manoeuvres go smoothly. There are virtually no opportunities for flotilla sailing in Britain; most companies are based in Greece and Turkey with some others appearing more recently in the Far East, the Caribbean and the Pacific.

There are currently over 200 charter companies in Britain alone offering in the region of 1,000 boats for charter. Some of these companies will also be large sailing schools. One of the biggest providers is the Sunsail Group based in Port Solent.

Although there is no formal control in the charter business the industry's association, the Yacht Charter Association, was set up over thirty years ago and promotes, not only specific trade association interests, but also high standards throughout the industry. The Yacht Charter Association sets minimum agreed standards for all of its member companies as below:

1.   All owners of yachts offered for charter undertake to ensure regular checks and servicing, cleaning between each charter and to equip the yachts with the minimum agreed inventory.

2.   All yachts for charter must be registered and listed in the YCA's register of Charter Yachts. These documents should be provided in the boat's file.

3. All yachts must have a current DOT certificate and should display a plaque informing customers that the boat complies with it's requirements.

4. All yachts must be thoroughly seaworthy.

5. Equipment, shown on the provided inventory list, must be supplied without extra charge.

6. All yachts must be clean and all equipment in good working order at the start of each charter.

7. If bed linen is not provided it must be available for hire and all bed linen should be freshly laundered for each charter.

8. All yachts should have adequate kitchen equipment.

9. Sea toilets should display simple instructions.   Spares and maintenance guides should be provided.

10. All rules set out by the YCA must be adhered to.

11. All yachts should be supplied full of fuel, water, with engine level at the correct setting and with spare oil.

12. All gas hoses and systems must be to high standards and a spare gas cylinder must be provided.

13. Checks must be completed before each charter on all electrical equipment and spare bulbs and fuses should be provided.

14. Before leaving a charterer must be introduced to all mechanical and electrical equipment. A manual should also be provided to ensure a reference is available.

15. The age of the yacht must be clearly stated in all of the literature.

16. Standard yacht charter agreements for bare boat, skippered, management and agency must be used as specified by the YCA.

When producing a brochure the yacht charter company must state clearly the registered number, length, beam (width) and draft (amount of water required to float), the make, model and many other details as shown in *Figure 9.1*.

Figure 9.1   **Example of brochure information**

Starvision II	Atlefolk Class Traditional Long Keel Sailing Yacht
Built	1967
Accommodation	Double berth in Fore Peak, 2 single saloon berths
Size	Length: 25', Beam 7' 4", Draft 4' 6"
Engine	Vire 7hp petrol engine 5 gallon fuel tank
Electrical Equipment	VHF radio service, Navstar Dinghy Decca, Walker Trailing Log, Echo Sounder
Call Sign	
Gas	Butane 2 ring cooker with grill
Sails and Rig	Masthead Sloop; Mainsail, Nos. 1,2 and storm jib, light weather Genoa.

Booking should be made using a booking form, an examples of the recommended content is shown in *Figure 9.2*. When a booking is received the company must send out confirmation which includes the name of the craft chartered, type of yacht, conditions for payment and return of deposits. The customer should also receive clear joining instructions explaining how to find the yacht, time of arrival, car parking and expected time of return.

Figure 9.2 **Yacht Charters Sample Booking Form**

Personal Details :
Surname (Mr/Mrs/Miss) ....
First name ....
Address ....
....
.... Postcode ....
Telephone................................. (day) .... (evening)

Existing qualifications ....
Sailing Experience ....
Yacht ....
Number of Crew..
Departure Date...
Return Date...
- - - - - - - - - -

Payment Details :
Charter fee   £ ....
[10%] Deposit (enclosed with booking) + insurance =   £ ....
- - - - - - - - - -

Terms of Business:
Yacht Charters Sample are fully insured against accidents and third party liability, but responsibility is not accepted for personal accidents, loss or damage caused by your negligence. The Deposit is payable on booking and is non-returnable. Final payments are due 8 weeks before departure. For cancellations made within four weeks of departure we reserve the right to withhold the full invoice amount. If we cancel, we will offer an alternative or refund all payments. Yacht Charters Sample reserve the right to charge additional fees if the boat is returned late, to refuse to hand over the boat to a skipper considered unsuitable and to take the charterer out for a short familiarisation cruise.
- - - - - - - - - -

Declaration:
I agree to the terms of business and I understand that I will be required to sign a charter agreement (copy available on request).

Signed ....

Date ....

When a charterer for bare boat charter arrives s/he should be met by a company representative and given a tour of the boat. This tour should include the stowage of equipment, the method of use of all emergency equipment on board, location of all seacocks and a demonstration of how they work, routine maintenance, and sail handling. Before leaving it is a good idea to ensure that the charterer checks that the inventory is correct. The company must also provide the charterer with the following documentation: registration papers, copies of insurance policies, details of permitted operating areas, instruction manuals, electrical and plumbing diagrams, inventory, stowage plans and a list of 24 hour contact telephone numbers.

On return the charter company should carefully inspect the vessel. A thorough check of the inventory should be completed and any damage, missing items and maintenance required should be listed. The details of this inspection should be noted on an appropriate form and signed by the company representative and the charter skipper. This is essential to avoid disputes over return of deposits.

The procedure for skippered charters is, of course, different from the bare boat charter as a company representative will be on board for the duration and should already be familiar with the physical aspects of the boat. However, the skipper should carry out a safety briefing as outlined by the YCA.

By insisting on the conditions specified above the Yacht Charter Association has successfully regulated the business for many years on a voluntary basis. Yacht charter companies need not be members of the YCA but increasing awareness on the part of charterers has led many companies to conform with these conditions. The Yacht Charter Association does not currently insist that yachts are marina based provided clients are met and taken to the boat, spares are available and a contact is given in case of emergencies. The British Marine Industries Federation, in their notes to would-be charterers, advise that companies who operate fleets from marinas, preferably with staff on hand throughout the week, may present a safer option for first time charterers.

Yacht charter companies sometimes operate a fleet of matched boats from a particular boat builder. For example, Westerly Sea School at one time operated a charter business using only Westerly boats. Other companies operate under a management agreement for individual owners. In the latter case owners agree to use a charter company's services to manage, maintain and charter their yachts and pay a commission to the company for charters obtained. Still more companies remain very small and offer either one or two boats for bare boat charter, or more frequently, offer skippered cruising sometimes on a much larger and traditional yacht.

Yacht chartering now forms an important part in opening the sport to people who either cannot afford to own a boat or who do not want the commitment. Flotilla and bare boat holidays in the sun are now becoming an important part of the summer activity package holiday market.

Corporate Entertainment and Management Training:
Other aspects of the sailing and charter business which have grown in popularity over recent years are corporate entertainment and management training courses. Corporate entertainment has become a particularly lucrative aspect of the charter business. Charter companies usually operating from larger and more luxurious motor or sailing yachts offer day and longer charters to businesses for the purpose of entertaining their customers. The charter company usually provides a full crew with waitresses serving buffet meals and drinks, allowing business companies the undivided attention of their customers in order to impress them, thank them for existing business and encourage new business in a relaxed and enjoyable atmosphere. Many major companies employ a range of regular corporate entertainment events to boost their marketing operation.

The charter company wishing to offer this type of corporate

entertainment needs a suitable boat and contacts with high class caterers. Some companies offer set packages per day or number of days, others tailor each event to the needs of their customers. Some companies use smaller skippered charter yachts as an incentive or reward for staff. Usually several yachts will be chartered and a corresponding weekend of entertainment arranged. This may include some match racing, picnics and barbecues. Larger companies, such as Marks and Spencer, have organised these events in the past using smaller yachts and arranging catering ashore at each meal stop.

To take this market further, some sailing schools and individuals offer on-board management training courses, similar in rationale to the use of outdoor pursuits for team building and management training. It is considered by advocates of this type of training that the small community environment on a sailing boat encourages better understanding and an ability to work together to solve problems. Sailing can be physically demanding and can place the crew in stressful situations. Team building helps members to identify and work to the strengths of their colleagues. There is, however, little market in this area although one British sailing school in the late 1980s did try to introduce the idea only to be hit by recession and companies subsequently cutting back on staff training. Although British based examples have not been a great success an operator from Gibraltar successfully launched this type of course on a medium sized yacht.

Sailing Schools:
A glance through the advertisement pages of sailing and yachting magazines will confirm that the potential sailing school customer has a large number from which to choose. Schools vary from substantial companies, with many matching yachts and power boats, to small one-person organisations offering sailing in their own yacht. Sailing schools should be approved by the Royal Yachting Association and offer a range of RYA courses that are designed to accommodate the complete novice right through to the skipper. The courses that are on offer are usually the RYA practical courses run over 5 days or 3 weekends on an approved yacht. However, these courses are

accompanied by theoretical courses designed for the classroom environment. During the winter months some sailing schools offer these as intensive courses, others as correspondence courses. The most popular way of attending these theoretical courses is through adult education classes normally provided close to home during winter evenings.

The cruising course structure allows clients to stay on the yacht for the duration of the course. Sailing schools, therefore, do not need to provide accommodation for the courses. For dinghy courses accommodation must be provided. Some sailing schools offer children's holiday camps under canvas or in dormitories but this is not suitable for many adults making water sports centres, such as Plas Menai, more popular for adult courses. Smaller schools suggest bed and breakfast accommodation close to the sailing base. The Island Cruising Club in Salcombe, Devon provides an ingenious solution to the accommodation problem. The *Egremont*, an ex-Mersey ferry, has been converted to provide accommodation, sailing base, catering and bar facilities. The ferry is permanently moored in the harbour and clients are transported ashore via a launch. The *Egremont* has proved a popular and unusual base for dinghy sailing, wind surfing and keel boat courses situated in the beautiful scenery of the South Hams.

In addition to approval by the RYA, sailing schools can become members of the National Federation of Sea Schools. This is the trade association for sailing establishments and is the only representative body of sailing and motor boat schools in the UK. The federation is represented on the RYA training committee and is organised by an elected committee. The federation offers providers the benefits of association with other providers in the dissemination of information and practices. For the customer, choosing a school which is a member of the NFSS assures that the school is RYA approved and will provide a quality product. Members of NFSS offer a range of courses including:

- Sailing cruising
- Motor cruising

- Dinghy sailing
- Power boating
- Shore based theory courses
- Radar, Decca, VHF radio operators, first aid

The NFSS organises an annual rally where participating member schools meet up for social events and cruising in company. The programme includes inter-school racing, barbecues, ferry trips and short cruises.

All sailing schools need to offer a varied programme and operate an efficient booking procedure. These aspects are considered for all water sports operations in Chapter 11. The sailing school must operate, as with any commercial boating operation, within the requirements of the DOT code of practice. This again is detailed in Chapter 11. The recession has hit sailing schools hard and, therefore, effective marketing and innovative new product development has become increasingly necessary.

Sailing schools, as with any business, need to ensure that terms of business are clearly stated. Yachts must be fully insured against accidents and third party incidents. Many sailing schools state that they do not accept responsibility for personal accidents and loss caused by customer negligence and advise that additional personal insurance should be taken out to cover these. The terms of business should also clearly state policy on deposits and cancellation, for example, deposits may be stated to be non-returnable. If cancellation occurs the sailing school should also clearly state their policy regarding the refund of course fees.

Sailing schools provide a voluntary opportunity for regulation within the offshore cruising world. Many other countries insist on potential customers having the relevant qualifications before they take boats out to sea. This policy has been strongly resisted in the UK as it is envisaged that this requirement would restrict the enjoyment of coastal recreation. Approved sailing schools allow customers to gain internationally recognised qualifications that cover requirements abroad, offer discounts on insurance and facilitate charter agreements. It is only through good marketing and these incentives that participation on these courses can be encouraged.

Sail Training and other Youth Organisations:

Many young people are introduced to watersports each year through membership of youth groups or by attending adventure holidays. One of the earliest providers of adventure holidays was PGL who has offered children-only activity holidays both in Britain and abroad for at least 20 years. Its courses include a range of exciting adventure training and other creative activities including canoeing and sailing opportunities. One of the more established projects included canoeing along the River Ardeche, in France, in Canadian style canoes. This experience was often combined with a week of water sports at a Mediterranean beach resort.

Now there are many children's activity holiday providers, both residential and non-residential, which offer the important initial opportunity for water sports participation. It has, however, proved hard to maintain this enthusiasm by young children unless their parents are also interested. Maybe this is an aspect to be addressed by future water based recreation managers.

Other children and young people experience the thrill of water sports through a club or youth group. The most obvious water based youth group is the Sea Cadets which caters for young people aged 12 to 18 years, with some units having a junior section for 10 to 12 year olds. Sea Cadets is open to both sexes although some Marine units exist only for boys aged 13 to 18 years. They have their own sail training ship *TS Royalist* which is a small square rigged tall ship. Members are also introduced to a range of water sports such as canoeing and sailing. There are 400 units throughout the UK that hold regular weekly meetings and offer young people not only an opportunity to try a range of water sports but also to develop team skills and experience other activities.

An important part of Scouting and Guiding activities is often outdoor pursuits including, in particular, canoeing. Many units own their own canoes and travel to compete in competitions and plan their own expeditions. The movement also benefits from the dedicated water sports facility on the River Thames at Marlow, Longridge. Here groups can try a range of sports including canoeing and sailing while spending a week or weekend under canvas. Good toilet and other facilities are provided.

Some youth service departments of local authorities also provide opportunities for sailing and other water sports. An example is the Kent County Council Youth and Community initiative - the Kent Sea Training Association. Sponsored by the Sally ferry company, Kent now runs a 55 foot sailing yacht the *Sally Endeavour* which accommodates mainly local groups from schools and youth clubs. In order to reach a wider audience the boat also allows special rates for Duke of Edinburgh Award Scheme participants and normal rate booking for adults and young people not in these categories. The venture is a sizeable initiative and could not be provided by local authority funds alone, the help of a local company is essential. However, similar smaller projects, for instance, the Avonquay project based in Bristol Docks, could be provided by local authorities offering urban water sports opportunities for young people.

There are many sail training organisations which operate vessels like the *TS Royalist* and *Sally Endeavour*. The main providers in the UK are The Sail Training Association and the Ocean Youth Club. The Sail Training Association, a registered charity, operates two schooners, the *Winston Churchill* and the *Malcolm Miller* that provide voyages for both young people (16-24 years) and adults (24-69 years). It has operated for over 27 years during which time it has taken over 30,000 young people to sea. Its purpose has been described by its patron HRH Prince Philip as:

a scheme designed to benefit young people, to give them a taste of fright, discomfort and adventure in an age where it is possible to live comfortably, securely and boringly.

The experience helps young people to develop team skills and understanding of other people. It also allows some tuition of basic sailing skills working towards the RYA Competent Crew (Sail Training) certificate or the Watch Leader qualification. The vessels are larger than most used for this type of training and require a crew of 55 to sail them, this includes climbing the rigging, setting and handling sails - a unique experience.

The Ocean Youth Club is one of the largest sail training organisations in Europe and operates 10 sailing vessels from ports all around the coast including Northern Ireland, Scotland and Liverpool. The objectives of the organisation are to help young people to develop:

- a sense of equality and fairness
- understanding of the needs of different backgrounds of others
- responsibility for their own decisions and actions
- teamwork and mutual trust
- awareness of the environment

(*Source*: OYC Annual Report 1993)

The boats are managed by professional full-time skippers but the remainder of the crew is made up of an average of 12 young people and supervisors or an afterguard of qualified volunteers. These volunteers are sometimes older OYC members who have gained qualifications, become watch leaders and, in time, some even become skippers. The OYC is significant because it operates boats close to areas of population and encourages young people to become involved in their own area boat, helping with maintenance work and participating in social events. Many of today's sailing instructors enjoyed their initial training on an Ocean Youth Club boat. The organisation is managed from central offices in Gosport and is a registered educational charity.

The RYA has also acknowledged the need for youth opportunities for sailing and runs the RYA Seamanship Foundation which was established in 1973. One of its prime objectives is to provide opportunities for young people, particularly from deprived areas, to go to sea. The scheme has helped youth groups and schools, particularly in deprived areas, purchase equipment. The Young Skippers Scheme allows young people to gain hands-on experience of skippering using small cruising boats without engines. The Foundation is governed by a management committee of 9 trustees who meet twice a year to make policy and financial decisions.

Other local authorities and borough councils run annual, one-off, events allowing young people to experience a range of water sports. One example of this is the Poole Youth Afloat Festival weekend, which started in 1984. Its opportunities cover a wide range of activities (see *Figure 9.3*).

Figure 9.3   **Poole Youth Afloat 1994 Activity List**

- Sub Aqua
- Dinghy Sailing
- Rowing
- Canoeing
- Surf Chasing
- Fishing
- Water Skiing
- Wind surfing
- Offshore Sailing
- Dragon Boat Racing
- Swimming

The activities are pre-booked at a price designed to be within the reach of young people - approximately £10 for three activities. Opportunities for camping and caravanning at the event are provided for a small fee. The festival has been very successful in introducing young people to activities available through water based recreation.

The British Marine Industries Federation is also aware of the need to attract young people into water sports and provides a free boating information service for young people called 'Schools Afloat'. The service provides Regional Schools Officers who can answer questions about the availability of all water sports in their areas and provides a list of organisations which provide water sports opportunities for young people - some examples of these are included in *Figure 9.4*.

Figure 9.4   **Youth Water Sports Providers**

NAME	ACTIVITY
The Astrid Trust	Sail training expeditions
Cirdan Trust	Sail training expeditions
Cockney Spirit Sailing Trust	Motor Sail
East Coast Sail Trust	Sail training expeditions
Excelsior Trust	Sail training expeditions
Fairbridge Drake Society	Sail training expeditions
Faramir Trust	Sail training expeditions
Island Cruising Club	Dinghies, day boats, wind surfing, cruising
Waterways for youth	Water way activities
Scouts Offshore	Sail training expeditions
London Sailing project	Sail training expeditions
Morning Star Trust	Sail training expeditions
Shaftsbury Homes and Arethusa	Sail training expeditions
RYA Junior Windsurfing	Windsurfing

Source: BMIF - 'Schools Afloat Service'

Overseas Holiday Packages:
Combining the joys of water sports with the guarantee of fine, warm weather has become increasingly alluring over recent years. A study of the national newspapers' travel sections or the charter pages of a

boating magazine will uncover a growing number of opportunities to learn to sail or participate in other water sports in the sun. Popular locations include the Greek Islands and Turkey where several tour operators (Mark Warner, Sunsail and Falcon) have created shore based water sports holiday centres offering novice and more advanced clients a range of activities including sailing, water skiing, wind surfing, cruising, and snorkelling. These operations could be seen as a threat to existing British water sports providers, tempting away potential clients to warmer destinations. A closer study may, however, reveal that these clients would not have considered a water sports holiday in Britain but, once hooked in warmer climates, return to Britain and continue participation, thus boosting participation growth and demands in the market.

Other sailing schools have benefited by providing the flotilla market with weekend preparation courses that cover basic manoeuvres.

SERVICES

Water based recreation requires many other professional services to ensure that participation opportunities are available and to provide recreational users with expert advice. The main services provided are specialist marine insurances, yacht and boat sales and surveying. Providers of these services are trained and regulated professionals who allow water users to enjoy their sports with peace of mind.

Insurance:
From the smallest canoe to the largest ocean going sailing yacht, owners require insurance to cover accidents and other events. As water craft ownership has increased with cheaper production techniques there has been an increased demand for suitable insurance polices. These have been provided by the expansion of large established companies to include marine departments and by the creation of small new specialist companies.

The owner needs to insure against the following risks:

1. Liability to third parties for injury or damage caused to another person or boat.

2. Damage or total loss caused by natural causes, fire, jettison, piracy, collision and other accidents.

3. Damage or loss caused to individual items of equipment.

Many clubs insist on third party insurance with membership. To ensure that their members get a satisfactory and well priced policy many governing bodies have arranged special discount policies for their members with the additional assurance that the policy is of an acceptable level of cover.

Individual policies are also provided for participants on sailing courses, charter, flotilla holidays and other events. Many of these are similar in nature to travel insurance covering loss of personal items and last minute cancellation. A need has been identified for special policies to cover the additional risks presented by water sports.

Brokerage:
There is a need to service the second-hand market, particularly for large yachts and motor boats. Most people buy their yacht second-hand and many first-time buyers prefer the security of negotiating through the yacht broker. The yacht broker is similar to an estate agent, selling boats and charging an agreed commission to the vendor. The benefits for the vendor are that the broker covers the advertising costs and, in some cases, is able to show people around the boat. For the purchaser the broker will act as an agent looking out for a suitable craft and ensuring that any paper work is correct and procedures are followed. Some yacht brokers are members of the trade association the Yacht Brokers, Designers and Surveyors Association.

Surveyors:
When a considerable sum is being offered for a second-hand boat most recreational users will want to assure themselves that the boat is

structurally sound. In these cases a surveyor's report is commissioned. Surveyors are sometimes specialist in one particular construction type, others are more general and are often contacted through advertisements placed in yachting and boating magazines. The surveyor will carry out an in-depth study of the safety of the boat and provide the potential buyer with a detailed report on its condition. The findings of this report are often used to renegotiate the sum paid for the boat. Older boats sometimes require a survey on a regular basis for insurance purposes or as part of a general maintenance review.

EQUIPMENT MANUFACTURE, DESIGN AND SUPPLY

Water sports participation is equipment intensive, from the basic essentials through to books, magazines and leisure clothing. Many water sports are fashionable and require new colours and designs to be launched each year. Through literature particular interest groups can communicate up-to-date information and magazines are important for publicising events and advertising goods and services. Many small craft are sold, and many job vacancies in the industry are advertised, in the classified advertisements in these magazines.

HERITAGE SITES AND VISITOR ATTRACTIONS

Around Britain's coast and attached to many inland water resources is an abundance of heritage sites and other visitor attractions. Although not usually the responsibility of water based leisure managers they require acknowledgement for several reasons:

1.   They offer large numbers of visitors contact with, and increased awareness of, water resources. Visitors to the many English Heritage and National Trust sites on the coast or near water will have the opportunity for water edge passive leisure - picnics, walks and art.

2.   In some cases they form an important income for water based leisure. Some sites are better viewed from the water and,

therefore, boating companies can use this as an opportunity to create special tours or excursions.

3. They may provide alternative activities to complement the activities of the existing water sports user, especially in the case of holidays. Plas Menai Water Sports Centre in North Wales can offer mountain activities in Snowdonia National Park or visits to associated attractions as part of the holiday experience. Individual visitors by boat to Portsmouth may stay extra days to see the *Warrior* and other museums. This gives the marina additional income for extra night stays.

SUMMARY

This chapter considers many of the background activities which combine to provide water sports opportunities for everyone. The work of youth agencies has been important in encouraging young people into water sports. The water sports holiday abroad has introduced many people to the sport who may not have enjoyed it if their first experience had been during cold weather. The professional services provided for recreational users help unskilled recreational participants to make safe decisions and their work in this field is backed up by the provision of water sports courses to encourage high standards of safety among recreation participants. Chartering both sea going vessels and water ways cruisers have opened the opportunities for water based holidays for millions of people who would otherwise be unable to take to the water.

CHAPTER 10

Recreation Management
of Water Resources

INTRODUCTION

Managing any business requires certain accepted skills including marketing, financial control, and human resource management. Many excellent text books have been produced on these subjects in general and, with the rise in popularity of courses in recreation management, specific leisure texts have been produced. This chapter does not, therefore, attempt to reproduce the information that is already widely available in detailed and specialist texts. A water sports manager wishing to study any one of these aspects in detail is advised to select a standard business or leisure management text devoted to the subject.

This chapter does, however, make the link between traditional recreation management theories and practice with the specific issues of water based recreation. In Chapter 2 the first and most important area was mentioned, accessibility of water sports. In this chapter, therefore, the main points about the accessibility of water sports are summarised. Awareness of opportunities is closely linked to accessibility and, therefore, the marketing of water resources for leisure is considered next.

Water sports providers, in public, private and voluntary sectors, are increasingly faced with demands to provide a range of activities and events. These demands can only be met through careful planning, programming and the application of zoning techniques to water resource management.

ACCESSIBILITY OF WATER SPORTS AND WATER BASED RECREATION

As explained in more detail in Chapter 2 there are four factors which, together, determine the accessibility of the water sports venue as shown in *Figure 10.1*.

Figure 10.1   **Factors which affect the accessibility of water based recreation**

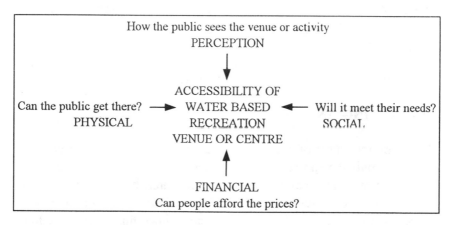

From this it can be seen that the recreation manager needs to consider perception, physical accessibility, financial aspects and social factors. The water based recreation manager reeds to evaluate the following factors when attempting to understand participation rates in water based activities:

- The way people see the activity.
- A range of social factors which may constrain people's ability to become involved.
- The knowledge and awareness of the water based activity.
- The location, ease of access and journey time to the facility.

Evaluation of these factors can assist the manager in improving participation in their particular water based activity. Social factors such as the special requirements of particular groups, often defined in terms of gender, age, class and ethnic groups, need to be fully understood by recreation managers of water based leisure venues in order to incorporate these requirements in product design. For a better understanding of perception and image local surveys can be used to discover what people think about the water based recreation on offer. Negative perception and images may prevent people from actually trying the sport. The water sports manager, therefore, needs to work with this information to create a positive image and to change existing perceptions of the sport. Physical accessibility can be improved by taking advantage of sites close to large populations and, for existing sites, by providing good car parking and sign posting. Financial accessibility can be achieved if managers carry out satisfactory customer research. Prices can be set to balance the rationale of the organisation with the needs of the customer.

MARKETING AND AWARENESS

An important aspect of the accessibility of any water based recreation site is the public awareness of the existence of the centre, the activities and levels at which they are available and interest in the sport itself. Marketing is a complex way of achieving this awareness and, therefore, a successful product. The process is sometimes mistaken for selling alone, however, marketing of a water based recreation site includes the product development, pricing decisions, promotion campaigns and the actual selling. Until recently restricted to private sector organisations, but now increasingly important, although under funded, in public sector operations, marketing of the water sports centre is essential to remaining in business and achieving a cost effective service or a healthy profit.

The water based recreation manager should be aware of the importance of having a marketing philosophy and not simply a marketing department or operation. Marketing philosophy means that the product on offer, whether tangible, such as a wind surfer, or intangible such as a visit to a water sports lake, is designed to meet customers' requirements. It is now accepted that product-led marketing is difficult to achieve and marketing should be based around a sound analysis of the needs of the market.

The leisure consumer is a discerning and unpredictable force in marketing decisions. It is, therefore, important that water based recreation managers take the advice of George Torkildsen (1992) and become *customer oriented*. To achieve this the water sports manager must understand the motivations which influence a participant's choice of leisure. To encourage repeated or regular use of a water sports centre the manager must ensure that an image or idea is created by the marketing effort. The message is important, as seen by television jingles which are remembered long after the product is forgotten. If images, promises and inferences can motivate or encourage people to take part in the water based activity then the same factors reversed can act as deterrents or demotivators. For example, poor customer care by any staff will alter a positive image of the centre and the user may go elsewhere. Hence, all of the staff employed by a water sports centre are essential to its marketing. The motivation to continue and to communicate satisfaction with the service comes from customers who have received a high level of customer care from all of the staff that they have contact with, i.e. reception staff, instructors, through to grounds staff. Staff attitudes in any leisure venue is the key to successful marketing.

This may appear to over simplify the traditional application of marketing in business which stresses the importance of the 'Marketing Mix'. The concept of the marketing mix has been explained in detail in texts such as Kotler's *Marketing Management* and in the leisure context by G. Torkildsen in *Leisure and Recreation Management*. It would, therefore, be a mistake to spend too long on the details of such a well documented concept. However, time is needed to assess its relevance to the management of water resources for leisure. To achieve this analysis a basic understanding of the concept must be developed.

The marketing mix is commonly defined in terms of four aspects of a marketing department described in terms of the four 'Ps' as shown in *Figure 10.2*.

Figure 10.2   **Marketing Mix**

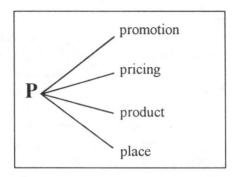

Product development:
Water based recreation products are the centre of a marketing effort because it is the product or service offered at a water resource which has the potential to give customer satisfaction. As with any leisure activity it is this level of satisfaction which is the deciding factor in whether the customer will make the purchase. A range of water based recreation products have been described in previous chapters, some of these products are in their early stages, such as jet skiing, others, like rowing, are more well established. Marketing theory suggests that any product experiences a life-cycle. The product life-cycle was explained by Kotler as four phases: *introduction, growth, maturity* and *decline*. The theory assumes that any product:

a.   has a limited life
b.   requires changes in management techniques at different phases
c.   profits in the case of commercial operations will vary during the life cycle
d.   from the point of view of sales each phase requires a new approach.

Many water sports and water edge activities are reaching their mature phase. For these sports, such as rowing, yachting and dinghy sailing, the recreation manager needs to modify the market in order to prolong the product life. This could be accomplished by attracting non-participants to the sport or encouraging more frequent participation among existing customers - these changes are in the customer base. An alternative is to modify the product, for example, to offer a new aspect of the activity such as a new style of yacht, thereby generating renewed interest and rejuvenating the product.

Very new activities, like dragon boat racing, are clearly at the introductory phase, which requires the manager to work hard to ensure high public awareness and to provide opportunities for participation in this new water sport. Jet skiing and wind surfing could be argued as being in their growth stage as illustrated by their rapid growth in participation.

Some water sports, particularly those which may be fashions or fads, will eventually decline unless effective marketing management, at the maturity stage of their development, can successfully maintain the market by altering the customer base, the product or the marketing mix. When this is the case it is important for water resources to diversify from single product bases thereby ensuring that while one activity declines another is in it's growth stage.

Marketing of water based recreation products presents other complexities for managers. Firstly, by comparing the purchase of a canoe to a visit to a water sports centre, it is possible to see that the canoe is something that the customer can see, touch, sit in, paddle and take away - in short, it is tangible. In contrast the visit will comprise an 'experience' which cannot be taken away, thereby, making the product intangible. A method sometimes adopted to overcome this problem of intangibility is to offer a certificate, course photograph, T-shirt or other souvenirs to provide a tangible aspect to the memory of the 'experience'. Water sports are also, in some ways, perishable. If a canoe course is not full or a booking for a water ski tow is vacant then

Figure 10.3 **Public Access - Free Provision**

Provides access for leisure free of charge - a subsidy by local authority providers

that opportunity will not occur again. If opportunities are not used then they are lost for ever and cannot be redeemed. Incentives for last minute bookings can be employed to overcome the loss incurred by 'lost opportunities'.

Product development is more than just providing a marina or water sports centre, it is the 'package' of activities or products available. The marina must, therefore, develop a range of products to suit a wider target group, for example, some have developed 'dry berthing' where boats are kept ashore and launched as required. The water sports centre may operate a variety of courses aimed at different levels, e.g. canoeing, wind surfing and sailing for the novice, the recreational user and the competitive athlete. Further product development can take place by varying the length of courses, for example, weekends, five days, a week or one day over a period of weeks. The opportunities are endless and depend on thorough market research.

Pricing:
Having developed a product or package which meets the demands of the market the water based recreation manager needs to decide on a pricing policy. The rationale behind the pricing policy is primarily affected by the type of management involved. By necessity, a private sector provider, such as a marina, sailing school or river boat company, has an underlying profit motive. That is to say that these companies will only provide water sports in the long-term if a profit can be achieved. On the other hand, a public sector provider may see the provision in terms of a service to the community and make no charge for access. An example of this can be seen in *Figure 10.3,* showing the tow path at Marlow in Buckinghamshire. This is part of a park which allows free access to walk along the river bank. It should, however, be noted that charges are made for more formal uses of the water, i.e. angling and overnight mooring. The club or voluntary sector centre only needs to break even, therefore, unless a fund raising event is planned, prices can be adjusted to cover both fixed and variable costs at the break even point. This summary has been further confused in the public sector by the introduction of compulsory competitive tendering

for leisure facilities. Now private management teams, if contractually allowed, may introduce new programmes in order to make a profit or at least reduce the subsidy required. The diagram in *Figure 10.4* illustrates this concept.

Figure 10.4   **Rationale for pricing in water based recreation**

Rationale for pricing	SUBSIDY	BREAK EVEN	PROFIT
Provider	Local authority sites	Voluntary clubs	Private companies
Prices	Free or lower than actual cost	Based on a calculation to cover total cost	Based on a calculation to cover costs and provide a return
Examples of Facilities	Tow paths, some water sports centres etc.	Any club or society, national governing bodies for water sports events	Marinas, charter companies, sailing schools

The water based recreation manager has to make other decisions on pricing tactics. As the product is perishable the manager needs to consider off-peak prices to encourage use in those times when bookings may be low. The manager may also wish to target certain groups in the market by offering special deals or concessions. Reduced prices for those groups identified as unable to participate at full cost is attractive for public sector and voluntary organisations who are aiming to achieve equal opportunity and mass participation. For the private company these concessions may be used to attract non-participants or to fill low-use periods. Price can also be used to consciously project an elitist image for a facility. High prices may be attractive to some water sports participants in the same way as an expensive five star hotel is for some people wishing to achieve exclusivity in their leisure time.

Place:

This is more easily applied to products where a distribution area can be defined. Water sports can only take place where water resources exist or can be created. The water based leisure manager, therefore, needs to consider the potential demand in the area and assess other opportunities within the catchment of the centre, if possible, before making final site selection decisions. It may be possible for local authorities to improve the distribution of water sports in urban areas by developing mobility schemes to transport urban populations to water resources by providing minibuses and trailers for canoes and dinghies or a central store for equipment. Alternatively, the philosophy could be to develop centres within cities that have docks, canals and/or rivers.

Awareness and Promotional Strategies:

Promotional campaigns are designed to communicate the benefits of a programme or activity and thus generate a willingness to buy or use the product. The promotion of a water resource for recreation can be achieved in a number ways:

1. Visits, talks and open days involving personal contact. All water sports operations can increase participation through the effective use of personal contacts. For clubs and specific interest groups, well publicised open days, where members of the public are invited to come along and see and/or participate in what the club has to offer, would probably succeed in attracting the local target group required. Clubs, societies and national governing bodies would also benefit from visiting other clubs and schools. For example, the Ocean Youth Club visits youth groups and schools showing a promotional video and explaining the opportunities on offer. This type of personal contact can help to enthuse new customers but is time consuming and difficult to set up initially.

2. Private companies may practice any of the activities listed above but could also offer events, such as buffets, lunches and parties to achieve contact with potential clients. These events allow companies to show off the best aspects of their service and gives a more vivid description than a brochure. Bigger organisations could also hire a stand at one of the major trade shows such as the London Boat Show at Earls Court or the Leisure Show at the National Exhibition Centre in Birmingham. Sailing schools and charter companies find these shows a particularly effective way of improving bookings.

3. Advertisements could be placed but require a marketing budget to cover the costs. If an advertising campaign is considered the water venue will influence the target groups. The small sailing club will have neither the funds nor the need to engage in an extensive national advertising campaign. Most clubs have a very small catchment area, often no more than a 10 mile radius, therefore, a poster campaign in local shops, libraries, sports centres, youth centres, schools and other venues would serve its needs. A poster campaign could be complemented by an advertisement in the local press.

Other companies which need to attract a wider audience, for example, sailing schools in the Solent need to attract customers from as wide a catchment area as possible, require a well planned advertising campaign using, most commonly, the relevant sections in the water sports press. Larger companies increasingly make use of the travel advertisement pages in the Sunday newspapers. The costs of these advertising campaigns may be high but are necessary to attract a nation-wide customer base. The average advertising costs in 1994 for a yachting magazine were from £30 for a 3cm by one column boxed advertisement of 30 words (*Classic Boat*, February 1994). Other forms of media advertising such as radio and television are usually beyond the means of water sports companies. Some trade organisations and governing bodies can help member companies by producing industry brochures containing advertisements from their members. The RYA produces such a brochure for approved sailing schools and during their Yachtmaster Instructor Conference in January 1994 Tim Bartlett identified some common failings by sea schools promoting themselves in the RYA brochure. Most common mistakes include:

i.   Not identifying clearly a unique selling point such as ladies only courses.
ii.   Confusing the opportunity by selling other services as well, for example charters available.
iii. Making comments which cannot be substantiated, for example the cheapest prices in the Solent.
iv.   Superfluous information, for example mentioning "RYA approved" in a brochure of RYA approved schools!
v.   Repeating information, for example sailing area or boats.
vi.   Poor grammar and spelling.
vii. Patronising statements which can cause offence to some potential clients.

Whether advertising is free or paid for it is essential that water sports managers carefully plan advertisements to make the most positive impact in a small number of words. It should be remembered that the advertisement will appear alongside rivals and needs to be different. To achieve this the manager could employ a specialist design company but, before this is done, s/he must have an idea of what image s/he wishes to portray. A bright colour action shot will give an image of challenge and excitement, while a yacht lying at anchor in a deserted bay will infer peace and relaxation.

4.   Publicity is basically free advertising through media coverage. It is particularly important to exploit its potential to the full and the organisation needs somebody to plan suitable press releases. The press release should inform the media, such as trade organisations, magazines, local and national newspapers, radio and television, of a new product, facility or event. The press release, it is hoped, will result in an article, report or even a short mention which will help to increase awareness locally and even nationally.

5. Incentives can be offered to attract new participants or to launch new products. For example, a discount on membership after an introductory water ski course. Regular customers can be offered discounts or free activities from the introduction of new members to the club. For example, two new berth holders introduced to a marina could result in a 10 per cent discount on next year's mooring fees.

The challenge for the manager of recreational water resources is to achieve the optimum combination of the factors described above. The idea of a mix, the way in which these items are combined, is crucial to the success of the product. In order to decide on the mix a manager needs to confirm a direction for the organisation. This is termed the mission statement. The mission statement for a canoe club may be to provide opportunities for participation, competition and social activity for local enthusiasts, whereas a luxury water sports club may set out to provide exclusivity, luxury and outstanding quality of service for the discerning water sports practitioner. Further to this the product may be 'positioned' by developing an image through marketing inferences, for example, the positioning of the luxury club may seek to infer class and sleek style by using associated images.

Finally, the market needs a policy for segmentation. There are three main accepted approaches. Firstly, the product could be undifferentiated and one product is sold to all customers. Secondly, the product could concentrate around a small number of traditional activities, such as a reservoir sailing club offering sailing and wind surfing. Finally, a different product could be offered to a different segment of the market, for example, a youth sailing club.

From this preparation the manager needs to construct a marketing plan ensuring that the process of marketing is ongoing and organised. *Figure 10.5* on page 227 shows a simple marketing plan for a new small commercial sailing school.

Figure 10.5   **Marketing Plan for a Sailing School**

No	Activity	Title
1	Aims and objectives specified	POLICY OF ORGANISATION
2	Investigate the potential customers' needs and existing provision	MARKET RESEARCH
3	Identify targets in terms of programming, social groups and attendances	MARKET STRATEGY
4	Design a programme to satisfy these criteria	PRODUCT/PROGRAMME DEVELOPMENT
5	Produce a price list and any discount or concessions	PRICING POLICY
6	Activities such as Boat show stands to launch the new programme, open days and follow up publicity in the local and boating press	PRE, DURING AND POST OPENING PROMOTION PLAN
7	How much will the promotion plan cost including brochures , posters, adverts and all other promotional costs?	COST CALCULATIONS
8	Measure booking obtained, enquires, actual attendances and customer satisfaction	RESULTS
9	Monitor performance and re-evaluate the promotions strategy	REVIEW PERFORMANCE

Programming and Planning:

An important aspect of product development in water sports is the programming of activities and courses. The success of the product will rely, in part, on a customer-oriented programme which meets the needs of the target market or markets. The importance of programming is often under-rated by water based recreation managers who fail to recognise its complexities. Programmes should be developed to make optimum use of the water resources, equipment and staff available. The process should involve scheduling, planning, time tabling and implementing the activity schedule. The programme should normally be produced from an initial regard to the policy or mission statement of the organisation. Many water sports programmes can be criticised for:

a.   *Always providing the same activities* - never introducing new ideas.

b.   *Not showing an innovative approach* - for example instead of an adults' sailing course why not try a restaurants and public house sailing expedition.

c.   *Lack of flexibility* - if a group or individual has a particular requirement try to incorporate it into the programme. Do not stick too rigidly to the original.

d.   *Programmes often concentrate on certificate courses* - many users want to learn in a less structured environment.

e.   *Lack of programme evaluation* - leads to stagnation and boredom for customers.

By devoting a little more time to evaluating the success of programmes and inviting comment from customers and staff for improvements and new courses, recreation managers would, perhaps, find that they could produce a more successful programme and product. The programme is often the first thing that the customer sees. Its presentation and user-friendliness are, therefore, very important as many potential customers are discouraged by dull, uninteresting programmes, lack of clear explanation and difficulty in finding all the relevant information.

Zoning of activities:
An important aspect of optimum programme design in water sports is

the concept of zoning. Zoning of activities allows a wide range of activities to be offered by a water resource. This is welcomed in terms of increased access to water based recreation and diversification of the product base, and, therefore, optimum potential profits. Zoning is practised to ensure that a range of activities can take place safely on a water resource where several conflicting demands have been identified. These demands could all be recreational, for example, the needs of sailing versus the needs of water skiing, or a combination of recreational demands and conservation as at Blakeney Point in Norfolk where zoning is used to allow birds and water skiers to harmoniously share the water resource.

One method of zoning, in small resources, is by time. This practice involves an evaluation of the demand in terms of hours for the water resource by each sport and time tabling accordingly. For example, dinghy sailors may wish to run a course on a Thursday evening and race on a Sunday, leaving the water unused for most of the time. Demands of other sports could be incorporated into the free time, thereby, making a more effective use of the resource. For example, a reservoir may be zoned by time to meet the competitive, recreational and training needs of a range of water sports as demonstrated in the sample programme for a gravel pit water sports centre (see *Figure 10.6* on page 230).

However, time is not the only zoning option, particularly on large resources. Where sufficient space is available it may be possible to allow activities to run concurrently, sharing the resource to suit their needs. Some water resources, such as country parks, could construct several different lakes for use by different sports who could share the central facilities. Alternatively, buoyed areas could be reserved for different sports (see *Figure 10.7* on page 231).

Figure 10.6 **Zoning by time - an example**

Time	Monday	Tuesday	Wednesday	Thursday	Friday	Saturday	Sunday
1000 - 1200	School Sailing	Wind surfing	Canoe Class		Wind surfing	Water Ski Club use	Sailing Club Use
1200 - 1400	Angling	Water Ski Club use	University Sailing Club		Angling	Water Ski Club use	Sailing Club Use
1400 -1600	Angling	Water Ski Club use	University Sailing Club		Angling	University Sailing Club	Wind surfing
Post 1600	Canoe Class	Water Ski Club use	Wind surfing	Sailing Club Use	Angling		

Figure 10.7   **Types of area zoning**

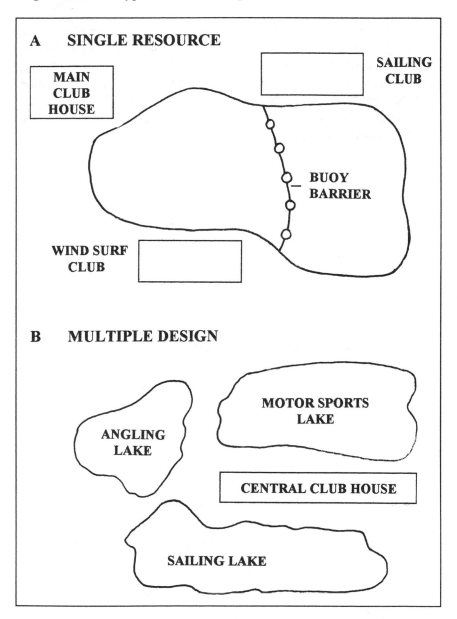

SUMMARY

This chapter coveres a range of marketing and planning issues, applying them to water sports providers. The same techniques can be applied to many other aspects of the water based recreation industry, e.g. marinas, beaches and other organisations. The water recreation manager must remember that these issues seek to achieve customer satisfaction. It is this level of satisfaction which delivers long-term loyalty amongst customers.

CHAPTER 11

Staffing Roles and Processes in Water Based Leisure Management

As water sports provision is a service industry, staff are often considered to be the most valuable asset. Therefore, it is important to identify methods of ensuring that water sports staff are selected and managed effectively to ensure customer satisfaction.

STAFFING

The management and motivation of staff is particularly important for the successful operation of a water based recreation centre as it is the staff who create the first impressions with customers and it is the staff who are responsible for the delivery of the product. Even when the product meets all of the customer's requirements, if the staff delivering it are unhelpful, poor communicators or unenthusiastic the customer is likely to find the product or experience unsatisfactory. Therefore, selection, induction, assessment and in-house training of water based recreation staff are essential to a successful organisation. This section considers the staff requirements for water based recreation, recruitment procedures and on-going staff development.

Staffing requirement for water based recreation :
Water based non voluntary recreation centres, depending upon their size and complexity in the range of courses offered, find that a major overhead is staffing. For all but the smallest centre, staff are required in managerial, administrative, instruction and maintenance work. The

nature of water sports, both in UK centres and Mediterranean areas, is that the season is usually restricted. Most customers use water sports venues during the spring, summer and early autumn months. The first problem faced by water based recreation managers, therefore, is planning for seasonal staff requirements. Whether the organisation closes for maintenance during the winter or chooses to run a skeleton programme, bookings and participation will be significantly reduced during these months and there will be a need for reduction or re-deployment of staff. Two main policies, therefore, operate. Some types of work in water sports and water based recreation is seasonal in nature and contracts are often offered from early March through to the end of October. The problem with this policy is that it can lead to instability. For example, if a water sports instructor knows that s/he will be out of work in November then it is only natural for him/her to be looking for work by September. This could lead to instructors leaving before the end of the season. It also makes it more difficult to justify investment in staff training because, although some staff will return the following season, many more will move on.

The natural transient nature of water sports work is widely accepted by instructors who, whilst young, enjoy the lack of long-term commitment and the flexibility of regularly being able to move to new areas and jobs. However, as instructors grow older the desire to settle and take home a reliable income can force many good instructors out of the industry to find more stable employment. It is, therefore, necessary for water resource managers to ensure that progression and full-time opportunities exist, particularly for senior staff. The employment of full-time staff usually comprises the core team who are involved with the day-to-day management of the centre. When instruction is not required flexibility on the part of teaching staff is needed to work in other areas, such as maintenance and administration. During the winter the work-load for maintenance tasks increases, therefore careful planning can lead to the benefit of retaining water based staff in maintenance work. The benefit of such planning is that staff training can be offered with long-term commitment and team-building will result from staff working together in other areas. Staff feel more settled towards the end of the season if they are assured of continued work.

An alternative to a seasonal staff employment policy, for some teaching establishments, is to make use of the many freelance instructors available. In this case the centre contacts qualified instructors and arranges to pay for their services on a daily rate. The benefits of this type of employment policy for the employer is that it allows flexibility in bookings and planning. When courses become full, an freelance instructor can be employed. Another advantage is that the freelance instructor is self-employed which reduces the centre's responsibility for payroll administration. The disadvantage of this option is that the freelancer, although qualified, may not be aware of, or share the objectives of the school and the centre will have little knowledge of their personality or suitability for a particular course. Also the freelancer will not be able to project the organisation's corporate image easily. These objections can be, to some extent, overcome by the centre maintaining a list of regular and popular freelance instructors so that, over time, they are able to get to know the freelance staff better. To improve the freelance staff's knowledge of company practice it is beneficial to invite all the freelance instructors for a pre-season briefing each year, thereby giving the management a chance to communicate the organisation's current policy and changes in practices, and to allow instructors to familiarise themselves with the surroundings. A suggested format for this type of event is shown in *Figure 11.1* on page 236. This programme can significantly help to reduce the potential problems which arise when employing freelance staff.

Before employing staff in any job, organisations need to decide what the job will entail and the responsibilities it carries, how it will fit into the existing structure and the conditions of work. This plan will form a job description. From the job description managers can decide on the type of person they are seeking, i.e. criteria such as age, personality, qualifications and experience. These points will be used to create a job advertisement.

Figure 11.1 **Agenda for annual pre-season induction for freelance instructors**

TIME	ACTIVITY	DETAIL
10.30	Welcome	Coffee and informal chat
11.00	Talk by management	Procedures: Arrival Departure Incidents/Breakages Reports
1200	Demonstration	Changes in equipment and practices
1230	Lunch	Informal chat
1330	Tour	Point out all important areas, location of office, maintenance etc.
1430	Water Sports	Possibly a chance to get out on boats and remind instructor of organisations equipment
1630	Close	A chance to give written instructions and make any booking required

In the water based recreation industry certain qualities are important depending on whether the person is to be employed on the water, in the office or in maintenance work. As staff contact and the resulting impression with customers are particularly important then the following qualities will be desirable in any position:

- cheerful disposition
- out going personality
- willingness to work anti social hours
- flexibility and genuine interest in the market

Further to these qualities recreation instructors or supervisors need to possess relevant qualifications. For example, a dinghy sailing instructor needs to have an RYA dinghy sailing qualification.

Staff Qualifications:
With the increasing pressure of diversification it may be desirable for a potential staff member to have several instructor qualifications, for example, dinghy sailing, canoeing and wind surfing. A combination of skills allows managers more flexibility in planning programmes and staff rosters. Some instructors have gained these skills through intensive courses. Plas Menai Water Sports Centre offers three and six month courses covering a range of water sports qualifications. The training course makes no guarantees on the number of qualifications gained upon completion though any combination of skills can be learnt from sailing, wind surfing, canoeing, power boating, cruising, rock climbing and mountaineering. Given a reasonable level of experience prior to the 6 months' course a candidate can achieve three instructor qualifications and proficiency certificates in several other areas. Candidates will also gain experience in large multi-activity water sports centre management. This type of experience is becoming increasingly attractive to water sports employers. Unfortunately, levels of participation may be restricted by the cost of such courses which, in 1994, was an estimated £4,600 for the 6 month training.

An alternative base for some water sports qualifications is the National Vocational Qualification (NVQ) which is currently being developed. The NVQ in Sport and Recreation will eventually be available at four levels as follows:

Level 1 - Non Sport Specific e.g. recreation assistant

Level 2 - Coaching e.g. sailing instructor

Level 3 - Managers e.g. sailing school managers or water sports centre management

Level 4 - Professional - not relevant for water based recreation

NVQs allow experience and existing skills to be assessed towards an accepted qualification. Assessment is based on performance evidence from natural observation and extracted examples and is backed-up with 'what if' scenarios and simulation of situations such as man overboard drills.

The Sport and Recreation qualification has been developed by individual project steering groups covering:

- Facility Management
- Facility Operations
- Outdoor Education
- Play
- Sports Development
- Coaching

The RYA has worked hard to adapt and include NVQs into its instructor qualifications for dinghy sailing. At the water based recreation conference in 1993 John Driscoll of the RYA identified the following perceived benefits for national governing bodies of water sports involvement in the introduction of NVQs:

a.   The result will be a clearly defined framework against which performance can be graded.

b.   It will be a nationally recognised qualification.

c.   The process will offer quality assurance.

d. Common skills developed will be transferable to other sports, reducing duplication when gaining more than one qualification.

e. Will fit into a European framework.

f. The qualification will improve the credibility of coaching and instructor qualifications.

g. Employers can contribute to the definition of the qualification.

h. National Governing Bodies will have the opportunity to influence standards in the future.

i. The process has encouraged additional Sports Council support.

The NVQ should help to reduce unnecessary duplication of skills training for staff. For example, one first aid qualification should cover all water sports and give water based recreation a clearer idea of levels of competency across the currently complex array of water sports instructor qualifications as listed in *Figure 11.2*.

Figure 11.2 **Water sports instructor qualification details**

SPORT	AWARDING BODY	QUALIFICATION
Yacht Cruising	RYA	Yachtmaster Instructor
Dinghy Sailing	RYA	Instructor and Senior Instructor
Wind surfing	RYA	Instructor
Water Skiing	BWSF	Instructor
Canoeing	BCU	Instructor
Rowing	ARA	Instructor, Bronze, Silver, Gold

Concerns about the lack of qualification among skippers of small commercial craft have led to the Department of Transport introducing the *Code of Practice* which sets standards for the safety of vessels and for the qualifications required by skippers. For coastal sailing schools, charter companies, sail training organisations and many others the affects of these new requirements were known in late 1994. By April 1994 all yachtmaster instructors required a commercial endorsement to their existing qualification. The new requirements include a five day ships captain's medical course for skippers on boats which go over 60 miles from a safe haven and a 2 day first aid at sea course for those who remain within 60 miles of safe havens. The qualification requires attendance on a Basic Sea Survival Course at a DOT approved centre and a medical fitness examination by an approved doctor. The initial problem with these changes is the time required for training (up to five days for the first aid) and the cost of course fees.

Further to these requirements sailing schools and other organisations will be required to employ more staff when planning long cruises, thereby making such cruises uneconomical for the small sailing school and so reducing the opportunity for participants. Details of the DOT manning requirements for small commercial vessels are listed in *Figure 11.3* on page 241. The RYA also requires an instructor endorsement for teaching RYA certificate courses. Where a sailing boat is used the qualification may be sail.

Water recreation instructors and providers are not the only staffing requirement of a water based recreation centre - office administration, reception and other shore based staff will be required. It is an advantage if these staff have knowledge of water sports as they often deal with initial questions from clients and need to be able to discuss suitability of courses and requirements in an informed manner. Indeed, during new staff induction it may be sensible to explain thoroughly all activities provided and give staff a checklist to assist in correct handling of customer enquiries. In addition to these skills staff are better prepared for the nature of the work in water based recreation if they hold a leisure management qualification, e.g. City and Guilds, BTEC First, National and High Diploma and Certificate Courses, General National Vocational Qualifications, undergraduate, post-graduate and diploma courses. Depending on the level of work, one of these qualifications ensures that the holder is aware of the activities within the leisure industry. It is now possible to employ staff with specific leisure management of water based recreation qualifications at HND and undergraduate levels from courses at Southampton Institute. Other colleges are providing course modules in outdoor recreation and water based recreation which will obviously offer useful specialist knowledge for the water based recreation employer.

Figure 11.3   **DOT manning levels and qualifications for small commercial craft under 24 metres in length or 80 tons gross**

Area category	Qualification	Number of qualified staff
¾ up to 20 miles	RYA/DTp Certificate of Competency as Coastal Skipper Motor	Coastal skipper
2 - up to 60 miles	RYA/DTp Certificate of Competency as Yachtmaster Offshore (motor)	Yachtmaster skipper plus one person deemed by the skipper to be experienced
1 - up to 150 miles	RYA/DTp Certificate of Competency as Yachtmaster Offshore (motor)	Yachtmaster Offshore (motor) and Coastal Skipper, one of whom must have engine maintenance course qualifications
0 - unrestricted	RYA/DTp Certificate of Competency as Yachtmaster Ocean (Motor)	Yachtmaster Ocean (Motor) and Yachtmaster Offshore (motor) one of whom must have an engine maintenance course qualification

Source: DOT Code Of Practice

Maintenance staff require a variety of specialist skills including countryside management for grounds maintenance, and boat building skills for boat maintenance. There is a wide variety of both types of course at all levels. City and Guilds and BTEC qualifications exist at several colleges in Britain for marine skills including marina and boatyard management.

Advertising for Staff:

Potential staff can be alerted to vacancies by advertisements, which should describe the vacancy and the requirements for potential applicants. Advertisements are normally placed in trade magazines, local newspapers and special interest magazines. Agencies offering recruitment services exist but they are often unsuitable for water sports staff. Alternative sources of potential staff include colleges that run suitable feeder courses and existing trained clients.

Processing Applications:

The manager must decide on the format acceptable for applications. Most popular formats are:

1. *Application Form*: By providing the applicant with an application form the company ensures that all information required in the selection process is collected. It is also less time consuming to read through several applications in the same format. However, production and distribution of application forms is expensive.

2. *Curriculum Vitae*: The applicant sends a resume of his/her qualifications, skills and experience. Although most CVs have a similar content the structure and the detail included is at the discretion of the candidate and could, therefore, contain insufficient information. However, requesting a CV is cheaper for the potential employer.

Once applications have been sorted a short list should be drawn up and the candidates invited for interview. Interviewing techniques vary from manager to manager but water recreation centres should consider holding a practical assessment of skills to assist in the final decision. If the potential employee is required to work with young people, particularly very young children, checks should be made into his/her past by taking up references and investigating whether s/he has any criminal record.

Employment Legislation for Water Based Recreation

There are many specialist reference texts on the subject of employment legislation. This section, however, briefly identifies the aspects most important to water based recreation managers. When employing staff, managers must ensure that an equal opportunities policy is followed in line with the requirements of the Sex Discrimination Act 1975, Equal Pay Act 1970 and Race Relations Act 1976. Many areas of water based recreation are dominated by white males, therefore water sports managers should promote opportunities for both women and ethnic minorities. Working conditions, together with the responsibilities of water based recreation centres as employers, are laid down in the Health and Safety at Work Acts 1974/1988, Employers Liability (Compulsory Insurance) Act 1969 and Employers Liability (Defective Equipment) Act 1969. Water sports centres wishing to employ young people on a part-time basis, for example Saturday jobs, must beware of the restrictions placed by the Young Persons Employment Act 1938 and the Employment of Children Act 1973. All contractual commitments are covered in further employment legislation in the Employment Protection Act 1975, Employment Protection Consolidation Act 1978, and Employment Acts 1982, 1988, 1989.

Training:

Training is an important tool in staff motivation and development, and in improving the value of the business. Training can be in-house or by external courses. By providing a good training scheme a water sports provider can improve the quality of service to customers and retain staff through the presence of a structure for progression. A particularly important aspect of training in the water based recreation industry is customer care. By training staff to understand the importance of good practice, the image of the organisation can be significantly improved. Training should include handling irate customers, customer enquires, telephone manner and general communication skills. Training should also include familiarity with the organisation's policy on customer care.

Communication:

Effecting good communication with all staff is a difficult problem for water based recreation centres. Many staff are out on the water, therefore memos can be an impractical mode of effective communication. A more successful method of communication can be achieved through regular staff meetings where management information can be passed to staff and staff have the opportunity to communicate concerns and questions to the management. Many water sports centres operate a daily meeting. However, in some situations this may not be practical, in which case a weekly meeting would be sufficient.

BOOKINGS AND RESERVATION OPERATIONS

Although the quality of facilities, equipment and instructors are important, often the first contact with centres is made over the telephone or by booking correspondence. The way in which the first contact is managed will dramatically affect perceptions of the organisation and the success of the product. As the product is perishable the management of bookings, to ensure optimum take up on every course, is a considerable task. There is a range of micro computer systems which can be tailored to assist in these tasks, produce automatic business status reports and record payments. A basic system can be invaluable for many large businesses, while small organisations are able to work effectively with a manual system. The manual system must, however, be able to remind staff to send out letters and invoices and should be arranged so that, at a glance, the booking staff can confirm availability. Most commonly the latter takes the form of a wall matrix bookings status chart. As bookings are taken the information is filled into the chart.

The beauty of computerised systems is that once client information has been entered into the computer it is stored and can be called up for repeat bookings, promotional mailings and contact details. Computer systems are also able to generate letters to customers at set intervals during the booking process. They can tailor booking status reports, overdue invoices and check in lists. All of these functions are essential in cutting down on man hours and allowing faster customer enquiry feedback. Whether a computer is used or not, an organisation must have a reliable bookings system (see *Figure 11.4*)

Figure 11.4 **Water Sports Course Booking System**

Telephone enquiry
Booking form received
Reserve place to avoid double booking
Send confirmation letter
Ten weeks before course send invoice for balance
Record payment
Send receipt and enrolment information letter

The booking form should be designed to collect all the information required such as personal details, course required, dates, second choice details and relevant water sports experience. A sample booking form is shown for water sports courses in *Figure 11.5* on page 245. The booking and receipt of the deposit must be acknowledged by letter. This may be followed up by a final invoice, often due 10 or 8 weeks before the course date. Once the balance has cleared, joining details should be sent, these should include :

- Directions and/or map
- Arrival times
- Equipment required
- Details of course (if available)
- Departure details

The smooth operation of a reservations department is essential for any water sports centre.

Figure 11.5   **Water Sports Booking Form**

Personal Details:

Surname (Mr/Mrs/Miss) ....
First name ....
Address ....
....
.... Postcode............................
Telephone (day) .... (evening) ....
Special Dietary Needs: ....
Existing qualifications ....
1st Choice : .... 2nd Choice : ....
Course : ....Course : ....
Dates : ....Dates : ....

Payment Details :
Course Fee :   £ ....
10% deposit + insurance (enclosed with booking) =   £........................

Terms of Business :
Watersports International are fully insured against accidents and third
party liability, but responsibility is not accepted for personal accidents,
loss or damage caused by your negligence. The deposit is payable on
booking and is non-returnable. Final payments are due 8 weeks before
the start of the course. On cancellation within four weeks of the start
of the course we reserve the right to withhold the full invoice amount.
If we cancel the course we will offer an alternative or refund all
payments.

Declaration :
I agree to the terms of business and declare that I am in good health
and fit for this type of course.

Signed ....
Date ....

MAINTENANCE MANAGEMENT

Quality services include quality equipment, and a successful water resource needs effective management of maintenance tasks to ensure customer satisfaction. If, for instance, the showers are faulty at the end of a day on the water, all enjoyment will soon be forgotten when masked by this type of problem. The management of resources calls for efficient identification of problems, communication of these faults to staff concerned and checks to ensure all tasks are up-to-date. Many problems can be identified by carrying out regular checks which should be recorded in a maintenance file together with a report on any work that is required. Other problems may be discovered by customers and staff and should be recorded centrally. This detailed information should be passed to the staff concerned as quickly as possible. When a problem is rectified the entry in the log or file should be completed so that managers can easily check the maintenance situation.

CHAPTER 12

Safety Policy and Practice

INTRODUCTION

Water as a resource for recreation and leisure presents the attractions of challenge and of being at one with nature. However, any adventure activity has an element of danger to offer these challenges; adventure infers that there is an element of the unknown and it is this which presents the biggest challenge. It is the responsibility of water recreation providers to manage the challenge and dangers presented by water based recreation. The problem is how to balance the need to offer excitement and the feeling of potential danger intrinsic in the sports with methods to ensure that the dangers remain a feeling in the minds of the participants and not a reality in terms of accidents. For most casual water users the requirement of danger is not important, a trip to the beach, a picnic by a lake or a walk by the river provides, for them, relaxation and enjoyment. In these cases the participants may be unaware of potential dangers and, as they are usually unsupervised, good water safety information and instructions are required.

What are the dangers?
The most obvious danger for both water's edge activities and water sports is the threat of drowning. It is possible to drown in anything from a shallow duck pond to the deepest ocean. The danger of drowning has led many education authorities to introduce 'drown proofing', a course of swimming lessons for junior school children.

The importance of learning to swim has been acknowledged by the National Curriculum and swimming has been introduced as a compulsory element of primary school education. However, will the ability to swim significantly reduce the possibility of drowning? A percentage of drowning accidents occur when another injury has been sustained prior to the victim entering the water, for example a knock to the head by a boom on a sailing boat could render the victim unconscious. Therefore, although the ability to swim is of vital importance, other precautions are necessary for water recreation safety.

Other common problems faced by water based recreation users are tides and currents. Some very strong tidal streams prevail around the British coast and in its estuaries. At its height the tide can sweep a boat past the Needles entrance to the Solent at over two and a half knots. It is impossible for many small pleasure craft to travel against this considerable force and they risk being swept out to sea. Tidal information is available in small local area booklets and national almanacs. Many water users are unaware of the power of tides so this must be stressed by clubs and centres. Strong currents also exist in non-tidal waters, particularly in rivers around locks and weirs, and when rivers are very full, the stream runs faster. This can be illustrated by a visit to a local river. After a heavy rainfall, a stick thrown into the water will be carried by considerable force downstream and will demonstrate how much effort would be required to paddle or swim against the current.

Winds and other weather conditions also create dangers for coastal water based recreation. Strong winds and gales present dangers to small pleasure craft at sea. High winds create a rough sea, making it difficult for small power craft to motor through. Strong onshore winds can sweep small craft ashore whilst offshore winds create difficulties in reaching the safety of a harbour. Light inflatable craft, often used by beach users, are frequently blown out to sea by the lightest of winds. Sea mist and fog also present problems for the navigation of small craft and increase the possibility of collisions.

Other incidents include equipment failure, personal accidents and sudden illness. Fire, sinking and loss of propulsion for a boat can present serious dangers, particularly when the stricken vessel is some distance from land.

What are the chances?:
Water based recreation presents a number of potential dangers for the water resource or water sports manager. S/he needs to identify and manage these dangers to reduce the possible risk of accidents as it is extremely bad publicity for any resource to sustain a serious accident. By studying statistics from casualty departments in hospitals and rescue services, recreaction managers can assess and understand the potential risk of accidents. Annual figures indicate that water sports account for 76,000 personal injuries that result in a visit to a casualty unit. National estimates, during the period May to October 1987, suggest that 9,000 accidents occurred on rivers, lakes and the sea whilst 10,000 occurred on the shore or waterside. These statistics formed part of the 1987 European Home and Leisure Accident Surveillance System which also indicated that 48 per cent of these accidents were sustained by 15 - 64 year olds.

As these accident statistics ignore boating incidents and drowning a second source of information is required to complete the picture. HM Coastguard produces annual statistics of the number and nature of incidents which they deal with around Britain's coast. The information for assistance rendered to recreational users is approximately 80 per cent of the total assistance given (see *Table 12.1* on page 251).

Managers must be careful when interpreting these statistics. Motor cruising and yachting have much higher participation rates and the majority of these rates are for coastal activity. Other sports have lower participation rates and a high proportion occur on inland water which are not covered by these statistics. Because power boating attracts more people (using the participation rates suggested in Chapter 2) it would, therefore, be inaccurate to conclude that it is more dangerous than other activities. The individual chance of an accident is less than

0.106 per cent based on a 1,000,000 participation rate per year. However, what can be seen is that pleasure craft require assistance more regularly than other water users, accounting for approximately 80 per cent of all assistance to coastal vessels.

Table 12.1   **Coastguard assistance to recreational users in 1992**

Type of craft	No. of incidents	Total recreational incidents [%]
Powered pleasure craft	1059	37.4
Sailing craft	873	30.8
Sail boards	366	12.9
Small craft	349	12.3
Inflated craft	185	6.5

Source: HM Coastguard - Positive Performance '93

It is interesting to consider the cause of a problem and the need for assistance (see *Table 12.2* on page 252). Machinery failure causes the greatest number of problems closely followed by adverse weather conditions. Many incidents could be avoided by more careful planning and better maintenance of boats and equipment. Water sports managers, particularly those involved in clubs and training, need to reduce the likelihood of incidents by educating all participants. All water based recreation providers should also ensure that equipment and vessels are maintained in line with the requirements of the DOT *Code of Practice* and that all courses and activities are planned with due regard to dangers.

The statistics above relate to incidents that involved vessels. However, many other incidents require assistance to people. Most commonly these are medical evacuations from foreign ships at sea. Practically all other assistance to people involves leisure participants and includes more shore based activities than water sports as shown by the information in *Table 12.3* on page 253. Although the figures appear high HM Coastguard summary indicated a 10 per cent fall in the number of shoreline or cliff rescues.

Table 12.2 **Reasons for incidents involving assistance rendered to vessels**

NATURE OF INCIDENT	NUMBER OF INCIDENTS	PERCENTAGE OF TOTAL
machinery failure	1344	37.1
adverse conditions	535	14.8
stranded	355	9.8
capsized	305	8.4
sail mast failure	257	7.1
taking on water	165	4.6
fouled propeller	190	5.2
other	192	5.3
out of fuel	70	1.9
overdue	62	1.7
fire	57	1.6
collision	46	1.3
sunk	34	0.9
abandoned	11	0.3

Source: HM Coastguard - Positive Performance '93

The Royal Society for the Prevention of Accidents (RoSPA) offer the most conclusive information on the risk of drowning presented by water sports. Their research, in 1990 and 1991, indicates that the risk of drowning during water sports participation fell by approximately 15 per cent with no drowning recorded in water skiing, snorkelling, wind surfing, jet skiing and surfing during 1991. Swimming and angling have the highest figures for drowning. Canals, docks and harbours statistically show the lowest percentage of drowning incidents with the highest rate (35 per cent) occurring in rivers and streams. When this figure is combined with information about lakes, reservoirs and canals it is easy to conclude that the majority of drowning incidents occur in inland waters (*source*: Dept of National Heritage: The report of the Watersports Safety Working Group).

Table 12.3   **Assistance to people by HM Coastguard in 1992**

TYPE OF INCIDENT	NUMBER OF INCIDENTS
cut off by the tide	696
cliff	240
swimmers	126
divers	129
missing persons	115
persons over board	43

Source: HM Coastguard - Positive Performance '93

How does this compare with other leisure activities?:
The risk of water based accidents are very low. However, when they occur they are often more serious than in other activities. The Consumer Safety Unit at the DTI examined statistics from 11 selected hospitals during 1989. These indicated that water sports accidents involving a visit to a casualty department are very much lower than for other sports. There were 4,025,000 accidents to football players in the survey versus 76,000 for water sports. However, water sports are minority activities with low participation rates whereas football, according to the Sport Council's research during 1986, enjoys participation by 6 per cent of the total male population - no figure was given for water sports. Although the total number of accidents was considerably lower for water sports consideration must be given to participation levels.

SAFETY ORGANISATIONS

There are three main organisations which are concerned with water safety and provide advice for recreational users and/or assistance with incidents. Many of the statistics compiled above were prepared by these organisations to help increase water users' understanding of the degree of risk and dangers involved.

HM Coastguard:

The structure and general role of the HM Coastguard is outlined in Chapter 7. Among its many responsibilities HM Coastguard is an important force in recreation user awareness campaigns. These have sought to improve the recreational user's knowledge of methods to prevent incidents and of procedures when incidents occur. Its interest in awareness and education is a direct result of the fact that the largest percentage of its work in search and rescue involves recreation participants. Its work in leisure education has taken many forms, the most widespread being the 'Be Safe' campaign which has generated a number of posters and leaflets covering the specific issues of different water recreation users. From 1991 to 1992 the number of incidents rose by 15 per cent, partly assisted by the increase in the leisure industry. During 1992 218 people lost their lives in British waters and HM Coastguard gave assistance to over 14,500 people though not all recreation participants. This indicates that HM Coastguard has a 98.5 per cent success rate and offers a considerable service for all users of coastal waters (*source*: HM Coastguard - Positive Performance '93).

Royal National Lifeboat Institute (RNLI):

The lifeboats provided by the RNLI are an important asset for the co-ordination of search and rescue operations by HM Coastguard and for the assistance given to vessels and people in trouble at sea. The organisation classifies its work in terms of callouts, people at grave risk and people assisted. Information boards displayed at lifeboat stations indicate that during the summer months a large percentage of call outs is to recreational vessels. A lifeboat station in an area of high recreational use is Lee on Solent where the recorded call outs, in 1992 were 186: 117 to people at grave risk and 64 people assisted (*source:* HM Coastguard - Positive Performance '93)

Royal Society for the Prevention of Accidents (RoSPA):
RoSPA is a professional body which receives grant aid from the Home Office and is concerned with safety in many areas. It has established a water safety department which serves the National Water Safety Committee. This committee is made up of representatives of the key organisations with a responsibility for water safety. The committee makes suggestions as to how the occurrence of water accidents can be reduced in the future. Initiatives by the committee, which meets four times a year, have resulted in such items as the national signage scheme for water safety. The committee has the sole and important responsibility for co-ordination of a wide range of organisations with concerns for water safety.

GOVERNMENT ORGANISATIONS WITH RESPONSIBILITY FOR WATER SAFETY

The responsibility for water safety legislation and control is confusingly distributed throughout a wide range of government organisations as described below:

Home Office:
As well as providing grant aid for RoSPA, the Home Office also has the power to control the safety of water based recreation through the use of bye laws allowed under the Public Health Acts of 1936 and 1961. The 1936 Act allows bye laws to regulate bathing areas which have been extended to include designated wind surfing areas. The 1961 Act allows the Home Office to create bye laws to control the speed and navigation of pleasure craft in order to prevent danger to bathers in tidal rivers and coastal locations.

Department of Education:
Swimming and water safety instruction prior to the age of eleven years is an essential element of physical education teaching under the 1994 National Curriculum. In this domain the Department of Education has

played a vital role in making water safety among school children a compulsory subject.

Department of the Environment (DOE):
The main interest for the DOE is the setting and maintenance of water quality standards under the provisions of the Water Resources Act 1991. The department has the power to designate areas safe for recreation and to ban activities, such as bathing, from those areas which do not meet the required standards. The Water Resources, Water Industry and Land Drainage Acts of 1991 lay down the requirement for water companies, the NRA and Internal Drainage Boards to provide recreational access to water resources where possible. A *Code of Practice* has been introduced by the Secretary of State and is monitored by a standing committee with representatives from the above mentioned organisations. The DOE controls the use of bye laws made by navigation authorities on inland waters.

Department of Trade and Industry:
The main area of control for this department, as regards water safety, is the power to ban dangerous equipment or products.

Department of Transport:
This department has the main control over water sports safety and, most importantly, the HM Coastguard forms part of this department. The department also controls international regulations, to prevent collisions, and the work of the Marine Accident Investigation Branch which is normally restricted to commercial incidents. The department also has a ports division which is concerned with the framework of general legislation such as the Harbours Act 1964. The powers of each harbour is set out in individual local acts and harbour orders.

SAFETY AND WATER'S EDGE ACTIVITIES

Safety on Beaches and for Bathers
HM Coastguard's assistance to people includes calls to people cut off by the tide and to swimmers. In 1992, although the extent of these

incidents decreased by 10 per cent from the previous year's statistics, good publicity, such as that provided by HM Coastguard, together with a clear management policy for preventing accidents on beaches would help to further reduce these figures. HM Coastguard produces leaflets and posters that promote awareness among beach users of the potential dangers and indicates what action is required should an an emergency occur. This campaign is called *Be Safe by the Sea* (*source* HM Coastguard - Positive Performance '93).

Beach users can reduce the risk of accidents on beaches by:

1. Keeping a careful watch over children while playing at the water's edge. Small children can drown in very shallow water.

2. Ensuring that members of a group know where each other are, especially if they go for a swim or leave the beach. It is easy to think that someone has gone home when they actually went swimming and have not returned. This delay could be a matter of life or death.

3. Making sure that they know how far the tide will come in and whether any part of the beach is likely to be cut-off off at high water.

4. Avoiding playing on rocks as they are often slippery and can be dangerous.

5. Watching out for large waves which may sweep young children off their feet.

6. Checking and *obeying* notices and flags displayed.

Codes of practice should be clearly displayed by beach managers together with an explanation of the flags used for beach safety, as shown in *Figure 12.1* on page 258.

Figure 12.1 Beach Safety Flags

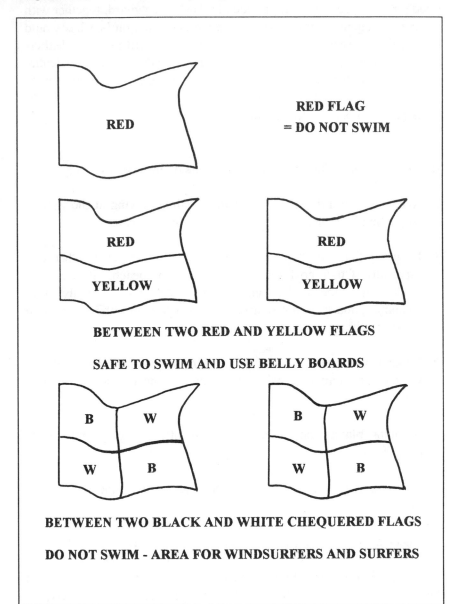

These flags should be used and updated regularly. Many beaches experience specific local currents and other conditions which should be clearly explained. A map indicating areas of the beach likely to be cut off in high tides also provides essential local knowledge for bathers. Life belts should be readily available and their positions clearly indicated together with advice as to the correct procedures in the case of an emergency, including the location of the nearest telephone box.

Swimming accounted for many incidents to people, some of which could be avoided if beach users were more aware of the following advice described by HM Coastguard:

1. Beach users should not swim if the red flag is displayed or if they feel unwell, cold or tired, or for two hours after a meal or drinking alcohol.

2. Swimmers should try to use areas patrolled by life guards.

3. Swimmers should not swim out to sea but stay near the beach.

4. Cold can kill and, therefore, swims should not be for too long.

5. Inflatable air beds are very dangerous on the water as they are easily blown out to sea.

6. Belly boards should be kept with the user at all times. An unattended board washed up on the beach could result in a search for the user.

7. Snorkelling is enjoyable but should only be attempted in calm water and not by people with breathing problems.

As with general beach safety information the above advice should be available at all beach areas. During the summer season popular beaches should be manned by a qualified life guard and safe bathing areas should be marked clearly by two red and yellow flags. Beaches displaying this information and providing a well managed environment for leisure and recreation are more likely to be awarded the European Blue Flag.

Safety on River and Canal Banks:
Many water based recreation accidents occur on inland water, possibly because the activities do not appear to present dangers and are nearly always unsupervised. To reduce the risk of accidents recreational water's edge users can do a number of things:

•   When selecting a spot for a picnic choose one which is slightly away from the bank

•   When walking by the water be careful of wet, muddy paths because it is easy to slip into the water

•   Children should be watched at all times and prevented from running or getting too close to the water

•   Make sure of the whereabouts of life saving equipment and from where help can be obtained

•   Do not swim close to locks and weirs

•   Obey any notices asking people to keep clear

The National Rivers Authority, British Waterways and water companies are the most frequent guardians of inland water resources. Although they have no legal responsibility for water safety they provide notices alerting water leisure participants to potential dangers. They also provide and carry out regular inspection and maintain life saving equipment (see *Figures 12.2a & 12.2b* on page 261) at popular spots.

Figure 12.2a   **Older-style life-saving ring**

Older style ring with floating line - can be subject to vandalism

Figure 12.2b   **Modern life-saving ring in sealed container**

SAFETY FOR WATER SPORTS

General Equipment:

Boats and other water craft should be equipped sufficiently to cover basic emergencies and attract attention. Obviously a wind surfer is limited to what it can carry in the way of equipment whereas an offshore cruising yacht has many options available. Personal flare packs are now produced which can be carried by all water users. Red flares (orange smoke for day time use) are the standard modern method of alerting other water users of an emergency. The number, size and type of flares carried depends upon the size of craft being used. It is recommended that a coastal craft up to 10 miles offshore should carry: 4 red hand held flares; 2 red rocket flares; 2 orange smoke signals; 4 white collision warning flares (see *Figure 12.3*). A water tight container enables the flares to be safely stored on cruising coastal dinghies and other open craft as well as cruisers.

Figure 12.3   **Recommended Flares**

All water sports participants should be properly equipped. Warm clothes are essential as British weather can change very fast. For water sports such as wind surfing, diving, dinghy sailing, water skiing and surfing the chance of spending some time in the water is much greater. In these instances a wet suit is needed in all but the kindest of conditions. Wet suits come in a range of designs and weights, the most popular being the long john version as shown in *Figure 12.4*. For colder weather, jackets and wet suit boots are a good idea. In warmer weather many participants prefer to wear the 'shortie' which offers protection to the torso and leaves the lower parts of the legs and arms free to get a tan! When selecting wet suits care should be taken to ensure that the thickness of material is sufficient for the water temperatures to be experienced. It may be necessary for centres operating winter courses and activities to purchase a second heavier set.

Figure 12.4   **Long John Basic Wet Suit**

In winter, outer clothing is usually worn to act as a wind break and to offer insulation, and suitable footwear can avoid accidents from slipping. The most essential piece of personal safety equipment is the buoyancy aid or life jacket. Either should display the British kite mark indicating its suitability for the job. Life jackets support the head and enable an unconscious body to float the right way up. Some models are filled with foam and are bulky to wear but more modern designs inflate automatically or manually, by gas cylinder, when the wearer enters the water and can, therefore, be worn flat (see *Figure 12.5* on page 265). Life jackets should be kept on all cruising boats but for other water sports a buoyancy aid is easier to wear and is more commonly used. All watersports venues should insist on buoyancy aids for sailing, water skiing, jet skiing, power boats, wind surfing and canoeing. Rowing and surfing enthusiasts rarely wish to be restricted by such an aid. Buoyancy aids should be the correct size for the wearer and children's sizes should also be provided by most centres. Aids help to keep a person afloat but, unlike life jackets, they do not support the head when unconscious. Buoyancy aids for sailing are shown in *Figure 12.6* on page 266.

Safety for Coastal Sailing
There are many pieces of high-tech safety equipment for the coastal and offshore cruising boat including radar reflectors that allow large vessels to 'see' small craft on their radar. All vessels should carry first aid kits, VHF radios and life saving equipment such as life rings and man-overboard markers.

Cruising sailors should also dress sensibly for adverse weather conditions and all crew members should have water proofs, a safety harness and a life jacket (see *Figure 12.7* on page 267). Hypothermia is a serious problem during coastal voyages; a hat, therefore, is essential. Even summer nights at sea can become very cold.

Figure 12.5 **Lifejackets:**

(a) before inflation

(b) fully inflated

Figure 12.6   **Sailing Buoyancy Aid**

Figure 12.7   **Full Coastal Sailing Wear [fitted with cuffs, hood and safety harness]**

The well equipped boat with a trained crew and skipper should come to no harm if a few extra precautions are taken. HM Coastguard runs a yacht and boat safety scheme where yachts are invited to register details with their local coastguard. The form plus a photograph is kept on file for three years. By registering the owner can ensure that, if over due or notified as missing, HM Coastguard will have enough information to co-ordinate a fast and efficient search.

Before setting out skippers should check the weather forecast which is available from many sources, including HM Coastguard. Adverse weather caused HM Coastguard assistance to 535 vessels in 1992. Finally, HM Coastguard will record passage details if transmitted by VHF. However, these are only recalled if the craft is reported late or missing by another person. For longer cruises crews should leave their plans with somebody ashore and remember to telephone them when they reach their destination.

Safety for sea divers:
Dives are led by a dive marshal who obtains advice on local conditions, checks safety equipment and knows where the nearest hyperbaric chamber is in case of emergencies. Dive plans should be logged with HM Coastguard together with information regarding the abilities of all members of the party. The boat skipper must check the safety and maximum carrying capacity of his/her craft and check that communication with HM Coastguard is working before allowing the dive to commence. Throughout the dive other vessels are alerted to the activities by the dive boat displaying a code flag 'a' as shown in the diagram in *Figure 12.8* on page 268.

All divers should be certain of the diving brief and emergency signals. During the dive the marshal should keep a regular check on the divers' location and communicate at hourly intervals with HM Coastguard. HM Coastguard should be notified once the dive is over and the boat has returned. Divers should be equipped with dry suits which afford better protection from cold water than wet suits.

Figure 12.8   **Safety procedure during diving activities**

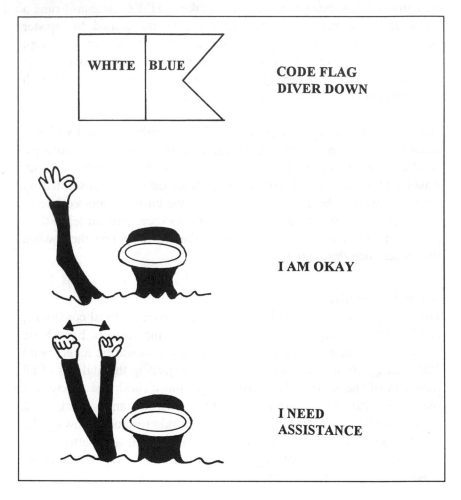

WATER BASED RECREATION SAFETY GUIDELINES AND POLICY ADVICE

Water sports Safety Code
Produced by RoSPA the Water Sports Safety Code gives general advice to all water based recreation participants.   The main recommendations are that participants should:

- be made aware of natural dangers and not take unnecessary risks
- be prepared for cold water
- find out local knowledge of any new area
- take advice on safety
- not to go alone
- be encouraged to learn life saving and to know what action to take in an emergency

The basis of this code is that most water sports accidents occur when participants either ignore dangers, such as adverse weather conditions, over estimate their ability, are not familiar with local conditions, go out alone away from patrolled areas or are unable to cope when an emergency occurs. Training is, therefore, essential for all water based recreation to ensure that all users understand the dangers that their sport entails and can judge their own limitation. Correct training can, therefore, be the difference between life and death.

Report of the Water Sports Safety Committee
In 1990 Colin Moynihan, the then Minister for Sport, commissioned a study into the provision for safety in water sports. The report was structured to study the generic issues in water use for recreation and the role of the governing bodies and the non-sporting organisations in the provision of safety awareness. The aim of the study was to decide whether levels of education advice and enforcement of regulations, then in place, were sufficient and to recommend areas for improvement.

The role of government departments and specific safety organisations was discussed earlier. However, much important training on safety issues naturally falls with the governing bodies of water sports as the safety requirements are slightly different in each sport. Safety training is co-ordinated by the governing bodies by their training schemes. Training advice through these schemes was identified in the report as:

- *Primary Safety*:   the safety of the individual
- *Secondary Safety*:   the safety of other water users
- *Tertiary Safety*:   the safe use of equipment
         Source: (Department of National Heritage)

Analysis of the availability and take-up of courses for individual sports showed that no major areas were left uncovered with an estimated 100,000 taking part in RYA training courses during 1993 (RYA Annual Report 1992-3). One area of improvement as demands on limited water space by different activities becomes more intense, is training in the needs of other water sport users to avoid accidents caused by conflict between water sports.

The report makes ten recommendations for improvements to the current situation as regards water sports and safety. These recommendations affect :

> Governing bodies of sport
> Central Council for Physical Recreation
> Department of Environment
> The Association of District Councils
> Local authorities
> Water companies
> RoSPA

To summarise, the report suggests the need for a more integrated approach with better consultation between groups and clear responsibility accepted by governing bodies to promote and liaise with all parties involved in the provision of water sports. The report also recommends that water quality guidelines, for recreation, should be developed and local authorities should adopt a more strategic approach to safety issues. A further suggestion was that all club leases should insist that the club operates to the relevant governing body's safety standards.

Code of Practice for Small Commercial Vessels:
The Merchant Shipping (Vessels in Commercial Use for Sport or Pleasure) Regulations 1993 is a code of practice which covers the level of equipment and manning on commercial vessels under 24 metres in length intended to improve levels of safety on boats used to carry passengers. Boats and organisations included should cover all charter

yachts. Sail training vessels and sailing schools are covered under the code of practice for Sail Training Vessels. The level of safety equipment and staff required varies depending on the nature of work and the distance travelled from the safe harbour. However, all vessels are to meet these standards and should, therefore, be equipped with sufficient fire extinguishers, first aid and emergency equipment. The physical construction of the vessel should be acceptable for safety requirements. Staffing requirements, under the code of practice, are covered in Chapter 11. The stability of the vessel and its safety for various types of work are controlled by these regulations.

The operators of these vessels need to obtain certificates for all vessels through any one of eight appointed Certifying Authorities including Lloyds, Yacht Brokers, Designers and Surveyors Association, The Society of Consulting Marine Engineers and Ship Surveyors and the RYA. The process involves a five year cycle of inspections and surveys as follows:

Year 1:   Full survey and inspection
Years 2-5:   Annual inspection by owners and a check at, at least, 3
                     year intervals by the Certifying Authority

The introduction of codes of practice are, for the most part, a way of insuring good quality of safety practice and have been accepted by the RYA.

SUMMARY

With sufficient care, training and awareness, water based recreation should be no more dangerous than other activities. The work of many government departments and organisations, although criticised for being spread across so many departments, has struck a reasonable balance between legislation and control and the desire for freedom in the sports. Individuals in Britain are still free to buy a boat and use it without training, insurance or other restrictions. This is now increasingly unusual across Europe and other continents where governments set individual standards to restrict the freedom of these activities. The national governing bodies of water sports have, up to now, resisted this style of legislation. In Britain safety remains a matter of personal choice, the degree of risk accepted by a recreation user can only be advised, except in specific areas and clubs where rules, such as the use of buoyancy aids, can be enforced.

Legislation and control has increased and will continue to increase for commercial ventures. Where people are paying to experience the thrill of water sports the operator must ensure that standards of safety are met as laid down by individual governing bodies and for coastal operations the legislation contained in the *Code of Practice*.

CHAPTER 13

Water Based Recreation:
An International Perspective

INTRODUCTION

Water based recreation in Britain draws many parallels to similar activities world-wide. The activities in water based recreation abroad can serve to create new markets for British products, bring new ideas and activities to British water resources and act as a reference for changes, policies and provision in Britain.

EUROPEAN COMMUNITY

With the opening of the Channel Tunnel in 1994 the biggest barrier between Britain and Europe has lessened in its importance. Britain's motorists are able to get in their cars and drive to France, Holland and other European countries. This is just one of the ways in which Britain is becoming closer to Europe. Over the last decade the work of the European Community has contributed to breaking down other barriers between these nations and their systems. Many European nations share the British tradition of seafaring which remains, to the present day, represented in high levels of participation in water sports and water based recreation. Many European countries experience high levels of provision and participation with examples in Holland and France being particularly important.

Opportunities for Sailing:
Holland enjoys extensive areas of inland water, a long coastline and a

network of well maintained and used canals. The water system is important to the Dutch in terms of trade and recreation. The network of canals brings water recreation opportunities right into the centre of most Dutch towns and cities. Wider areas of flat inland water provide important locations for wind surfing, water skiing and many other activities. Canal tow paths weave an interesting network of footpaths and cycle ways through cities. Dutch water sports are dominated, as in Britain, by the existence of numerous clubs and societies. Provision for recreation in the form of moorings and marinas reflects and blends with the traditional towns although some marinas have been developed in particularly busy areas, such as Amsterdam and the main seaports. The extent of Holland's water resources is illustrated in *Figure 13.1* on page 275.

During the summer months France offers a popular cruising ground for British yachts and boats. (See *Figure 13.2* on page 276.) Its coastline has many traditional ports and harbours, the older harbours have now been supplemented by the creation of many marinas. The French government and local authorities support marina development by providing financial aid, where appropriate, allowing them to charge considerably less than their British counterparts. Many British boat owners now keep their craft in French marinas, allowing them a saving of up to £1,000 per annum. It has been suggested that this trend may increase with the opening of the Channel Tunnel.

France, however, is famous not only for its superb cruising waters but also for its opportunities for youth water sports and methods of instruction. One of the most successful enterprises in the French style of sailing school is the Glenans project. This proved so successful that a sister project has operated for some years in Ireland and a book describing the technique is a best seller world-wide. Boats, upon entering a French harbour, can witness a parade of young people learning to sail in small basic single-handed dinghies and wind surfers. The existence of many sailing schools allows thousands of French

Figure 13.1   **Main Water Resources in Holland**

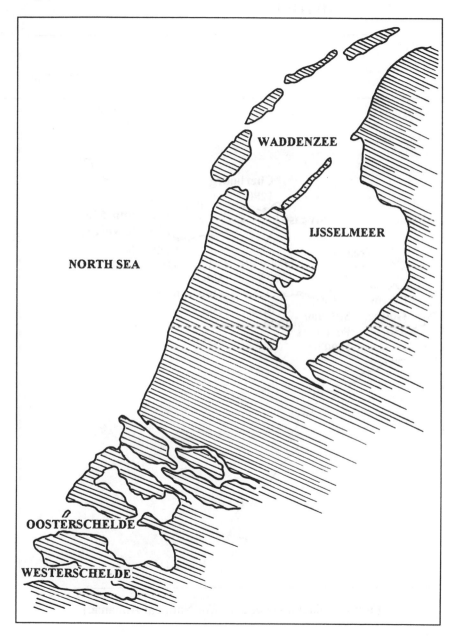

Figure 13.2   **Major marinas in northern France with number of berths (1993)**

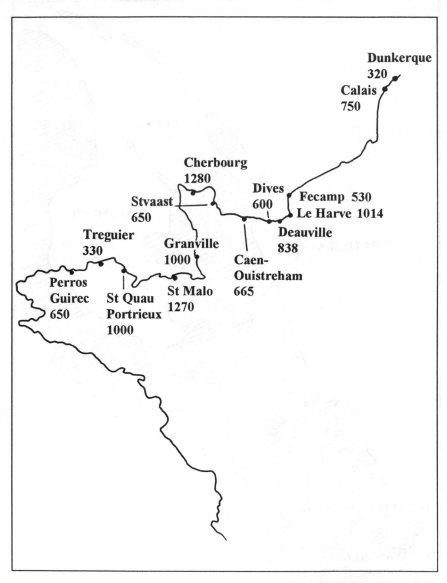

(*Source*: Macmillan & Silk Cut Nautical Almanac)

European Directives:
One important aspect of water based recreation in Britain has been the legislation resulting from European Community agreements. Some aspects of these policies have been discussed earlier. Water quality directives have been received with mixed feeling in Britain but for recreation water users they ensure safe water resources. Water quality, however, is not the only directive which affects water based recreation. The VAT Directive of 1992 has caused some confusion for boat owners who keep their boats abroad and the need for certificates proving that VAT has been paid on all European boats has led to many boats requiring VAT clearance in France and Spain.

Proposals for a European directive on the construction of pleasure craft to maintain standards were lobbied by the European Boating Association. These have now been introduced to ensure a level playing field for boat builders and to set standards for all of Europe. Concerns have been raised over the cost of compliance certificates, particularly for small operations. The result of the proposal may be that all boats will be produced in Europe with a plaque specifying certain safety information. However, there are fears in Britain that this information will be used to restrict areas of use.

A final European directive, already in force in some European countries, is to make sport VAT exempt, thereby reducing the cost of essential equipment.

Legislation and Regulation of Water Users:
Traditionally, water based recreation in Britain has enjoyed freedom from compulsory registration and regulation, a philosophy held dearly by many governing bodies of water sports, including the RYA. However, many European countries bordering the English Channel have imposed regulation, control and registration on their recreation users. France and Holland have strict policies on the licensing of certain users of their inland waterways and, in recent years, these regulations have been extended to cover all overseas vessels. In Holland a skipper or helms person of a boat greater than 15 metres in

length and capable of speeds over 20 km per hour, requires the equivalent of the Helmsmen's Overseas Certificate of Competence. The boat must also carry the rule book for use of the Dutch waterways and volume one of the ANWB Almanac. For cruising on the major inland waters such as the Isjjelmeer, skippers need the equivalent of the Coastal Skipper Certificate of Competence. In France similar guidelines apply for vessels under 15 metres that travel at 20 km per hour. However, no such equivalents exist for the higher standards set for larger or faster vessels. These types of restriction do not appear to significantly affect participation in water recreation on inland waters. British organisations see them as a further tax on enjoyment and continue to resist such regulation. Regulation and registration also cover some coastal vessels in some European countries, setting prescribed cruising limits based on the type and size of boat and the level of experience and qualification of the skipper. This has been implemented to improve safety for water users but again is not favoured by British enthusiasts. *Figure 13.3* shows the regulation for qualification on Dutch and French inland waterways.

Figure 13.3   **European Inland Water Licence Requirements**

Country	Vessel	Requirement
France	< 15 m length	French Cat. C
	< 20 kph	
	> 15 m length	French Cat. PP
	> 20 kph	French Cat. S
Holland Rivers, Lakes and Canals Schelde, Ijsselmeer and Waddenesee	> 15 m Length >20 kph	Klein Vaarbewijs 1 Klein Vaarbewijs 2

THE INFLUENCE OF AMERICA IN BRITISH WATER BASED RECREATION

Fashions and Activities :
Many new water sports originate in the USA. British leisure patterns have, for some time, acknowledged the Americanisation of leisure together with the important influence of American leisure patterns. Outside of water sports this can be seen in terms of the popularity of American football, basketball and baseball in Britain. American fashions also have effect on Britain's young people who are strongly influenced by media images of American products.

This, therefore, explains some of the fashion influences in younger activities such as surfing, wind surfing and water skiing. Here many of the key designs for clothing and equipment are originated by American companies. In the more mature sports the American influence has introduced pressure for better facilities in marinas and more comfortable designs in boats.

For the water's edge user several influences can be determined, and include the development of shopping malls and boutiques as leisure venues around yacht marinas. Exclusive housing developments and marinas can also be traced back to America. It should be possible for British managers to learn from American examples and thereby achieve a more effective approach to water based recreation provision.

Similarities in trends for participation and population growth from American examples, such as California, and the dominance in both countries of boating, with the new important sport being jet skiing, led analysts to believe that reference to American examples will closely match British situations in the future. Indeed, even the regional importance of some sports, such as surfing, is matched in both examples. Therefore American and Canadian examples could be used by British water based recreation managers to predict future trends in participation and demand, and to identify changes in the relative importance of activities and products.

To avoid regulation, an important reference for Britain is the successful development of codes of practice, voluntary agreement and partnership. In the USA co-operation exists between conservation and recreation, as illustrated by the Code of Practice for boat pollution produced by the environmental group in Chesapeake Bay. Agreement has also been reached in many areas concerning water use by various activities. In Vancouver, Canada, for example, rowers and water skiers have agreed voluntary time zoning for their use of a shared river. The need for regulation in Britain could be avoided if these and other examples were fully developed to provide similar practices.

Another interesting phenomenon in North America and Australia is the designation of marine parks on a scale dictated by their allowed uses, from predominantly recreation to conservation. These developments demonstrate how management of water resources can achieve a balance by protecting conservation areas and allowing sustainable development of recreation areas. The protection in these areas, unlike Heritage Coasts, includes both the foreshore and the sea bed. The provision of such areas in Canada has been achieved through a partnership with the BC parks and the Canadian Yachting Association. The Canadian Yachting Association ran a campaign to raise money to purchase land associated with new parks called 'Marine Parks Forever'. Once purchased the land is leased to the BC parks for designation and management. This type of protective ownership has yet to be established in Britain.

IMPORTANCE OF INTERNATIONAL COMPETITION

As with all sports the existence of competition at an international level is important in terms of recognition and excellence. Most water sports mentioned in this book have important international competitive structures. Success in international competition wins media coverage which, in turn, influences the popularity of the sport in the winner's country and can assist in claims for government financial assistance. Britain is, traditionally, successful in all forms of water sport enjoyed in competition with many European countries, America, Australia and

New Zealand.

International competition also calls for partnerships and voluntary standards of competition to be set. The Olympic Games is an important venue for sailing and rowing. These events allow rules to be negotiated and accepted at international level. Ideas and new sports can also develop faster with input from these partnerships.

INTERNATIONAL RALLIES AND FESTIVALS

International events and rallies help to promote the interests of water sports on an international scale. These events often have a high media profile and attract many visitors to view the activities and enjoy the atmosphere. The arrival of major racing events in harbours around the world, together with their associated programme of events, form an important part of the market.

The annual *Cutty Sark* Tall Ships Race, often within European waters, and major events such as the *Columbus* Voyage to America attract large numbers of sightseers. These events have taken place in many European cites over the last few years (see *Figure 13.4* on page 282). Youth sail training organisations promote international understanding and provide the opportunity for socialising and competition. All the main sail training organisations mentioned in this book, together with other sail training groups, compete regularly. The scope for sail training throughout Europe varies considerably from country to country with many areas having a mainly naval cadet approach. Scandinavian countries have more a informal organisation and often use the traditional Colin Archer design of large yachts. Many Polish sail training boats, where the organisations tend to be attached to youth groups such as scouts and colleges, enter competitions. The mix in size and objectives of these vessels make such events interesting for spectators and participants alike. Most impressive is when the ships leave port in a parade of sail. Many organisations also open their boats to the public and use the event to create greater interest in these opportunities and organisations.

Figure 13.4   Cities which host *Cutty Sark* tall ships races

Smaller scale festivals are also important to celebrate and promote interest on an international basis. The festivals at Douarnenez in France are important sailing events that attract traditional boats from around Europe which compete in traditional sailing skills. In minority interest areas these events are particularly useful in ensuring the continued enthusiasm for traditional skills.

The Whitbread Round the World Yacht Race attracts large crowds at every stopping stage. The course takes the international crews to ports in Australia, South America, New Zealand, America and England. Television coverage of the race is transmitted to many nations and affects fashions together with the image and popularity of the sport world-wide.

INTERNATIONAL AGREEMENT

Since coastal resources are shared by many nations there is a necessity to reach agreement on several critical issues including navigation, services and pollution. Issues of pollution are complex as the effect cannot be restricted by geographic border. Recent studies have revealed that contamination from Cap de la Hague in France may be affecting British beaches. North Sea Conferences were set up to agree marine environment protection policies. The second conference, in 1987, agreed to limit the number of red list substances contaminating the sea by 50 per cent in 1995. The third conference, in 1990, agreed tighter controls on the discharge from ships to protect the marine environment. These controls also include pleasure craft and it is now illegal to dispose of any waste from boats, with fines and penalties imposed on culprits. The International Council for the Exploration of the Seas acts in the interests of marine science and gives advice to conferences and other interest groups on developing sustainable uses of our seas. The International Maritime Organisation is concerned with the safety of the seas and control of pollution from ships, thus protecting marine environment. These organisations help to reach a consensus opinion in the field of international pollution.

International agreement on navigation practice has been formulated by the Inter-Governmental Maritime Consultative Organisation that provides the International Regulations for Preventing Collisions at Sea. These regulations specify agreed international standards for buoyage (see *Figure 13.5* on page 285) and rights of way between various water users. It is now possible for pleasure craft to cruise anywhere in the world and to be able to take the correct action in terms of giving way and navigation into harbours and within channels.

Services, including coast radio stations and navigation beacons, are manned and provided by international agreement. For example, HM Coastguard shares responsibility for incidents in the Atlantic with similar organisations from other countries by zoning areas of responsibility. The coast radio station services are manned by various area radio stations and provide information and other services to maritime craft. Many pleasure craft also rely on the system of navigation beacons for electronic navigation such as Decca which is maintained by some countries.

SUMMARY

International comparison and co-operation is both desirable and necessary for the further development of British water based recreation. By researching and sharing experiences with similar managers abroad British recreation managers can gain new ideas for products and management techniques. Liaison of this type enables many problems to be solved quickly or be avoided altogether.

Co-operation in the management of coastal and marine resources is essential in order to provide British water based recreation with a wider scope of opportunity, compatibility and agreement on policies between international powers.

Figure 13.5   **International Buoyage**

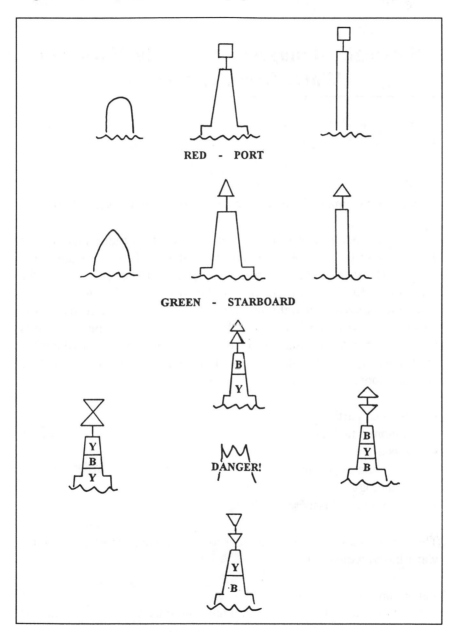

CHAPTER 14

Strategic Management and The Future of Water Based Recreation

How can we estimate the market for water sports in the year 2000?

As with any estimate of future trends there are no certain answers. In 1988 Leisure Consultants produced a detailed analysis of boating and watersports which made an assessment of the market structure in the year 2000. Even as that date approaches it is still difficult to be sure about the expansion of water based recreation. Water based recreation continues to grow steadily and has been an increasingly important area of analysis for leisure industry investigation. The extent to which the market will grow over the next couple of decades will be affected by several important factors:

- levels of participation
- economic factors
- legislation
- space and opportunity
- technology
- environmental issues

These factors are considered in order to evaluate the potential future for water based recreation.

Participation:
Participation in water sports overall has continued to grow over the last

decade. The major market has been in boating. With the expansion of opportunities for charter and a more even take-up in terms of age and gender this may continue to dominate the market. The leisure industry is increasingly aware of the growing population aged 50 and over who, having retired early, often with a considerable nest egg, are looking for enjoyable leisure opportunities. The boating industry, both motor and sail but predominately cruising, may enjoy some growth in this area. However, this may be limited to groups already participating if suitable training courses and holidays do not target the older age group.

Water sports are dominated by young people, which could explain some of the more rapid growth experienced in the 1980s when the children of the 1960's baby boom reached their late teens and early twenties. If similar levels of participation are to be experienced during the coming decade a concerted effort is required to increase participation by all age groups.

Another key factor affecting the growth of water based recreation is the perception, desires and values of future participants. The 1990s have, so far, witnessed a continued concern by the public to maintain a healthy lifestyle. As a result, participation in outdoor activities and the demand for activity holidays has increased. Both of these increases are beneficial to growth in water sports participation. Growing environmental awareness affects leisure participation patterns and it is therefore important for water based recreation to project an image of 'green', environmentally friendly, activities. This can be successfully achieved by liaison with environmental groups.

Fashion and image also continues to be important factors in the growth of water based recreation with many television serials from America and Australia projecting a positive image of water sports. Work in Britain has significantly reduced the elitist image of some water sports. If growth is to be maintained, organisations must ensure that sufficient awareness exists about opportunities for all in water based recreation. This will harness the interest that is created by media programmes and holiday experiences.

Economic Factors

Economic prosperity has a dramatic affect on the growth rate in water based recreation. When standards of living and wages increase people are more able to spend money on luxury goods, which most water sports experiences are part of. In times of economic insecurity many aspects of the British water sports market suffer, for example second holidays at sailing schools diminish when financial difficulties occur. Many businesses also find a need to diversify or amalgamate, when recession occurs, in order to secure a stable base. In this way larger companies then push out the smaller ones. Following the recent economic depression, the future, therefore, may see the market increasingly dominated by a few large companies.

Legislation

Prior to 1990 there was little legislation to control the activities of the water sports market. Growing pressure caused by a large number of water sports in crowded areas, together with a growth in the number of commercial providers, has resulted in calls for tighter regulation and control. This has affected many commercial operators under the requirements of the Code of Practice for the Department of Transport. There are now strict regulations for the quality of boats and for staff employed by commercial operations. These standards have proved costly for many organisations and have resulted in an increase in price and a fall in the number of providers.

Further calls, helped by the use of similar controls in France and Holland, have been made for the registration of private pleasure craft. Under a registration scheme recreational users are required to meet certain standards of proficiency and be covered by third party insurance. The benefit of such a scheme is to prevent novice users endangering lives. However, with very low levels of incidents, these proposals have been resisted by the governing bodies of water sports who see registration as detrimental to the freedom of recreational activity.

Space and Opportunity

Increased variety of demands for water based recreation could result in a lack of resources for activities and create pressures upon the environment, bringing about further problems of safety and more latent demand. Management of water resources needs to optimise the use of all water resources for recreation. To serve the needs of large populations it is necessary to create water parks and docks in urban areas.

In areas where only one water resource exists it is necessary to consider the development of a multi-activity centre. This can be achieved by well co-ordinated zoning policies. Careful management and increased environmental awareness within water sports participation allows co-ordination of growth and harmony with other activities and the environment.

Coastal Zone Management

The work of balancing the growing recreation demands on the already crowded coastal fringe will probably be undertaken by coastal zone management techniques. The concerns for coastal zone management, as identified by Portsmouth University, Coastal Zone Management Unit, will include:

1. An assessment of the economic value of coastal resources
2. A strategy for legal restrictions and planning rights in the coastal zone
3. A study of property rights and ownership
4. The planning and management techniques for coastal zoning
5. Methods to monitor the success of coastal zones
6. Methods to manage growing recreational use of water resources
7. Development of economic techniques for marine pollution control
8. A strategic approach to environmental protection of coastal and marine habitats

Technology

Technological advances throughout the 1970s and 1980s have led to the production of financially accessible craft for recreation. The use of GRP moulding for many boats has resulted in the production of a cheaper, low maintenance cost option. Many GRP boats are now available and it is possible that this market will show little further growth as many people entering the market buy from the wide choice of second-hand boats and a growing number of foreign craft. Growth in technology is likely to be predominately in new clothing and accessories, particularly electronics and fashion.

Environmental Issues

As the potential market becomes increasingly environmentally aware and the voice of conservation groups becomes stronger it would appear that the only way for water based recreation to grow in harmony with 'green' ideas is to form an alliance with environmental groups. To succeed in this water based recreation needs to ensure that its activities are not a cause for environmental concerns. Intensive educational campaigns are required to explain the importance of environmentally-friendly practices amongst participants and providers. If environmental and conservation groups do not see the activities of the recreation user as a threat, then common desires for a pleasant environment will lead to a strong and lasting partnership.

HOW CAN THE FUTURE OF WATER BASED RECREATION BE ASSURED?

Many recent policy documents, like the Sports Council's *A Countryside for Sport,* and recommendations, such as the Report of the Water Safety Committee, suggest that an important management issue for future water based recreation is to offer a more integrated approach by planning with wide considerations in mind. This can be summarised as the need to create partnerships which effectively manage water resources for leisure and to adopt strategic management techniques in the work of these partnerships and within individual organisations.

What is strategic management?

Strategic management has become an increasingly popular term. Many books offer strategic approaches to management issues and courses are now available to produce not just a business manager but a *strategic* manager. Despite its common usage the term strategic management is unclear in many people's minds. It is important, however, that the potential recreation manager needs to fully understand the meaning of this concept if a strategic approach is what the water based recreation industry requires.

Strategy is defined as the planning and directing of an entire operation - a plan or policy to achieve something. Strategy is concerned with the ability to produce and carry out an organised approach to a problem or activity. Strategic management is, therefore, the skill involved in the development of policies and plans of a whole business not just one area. In the past many organisations have consisted of departments or staff involved in the planning of one part of the business, for example, new product design or marketing. The inevitable result was an unco-ordinated approach to business management. By introducing the strategic approach an organisation can seek to co-ordinate a range of different operations or enterprises and achieve a single goal or objective. The strategic manager of water resources for recreation needs to have the knowledge and foresight to consider all aspects of the business.

Why do water resources require a strategic approach to management?

Previous chapters have shown how complex the types water resources and the demands placed on them are. If the manager of a sailing club plans only for the needs of its own members then the impact of these activities may be detrimental to the water environment and to the exclusion of all other demands. If, however, the same manager adopts a strategic approach the plans would include the needs of the water environment, the sailing club and other demands made upon the resources. By planning from the outset to satisfy a whole range of needs, the sailing club manager is able to achieve a more sustainable approach to water sports provision. In order to fully achieve a strategic approach the sailing club manager may first need to form partnerships with other organisations. For example, if the sailing lake is owned by a water company and contains a nature reserve and an angling club, a truly strategic approach involves planning in partnership with all of the other organisations. For example, by creating specific sites for anglers, species in the nature reserve would not be frightened away and, in turn, sailors kept from sailing too close to banks would cause less disturbance to anglers, and so on. Mutual agreement and understanding can be converted into actual development plans and serve the interest of all groups.

A strategic approach allows wider ranges of issues and needs to be considered for specific water resources, leading to a more positive approach to planning and providing recreation, as illustrated in the development of the Coastal Recreation Strategy by the Southern Council for Sport and Recreation. The strategy sets out to achieve six clear objectives:

1. A clear understanding of recreation which exists on the coast
2. Obtain data about the current level of demand and future predication for demand
3. An assessment of the ability of the coastal resource to meet these demands
4. An up-to-date investigation into the issues and concerns of coastal recreation
5. Ideas for new facilities and developments for coastal recreation
6. Objectives for the planning and management of coastal recreation

This water resource strategy is a positive management approach for the development of coastal recreation, attempting to increase participation and opportunity without adversely affecting commercial operations or the environment. By using a central strategic approach to management of both water's edge recreation and water sports in coastal sites many different needs and demands are met. It will increase opportunity and reducing conflict and is an important management issue in achieving a balance as pressure increases on water resources.

Strategy Development:

As a strategic approach is the way forward for the development of water based recreation it is important that potential managers understand its process. The formation of a strategy involves an overall evaluation of the demands on the water resource, the physical resource, access and conservation needs. The appraisal, in the form of a report, should include the details of all user groups, their needs and concerns, the resource available, access to the resource by all user groups and an environmental impact assessment to ensure that the strategy will offer a sustainable solution.

Once completed, the appraisal or initial investigation can be used through partnership with all users to form some strategic aims. The aims of the strategy will be a statement of general intent. From this philosophical aim, management will require objectives, which are quantifiable and achievable goals for the management of the resource.

To achieve these agreed objectives a policy statement is required. Policies may be general, for example, developing an open access policy for the general public. Alternatively they may be sport or area specific, for example, to provide sailing tuition for local schools through the development and management of a sailing centre, or an area of particular environmental interest may be selected to be developed as a nature reserve. These policies will need specific management activities such as marketing plans, programming, interpretation and visitor management. All of these management activities, unlike previous methods, work towards strategic objectives and policies. The key to success is working effectively together to achieve a balanced approach to management. With strategic management there may be a need to introduce alterations into an organisation to reflect new partnerships or policies. These changes may simply be a change of name or a more structural organisation change. The diagram in *Figure 14* on page 294 shows an approach to strategy development.

Figure 14.1   **Strategy Development**

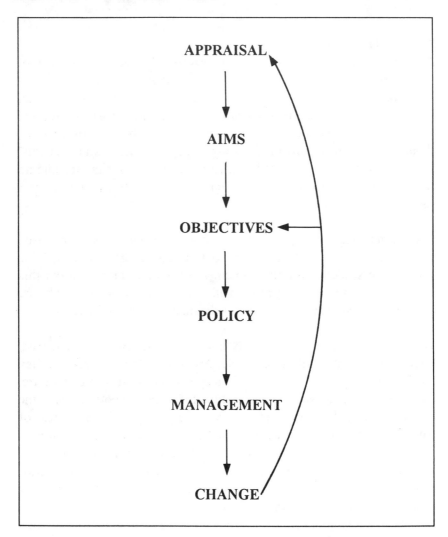

Managing and Assessing Strategies

In a large site it may be necessary to appoint one person to evaluate and co-ordinate its strategy. For the Coastal Recreation Strategy a Coastal Recreation Officer was appointed by a joint initiative with the county council and the Sports Council. In areas where strategy covers many different owners and clubs there may be a need for a central person to ensure that a balance is achieved between the different goals of the organisations. In the Coastal Recreation Strategy the concern was for the entire coastline of the Solent, not just a lake owned by a single organisation and used by a few easily identifiable parties. The development of a county or regional strategy benefits water based recreation by encouraging a large number of parties that the strategy can attempt to balance. Large scale regional strategies require central management and assessment. Their weakness is that they can only suggest policies and encourage the introduction of many of their ideas.

The management of a strategy for a single resource is more successful in achieving objectives because within a smaller partnership it is easier to control and evaluate policy decision. For smaller strategies, management and control is carried out through regular meetings with all involved partners to evaluate progress and agree methods to continue with objectives.

Whether a strategic approach is adopted regionally or by individual sites the Sports Council suggests several ingredients for success. Firstly, it is essential that all parties are committed to long-term planning as the results of strategies are not realised overnight. Secondly, partnerships are the way forward and essential to strategic planning. Finally, it is important to consult and actively involve the community; consensus and agreement facilitates policy implementation. The strategic approach to water based recreation has been adopted in several areas already. Some examples of this are shown in the information in *Figure 14.2* on page 296-7.

Figure 14.2   **Strategies for water based recreation**

Strategy	Organisations involved	Summary of Objectives
Coastal Recreation Strategy	Hampshire County Council Sports Council Southern Region	1. A clear understanding of recreation which exists on the coast. 2. Data about the current level of demand and future predication for demand. 3. An assessment of the ability of the coastal resource to meet these demands. 4. An up to date investigation into the issues and concerns of coastal recreation. 5. Ideas for new facilities and developments for coastal recreation. 6. Objectives for the planning and management of coastal recreation.
Hampshire County Council's Coastal Strategy	Hampshire County Council	1. Oppose new marinas 2. Encourage visitor moorings where environmentally acceptable. 3. Liaison with agencies to improve overall management 4. Lobby central government for a national policy for water sports provision 5. Maintain and improve access routes 6. Normally require future coastal development to offer public access to shore line

Continued over

Strategy	Organisations involved	Summary of Objectives
Leisure and Tourism Strategy	British Waterways	1. To become an established market leader in the provision of inland waterways for recreation in the UK. 2. Provide information and support research. 3. To obtain a financial contribution from leisure and tourism. 4. To create partnerships with public and private sector.
River Thames Recreation Strategy	National Rivers Authority (Thames Region)	1. Liaise with all Local Authorities concerned. 2. Consultation with user groups. 3. Consultation with other interest groups. 4. Research levels of demand and carrying capacity. 5. Investigate the potential of a database information system.

SUMMARY

This book identifies many diverse issues for the management of water based recreation. Indications show that participation continues to rise whilst the amount of water resources remain steady thus creating pressure on water resources. There are many ways to reduce this pressure and ensure that water resources continue to offer opportunities for all the activities identified and welcome new uses and activities. These methods include the need for more effective use of single purpose sites by encouraging multi-activity centres and clubs. There is also a need for better education among water users to create greater understanding of the impact of their activities on the environment and other users. The responsibility for this education firstly rests with the national governing bodies of water sports.

A balanced approach will be achieved through the creation of active partnerships and a strategic approach to water based recreation management. As the Southern Region Council for Sport and recreation identified:

The need for a more co-ordinated and integrated approach to planning and management of coastal recreation and conservation.

This final message is equally important for the management of all water resources for water based recreation, coastal and inland, man-made and natural.

Additional Reading and References

Amateur Rowing Association, 1993, *Rowing is Fun*

Boat and Yacht Harbour Review 1990/91

British Canoe Union, 1981, *Canoeing Handbook*

British Disabled Water Ski Association, *Water Skiing for the Disabled*

British Marine Industries Federation, *A guide to getting afloat: Sports Boating*

British Marine Industries Federation, *Schools Afloat*

British Waterways, *Environmental Policy and Mission Statement*

British Waterways, *Something for Everyone*

British Waterways, *Try out the Trent*

British Waterways, 1992, *Media Information MI/3, A Brief History Of Inland Waterways*

British Waterways, 1992, *Media Information MI/5, British Waterways Current Organisation*

British Waterways, 1992, *Media Information MI/6, Waterways: mileages, classification and restoration*

British Waterways, 1993, *Waterways Code*

Broads Authority, *The Norfolk and Suffolk Broads Act 1988 - Summary of main provisions*

Broads Authority *The Norfolk and Suffolk Broads: Know Your National Parks*

Broads Authority, 1993, *No Easy Answers: Draft Broads Plan*

Brown, A., 1992, *The UK Environment,* HMSO, London

Centre of Leisure Research, 1991, *Digest of Sports Statistics* Sports Council, London

Chenevix Trench, C., 1974, *A History of Angling*, Hart-Davis, MacGibbon

Cook, P., 1992, *A Guide to Boating and the Environment,* British Marine Industries Federation

Countryside Commission, 1983, *Annual Report*

Department of the Environment, Ministry of Agriculture, Fisheries and Food, Welsh Office, 1989, Water Act: *Code of Practice on Conservation, Access and Recreation,* Dept of the Environment, London

Department of the Environment, 1993, Water Industry Act 1991,

Water Resources Act 1991, *Code of Practice on Conservation, Access and Recreation: First Standing Report by the Governments Standing Advisory Committee*, Dept of the Environment, London

Department of National Heritage, 1993, *The Report of the Water Sports Safety Working Group*

Department of Transport, *Transport Statistics Report: Cross Channel Passenger and Freight Traffic*

Department of Transport, 1994, *Code of Practice*

Dumazider, J., 1974, *The Sociology of Leisure* Elsevier, Amsterdam

Environmental Protection Act, 1990, *Chapter 43*

Fairplay Information Systems, 1990, *World Shipping Statistics*

Gagg, J., 1989, *Canal and Inland Cruising*, Haynes

Glyptis, S., 1993, Leisure and the Environment (IN M F Tanner, *Recreation, Conservation and the Changing Management of Water Resources In England and Wales*), Belhaven Press

Green, B., 1985, *Countryside Conservation,* E & F. N. Spon

Gundrey, E., 1971, *England by the Sea*, Severn House Publishers Ltd

Hampshire County Council, 1992, *Coastal Planning & Management*

Haywood, L., *et al*, 1989, *Understanding Leisure,* Stanley Thornes

Henley Forecasting Centre, 1991, *Consumer Spending on Sport related Goods and Services in the UK*, Sports Council

HM Coastguard, 1990, *Co-ordinating Search and Rescue,* Oakfield Press

HM Coastguard, 1990, *Safety at Sea: Safety Guide*

HM Coastguard, 1990, *Yacht and Boat Safety Scheme*

HM Coastguard, 1993, *Positive Performance '93*

HM Customs, 1992, *Customs News*

Information Service, 1993, *Channel Navigation,* HM Coastguard CNIS Dover

Johnson, P., 1989, *The Encyclopaedia of Yachting,* Dorling Kindersley, London

Journal of the Institute of Biology, 1994, Volume 41 Number 1, Making Waves: Recreational Water Quality

Jubilee Sailing Trust Newsletter, 1993, The Nelson Touch number 24

Kolter, 1988, *Marketing Management*, Prentice Hall

Lavery, P., 1989, *Travel and Tourism*, 2nd edition, ELM Publications

Macmillan and Silk Cut Nautical Almanac 1993
Marine Conservation Society, *Seas Fit For Life*
Martin, Mason and Smith, 1989, *Boating and Water Sports in Britian,* Lesiure Consultants
McIntyre A.D., *et al*, 1994, *Marine Conservation in Scotland,* The Marine Conservation Society Scottish Panel
Money, D.C., 1987, *Foundations of Geography for GCSE,* Evans Brothers Ltd
National Rivers Authority, *Guardians of the Water Environment*
Plas Menai, 1994, *brochure*
Port of London Magazine, 1993, 4th Edition
Rivington, R.T., 1983, *Punting its History and Techniques,* Midas Publishing
Royal Yachting Association:
1992-3, *Annual Report*
News Sept., 1993, *Legal Desk*
News Dec., 1993, *Legal Desk and Cruising*
News, No. 63, 1993, *Code of Practice for Charter Vessels*
Seamanship Foundation Year Book 1993-1994
Notes from the Yachtmaster Instructor Conference, 1994
Scottish Natural Heritage, *Scotland's Natural Marine Heritage*
Sea Cadets, *Serious Fun* Promotional Leaflet
Sharpley, R., 1993, *Tourism and Leisure in the Countryside,* ELM Publications
Sidaway, R., 1988, *Sport, Recreation and Nature Conservation,* Sports Council and Countryside Commission
Sidaway, R., 1991, *Good Conservation Practice for Sport and Recreation,* Sports Council
South West Water, 1993, *Clean Sweep for Lyme Regis*
Southampton Institute, 1993, Notes taken at Water Based Recreation Conference
Southern Council for Sport and Recreation, 1993, *Coastal Recreation Strategy*
Sports Council, 1992, Factfile 3: *Countryside and Water Recreation*
a) Heritage Coasts
b) The Amenity Reclamation of Mineral Workings

c) Urban Outdoor Activity Centres

d) Planning and Managing Water Sports on the Coast

Sports Council, 1992, *National Centres Directorate Annual Report 1991/1992*

Sports Council Fact sheet, *Holme Pierrepont,* National Water Sports Centre

Sports Council Fact sheet, *Five National Sports Centres*

Stiles, R., *et al,* 1991, *Environmental Assessment,* Countryside Commission, Manchester

Tanner, M.F, 1973, *Water Resources and Recreation,* Sports Council, London

Thames Region NRA, *Guardians of the Water Environment*

Torkildsen, G., 1992, (3rd edition) *Leisure and Recreation Management,* E & F.N. Spon, London

Ward Lock & Co, c.1950, *Lyme Regis and South Dorset*

Wigglesworth, N., 1987, *Victorian and Edwardian Boating,* BT Batesford Ltd

Yacht Charter Association, 1994, *List of UK Companies*

Index

INDEX

INDEX

INDEX

INDEX